THE DEVELOPMENT OF EUROPEAN LAW

BY

MUNROE SMITH

DOCTOR OF LAWS, AMHERST, COLUMBIA, GÖTTINGEN AND LOUVAIN
LATE BRYCE PROFESSOR OF EUROPEAN LEGAL HISTORY
COLUMBIA UNIVERSITY

HYPERION PRESS, INC.
Westport, Connecticut

Published in 1928 by Columbia University Press, New York
Copyright, 1928, by Columbia University Press
Hyperion reprint edition 1979
Library of Congress Catalog Number 79-1621
ISBN 0-88355-925-0
Printed in the United States of America.

Library of Congress Cataloging in Publication Data
Smith, Munroe, 1854-1926.
    The development of European law.
    "A series of lectures delivered at Columbia University."
    Reprint of the 1928 ed. published by Columbia University Press, New York.
    Bibliography: p.
    Includes index.
    1. Law—Europe—History and criticism.
2. Law, Germanic—History. 3. Roman law—History. I. Title.
Law   340'.094   79-1621
ISBN 0-88355-925-0

EDITOR'S NOTE

These lectures as they appear in the present volume include the most recent corrections made by Professor Munroe Smith.

Where corrections have been made by the Editor, they are made in the form in which they were left by the author, or as suggested by his notes.

CARL L. W. MEYER

Library of Congress
September, 1928

FOREWORD

THE author of the present volume belonged to the class of foundation builders. In the highest and best sense he was a scholar. He did not undertake to popularize knowledge in the sense of making it easy to become learned without prolonged study and reflection. He was preëminently thoughtful. When he entered upon the examination of a subject, no matter what it might be, he proceeded carefully to analyze it, to resolve it into its component parts, to discover underlying principles and their operation, and thus to introduce order, system and certainty where superficial experimentation and uninformed imitation might produce chaos. With him this process was instinctive. Although he pursued it consciously and deliberately, it was the natural bent of his mind. Thus it was his high prerogative to serve as a guide to serious and earnest men, to explain to them the essentials of the problems with which they were called upon to deal, and to furnish them with the elements on which a safe and durable structure might be made to rest.

He had just been engaged in a work of this kind when I first met him. In saying this, I particularly refer to his essays on "State Statute and Common Law," published in the *Political Science Quarterly* for March, 1887, and March, 1888, and lately reprinted (1927) in the collection entitled *A General View of European Legal History and Other Papers*. The essays in question related to a civil code, a codification of the substantive law, which it was then proposed to enact in the State of New York. Although this code, popularly known as the "Field Code," had, after passing the legislature, been twice vetoed by governors of the State, and had been rejected by the legislature in 1885 and in 1886, its adoption was still strenuously advocated and the issue was uncertain. It is no exaggeration to say that when Munroe Smith entered the lists as an opponent of the projected measure, on the ground that it was unscientific in structure, inaccurate as a presentation of existing law, and disregardful of the theories on which all sound codification must be based, he contributed to the controversy a store of scientific information, a comprehensive knowledge of general jurisprudence and legal experience, ancient and modern, and a penetrating elucidation of elementary considerations, which enlarged the bounds of the discussion and exerted a powerful influence in bringing about the result he desired to accomplish.

The appearance and manner of Munroe Smith were exceptionally indicative of his character and his habits of mind. Modest and unpretentious in his demeanor, his expression was singularly intellectual, and he had about him an air of distinction that was as unmistakable as it was unaffected. He gave, besides, the impression of thoughtful preoccupation. If there were moments when he had "nothing on his mind," I cannot recall that I ever saw him in that condition. This by no means implies that he was wholly self-absorbed and incapable of diversion. He was highly appreciative of humor, of which he had a keen but refined sense, and was ever ready to take part in general conversation, be it heavy or light. But, no matter what the subject might be, his rare intelligence, his power of discrimination, and his skill and precision in the use of language, enabled him to give to the discussion an instructive and helpful turn and to add to the interest of the occasion.

I have spoken of his rare intelligence, and it is by reason of this quality, united with a passion for perfection in form as well as in substance, that the products of his pen, although he published anonymously many painstaking reviews of legal, historical and other works, are distinguished by excellence and variety rather than by quantity. Productivity is often developed at the expense of general intelligence, and this must continue to be the case, so long as time is an ingredient of human endeavor. But Munroe Smith never, I think, could have brought himself to the point of definitely restraining his quest for knowledge. His information covered an extraordinarily wide range, and he read, not superficially, but as a student of the causes and relations of things. This propensity to go afield was not compatible with exclusive preoccupation with a single subject, but it had its rewards, which posterity will share with his contemporaries, in enjoying the delights and the example of his enriched and exquisite workmanship.

I first met Munroe Smith forty years ago, in the office of my friend and colleague George L. Rives, then Assistant Secretary of State, at Washington. Three years later we became, unexpectedly, associated as members of the same faculty in Columbia University, at New York; and the casual acquaintance begun at Washington thus ripened into a lifelong and unbroken friendship, the memory of which I deeply cherish.

JOHN BASSETT MOORE
*Judge of the Permanent Court
of International Justice*

CONTENTS

FOREWORD
INTRODUCTION

BOOK I. EARLY GERMANIC LAW

Section	1. Historical Data	3
	2. Economic Conditions and Social Classes	8
	3. Military and Political Organization	14
	4. Crimes	24
	5. Torts	29
	6. Courts and Procedure	34
	7. Forms of Legal Acts	45
	8. Family Relations	47
	9. Movable Property	54
	10. Real Property	57
	11. Contract	61
	12. The Spirit of Early Germanic Law	66

BOOK II. INTERPENETRATION OF ROMAN AND GERMANIC LAWS

Section	13. Relations between the Germans and the Romans	71
	14. Germanic Kingdoms Established on Roman Soil	78
	15. Ostrogothic, Langobard, and Burgundian Legislation	85
	16. The Visigothic Kingdom: Historical Data	89

Contents

BOOK II. INTERPENETRATION OF ROMAN AND GERMANIC LAWS (*continued*)

Section 17.	Visigothic Legislation	94
18.	The Frank Empire: Historical Data	101
19.	The Frank Empire: Economic and Social Conditions	106
20.	The Frank Empire: Legal Development	115
21.	The Frank Empire: The Written Laws	124
22.	The Frank Empire: Courts and Procedure	134

BOOK III. DISINTEGRATION AND REINTEGRATION (887-1500)

Section 23.	Historical Data	149
24.	Roots of Feudalism	154
25.	Feudal Tenures in the Frank Empire	161
26.	Fully Developed Feudalism	166
27.	The Christian Church in the Roman Empire	176
28.	The Christian Church in the Frank Empire	180
29.	The Later Middle Ages: Ecclesiastical Jurisdiction and the Canon Law	191
30.	Influence of Canon Law upon Modern Law	208
31.	Development of Self-governing Cities	213
32.	The Law Merchant	217
33.	Local Law	227
34.	France in the Later Middle Ages	236
35.	Spain in the Later Middle Ages	240
36.	Italy in the Later Middle Ages	244

Contents

Book III. Disintegration and Reintegration (*continued*)

Section 37.	Germany in the Later Middle Ages	247
38.	Reactions against Lawlessness	253
39.	Revival and Reception of the Roman Law	258
40.	Roman Law in Italy	263
41.	Roman Law in France	271
42.	Roman Law in Spain	274
43.	Roman Law in Germany and the Netherlands	279
44.	Roman Law in Other European Countries	288

Literature and References for Collateral Reading 293

Index 301

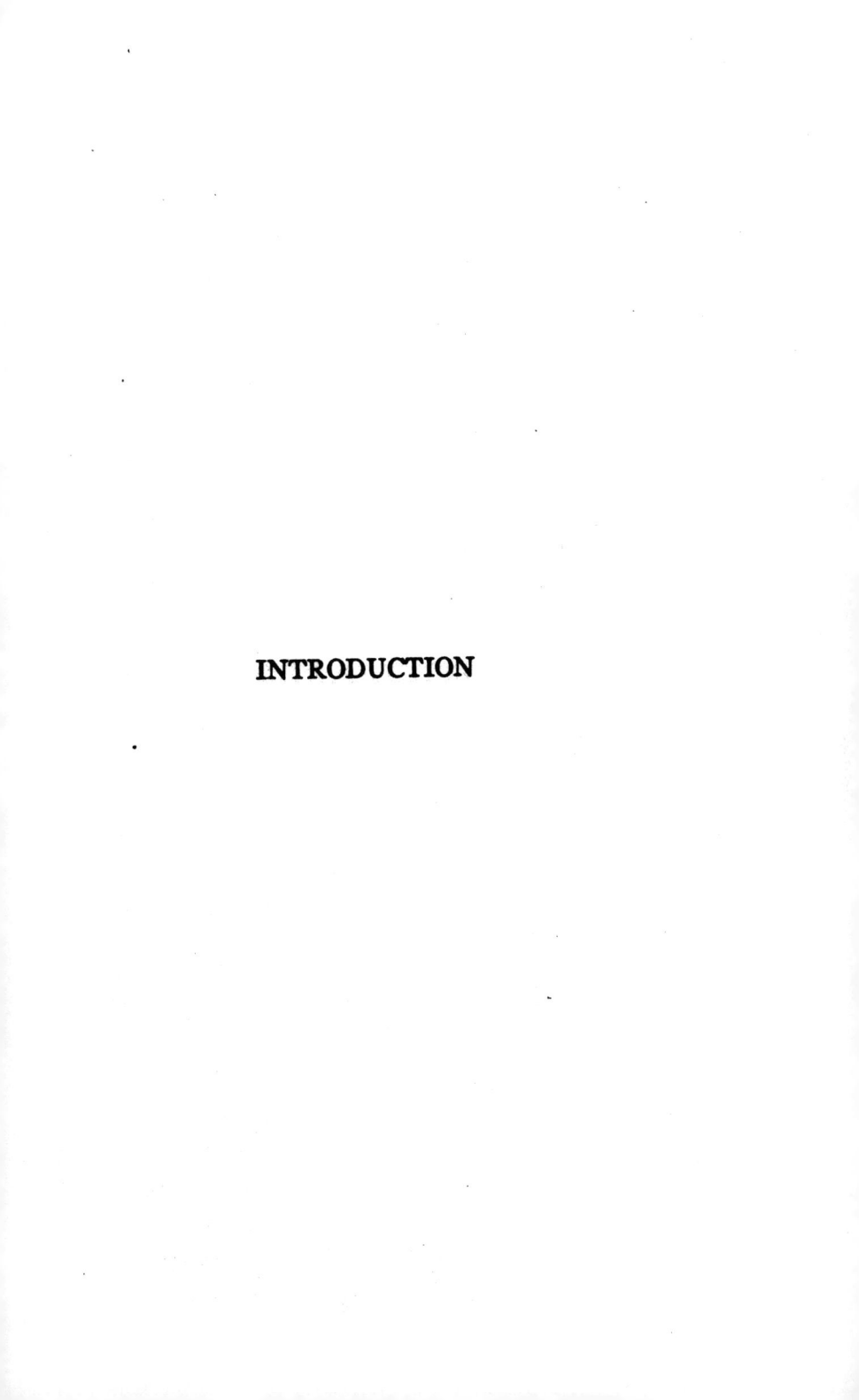

INTRODUCTION

INTRODUCTION

The subject of these lectures is the development of private law in western continental Europe from the fall of the West Roman Empire until the present time. We shall concern ourselves with public law only in so far as is necessary to understand the agencies and methods through which the private law was developed.

In this first lecture I shall indicate the main lines of this entire development in order that you may understand my point of view and plan of treatment.

The first century of the Christian Era witnessed the full development of the Roman Empire. In its greatest extent this included the larger part of Britain and western and continental Europe west of the Rhine and south of the Danube, including the territory between the headwaters of the Rhine and the Danube. It also included a large part of Asia Minor and the northern part of Africa. This was the area of early western civilization, and beyond the boundaries of the empire were only barbarous peoples.

In the first century of the Christian Era this Mediterranean civilization had reached a high stage of economic development, and in this empire there had been developed a highly refined and singularly modern system of private law.

Of the barbarians living beyond the Roman frontiers, the most important for our purpose were the various branches of the Germanic race. In the fifth and following centuries these barbarians, particularly those who had been living along the Roman frontier and had come into more or less intimate contact with the Roman civilization, broke through the frontier in all directions and occupied, to some extent peaceably and to some extent as conquerors, pretty much all southern and western Europe. The Angles, Saxons and Jutes invaded and settled in Britain; the Burgundians and Franks established themselves in Gaul; the Vandals, in northern Africa; and the Visigoths, in southern Gaul and in Spain. The Ostrogoths, and later the Lombards, overran northern and central Italy and the northern and eastern coast of the Adriatic. About all that was left of the old Roman Empire was the eastern part, with its capital at Constantinople. This East Roman Empire continued to exist with varying boundaries until the middle of the fifteenth century when Constantinople fell into the hands of the Turks.

The history of this East Roman Empire after the fifth century was singularly separate from that of central and western Europe, and the Roman law that survived in the East exercised little direct influence on the legal development of western Europe. Chief among the causes for this separate development was the split between the eastern and the western churches.

In these lectures I shall accordingly confine myself to the development of private law in France, Germany, Italy, Spain and the other western countries of the continent.

In the first centuries of the Christian Era, before the overthrow of the West Roman Empire, we find among the Germanic tribes in immediate contact with the Roman Empire some infiltration of Mediterranean Roman institutions and ideas. This was due primarily to the invasion of central Europe by Greek and Roman traders. Then before they overran the south and west of Europe all these tribes that were in close contact with the Romans had been converted to Christianity, and the church had succeeded in getting them to recognize as part of their various tribal laws some important principles, particularly in family law.

With the overthrow of Roman imperial authority, the German conquerors carried into Latin territory many of their institutions. At first they lived according to their own tribal customs and permitted their Roman or Romanized subjects to live according to Roman law. When there was a conflict the Germanic law regularly prevailed, but, as regards relations among themselves, the Romans were left pretty much to their own law. Some of the institutions, however, which the Germans brought with them sensibly influenced the development of law in western and southern Europe.

Out of the states established by the German conquests, there emerged three empires. An Ostrogothic Empire, with its capital at Rome, included for a time the Danubian provinces, the northern part of Italy, and southeastern Gaul. This empire was short-lived and had little effect on the development of European law. A second empire that lasted longer was that of the Visigoths, at first in southwestern Gaul and Spain, finally in Spain only, where it maintained itself until Spain was overrun, about the year 700, by the Mohammedans, who had previously broken the rule of the Vandals in Africa. Only gradually did the Christian kingdoms that survived in northern Spain fight their way south and reconquer the lost territory. During the period of Visigothic rule there was a blending of Visigothic law and Roman law, and a compilation of law was made which is regarded as the starting point of Spanish legal history.

The most important of these empires, however, was that of the Franks, which was to include practically all the Christian territories of continental Europe in which the spiritual supremacy of the Bishop of Rome was recognized. This empire ultimately included not only what is today France but the territory of the present Belgium and Holland, western Germany and Austria, half of Italy and northeastern Spain. This empire lasted until the latter part of the ninth century, and many of the most characteristic medieval European institutions took shape within this empire.

Broadly speaking, the legal history of the Frank Empire, like that of the Visigothic Empire, shows a blending of German tribal law and Roman law. Until the Empire of the Franks went to pieces, there seemed to be a possibility that a body of west European law would be developed by methods similar to those by which a uniform national law was developed later in England. With the dissolution of this empire, however, western Europe became a chaos of independent secular and ecclesiastic principalities. With the decentralization of political power, central lawmaking organs vanished, and western Europe was governed primarily by local customs. With the growth of cities there developed new areas of autonomy and varying city laws.

In medieval Europe after the dissolution of the empire of the Franks the development of law was wholly different from that which occurred in England. In England the power which the crown gained through the Norman conquest enabled it to develop central lawmaking organs centuries before such organs were developed on the continent of Europe. In none of the continental countries, at the close of the middle ages, had the crown obtained the degree of power which was exercised by the king of England; and organs such as those through which English national law was chiefly developed, royal courts of supreme jurisdiction, had nowhere else been established.

In continental Europe there grew up beside and over the various local systems three great bodies of European law — feudal law, ecclesiastical law, and the law merchant — administered by courts that were distinct from the ordinary local courts.

A great body of feudal law was developed. Some of the roots of the feudal system are to be found in the late Roman Empire, some in Germanic customs, but the feudal system was essentially a new and medieval product. Feudal law determined not only the political organization of Europe during the middle ages but also to a large extent land tenures and the law of real property. It reached very far into the lives of even the agricultural population, for the feudal manor ate into the jurisdiction of the ordinary local courts, and it was distinctly a feudal court that administered justice to the dependents within the manor. In feudal law, accordingly, we have a system of law which governed to a large extent the land of Europe, and also a system of manorial law which largely governed the life of the dependents within the manor. This manorial law, in spite of local variations, was more or less uniform throughout Europe. In the development of feudal law similar conditions produced a general similarity of institutions and rules throughout Europe. There was also a great deal of borrowing of law, each jurisdiction being more or less influenced by the development in neighboring jurisdictions. Furthermore, a compilation of feudal law was made in Lombardy which came to be regarded in other European countries as a correct general statement of the feudal law of the time. This compilation was in fact received as an authentic statement of the general feudal law of Europe.

Another great body of European law was the canon law — that is, the law developed and administered by the Roman Catholic church. The church inherited some of the power of the Roman Empire, and on the church rested in the main the task of perpetuating the civilization of the old world and adapting it to medieval conditions. After the dissolution of the Frank Empire the courts of the church began to absorb many fields of jurisdiction which had not previously been regarded as ecclesiastical. We may say roughly that from the tenth century to the Reformation the ecclesiastical courts, with a fairly well-defined jurisdiction, especially in the field of family law, met the needs of a developing society. The jurisdiction of these courts extended over marriage and the family relations, over wills or testaments, and in many parts of Europe over the distribution of personalty *ab intestato*.

The European system of ecclesiastical courts was a centralized system. From all the lower courts appeals could be and were taken to Rome.

So grew up the canon law, which of course contained a large body of rules governing what we may call the political organization of the church, but which also included a vast number of rules which we must call private law. Even in the Protestant countries ecclesiastical courts maintained much of their civil jurisdiction after the Reformation — in England until the early part of the nineteenth century.

With the growth of cities and the increase of trade, Europe began to emerge, in the eleventh and following centuries, from a long period of economic decadence. Even before the Roman Empire broke up, there was distinct economic retrogression in the south of Europe, and in the fifth century of the Christian Era economic conditions within the Roman Empire were far cruder and simpler than they had been in the first century. It may safely be said that Europe did not reattain an equal complexity and refinement of economic development until the nineteenth century. The beginnings of a new advance came with and after the crusades, and there was gradually rebuilt, chiefly through the decisions of mercantile disputes in city courts, a system of European commercial law. This law was necessarily more refined than feudal law or local customs. In its development there was to some extent a revival of principles and rules that had been embodied in the Roman law. Through the decisions of city courts, and to some extent by treaties between cities, a great body of substantially uniform commercial law was developed, and this law spread into England. This Law

Merchant was administered by special courts, just as feudal law was administered by feudal courts and the canon law by ecclesiastical courts. In England jurisdiction over commercial matters was not taken over by the royal courts until the time of the Tudors. English national law started with a centralized administration of feudal law and of the law of crimes. At a later period the royal courts took over admiralty law, and still later, general commercial law. In accepting the commercial law of Europe and making it a part of the English common law, England went further than any of the continental countries, for throughout continental Europe, commercial law is still regarded as a distinct system and is largely administered in first instance by distinct courts.

Throughout central and western Europe in the eleventh and twelfth centuries, there was need of new and more refined law which was not met by any of the established European systems. Almost everywhere, in city and country alike, new questions were arising as a result of increasing wealth and particularly of the increasing importance and variety of personal property. Where adjudication of disputes concerning personal property arose between individuals not engaged in trade, the commercial courts had no jurisdiction. The ecclesiastical courts had little to do with personal property except in the settlement of estates. The local customs were crude and could not meet the new problems that were arising. Even in the city courts all the needs of the new economic order were not fully met. Finally, as we have already seen, there existed nowhere in western Europe central royal courts with apellate jurisdiction such as were being developed in England.

It was under these circumstances that a singular phenomenon occurred. This has been called the revival of the Roman law. It may more accurately be described as the revival and acceptance in western Europe of the law books of Justinian. In endeavoring to meet problems that were within the exclusive jurisdiction of the local courts in city and country, the local law-finders had no general body of law to which they could resort — no reservoir of subsidiary law from which new rules could be drawn. This was the reason why lawyers began to study the highly developed system set forth in the digest and code of Justinian, and why they began to treat it as a body of positive law from which rules could be drawn. Finally, in most parts of Europe, the theory appeared that the old Roman law was a living law to which recourse was to be had whenever a problem could not be solved by reference to any of the existing medieval systems.

As a result of this whole development, the law of every continental European country consisted even in modern times of a great variety of local customs, in many cases reduced to writing, supplemented by provincial customs, also in most cases written, with hardly any national law anywhere. Earlier than in other continental countries a certain control of legal development was established by the monarchs of Spain and France. Even in these countries, however, there was no national law comparable with that developed by the royal courts and by Parliament in England. Beside the local systems of law, European countries still had great bodies of European law, feudal, ecclesiastical and commercial, administered by special courts, and back of all these different systems the great reservoir of Roman law.

Uniform national law had not been developed in the eighteenth century in any continental European country. Such law, therefore, had to be created by legislation; and as the national states took form and asserted supreme authority, we find national law developed by legislation and set forth in codes.

The first code that can properly be called national was

the Code Napoleon. Before it was compiled France was governed by hundreds of written local customs and scores of provincial customs which were subsidiary to the local customs. Across the customary law ran feudal law, ecclesiastical law, and commercial law, and behind all these systems throughout the greater part of France lay the Roman law as set forth in the law books of Justinian.

The French revolution swept away feudal law. Then France had to rid itself of ecclesiastical law and desired to rid itself of the direct rule of Roman law. But, above all, France wanted to get rid of its various local customs and to establish uniform law for all Frenchmen. This problem was solved by the Code Napoleon.

Some of the more important European countries achieved national organization only in the nineteenth century. The kingdom of Italy was not established until 1860, nor was Italian law nationalized until 1865. In Spain the laws of the different provinces varied even in the nineteenth century. In 1887 a Spanish civil code was adopted, but this did not replace provincial law in all the provinces. In general, however, the nations of continental Europe now have national law embodied in codes. They had to solve the problem of developing national law through legislation because it would have taken too long to create national law as in England by the slow process of decisions on appeal.

I have been sketching the development of law in western Europe as a single great movement. Oddly enough, there is no book in any language that treats this development as a European movement. There are good histories of and systematic treatises on canon law. There are good books on the history and institutions of feudal law. There are many treatises on commercial law, and there are good histories of Roman law in the middle ages. Beside this special literature we have separate histories of Spanish law, French law,

German law, Italian law, etc., in all of which a great deal of European development has to be noted, but all of which are written from a purely national viewpoint. Yet if we compare these different histories we can see in every case how very new is really national law. To a large extent, these national histories lay chief stress on the development of local customs, because the various systems of European law are dealt with in other treatises.

Books dealing with the history of European continental law as a whole do not exist in any language. In English we have translations of several good histories of the law of different countries, made under the auspices of the Association of American Law Schools. These form part of what is termed the Continental Legal History Series. In this series there is one volume which is termed a General Survey of Continental Legal History. It consists largely of extracts from different national histories. As a first attempt to deal with west European law as a whole, this volume is creditable, but it is not very satisfactory. It is, however, the best single volume that I can suggest for collateral reading.

BOOK I
EARLY GERMANIC LAW

SECTION 1

Historical Data

For our immediate purpose — the study of the development of continental European law — early Germanic law is of importance because it is one of the basic elements in that development. For the study of the history of English law, early Germanic law is of even greater importance. Modern English law, like the modern civil law of continental Europe, represents a fusion of Roman and Germanic institutions together with other independent institutions developed in the middle ages and in modern times. In the English law, however, the Germanic element is greater than in the modern law of Spain, Italy, France or Germany itself.

For the study of beginnings of law in general, from the comparative point of view, early Germanic law is of particular interest because in it we find notions and customs more primitive in their character than we find in any other branch, ancient or modern, of that group of scattered peoples whom we used to describe as Aryan and now describe as Indo-European. The oldest legal institutions of the Hindus, the Greeks and the Romans of which we have any knowledge represent a more advanced stage of civilization than any branch of the Germanic race had attained in the early centuries of the Christian Era. The Germans whom the Greeks and Romans knew were barbarians; and to compare their institutions with those of other races equally backward, we must study the institutions of modern barbarians.

Much of the comparative study of early law in recent times is in fact based on investigations of the institutions and customs of modern barbarians and even of modern savages — the Polynesians, the American Indians, and the peoples of darkest Africa. There is, however, an increasing skepticism concerning the value of such investigations for the student who wishes to discover the "seeds and weak beginnings" of the real systems now obtaining among the civilized peoples of the world. There is room to doubt whether races that have lagged behind in the march of civilization did not start wrong or turn at a very early period into blind alleys. As Maitland puts it, it seems probable that backward peoples are backward because they have failed to get in the right track. As a result of these doubts, there is a growing feeling that we may more safely base our studies of legal development primarily on the beginnings of law among those peoples whom, on the basis of language, we recognize as belonging to the Indo-European group. Today we do not think of that group as representing any modern or even ancient community of race or blood, but as representing a prehistoric community of culture only; the Indo-European peoples seem to have had common starting points, at least, in speech, in religion and in customs.

Early Celtic institutions and laws are of course to be included in this narrower field of research. But for the purpose of tracing the evolution of European law, they are of less importance than the early Germanic institutions and laws. Apart from the fact that Celtic law has exercised far less influence than Roman or Germanic law on the development of modern European law, the data we possess regarding Celtic law represent, as compared with those we have for early Germanic law, a less primitive stage of culture. The Celts came earlier under Roman influences, civil and ecclesiastical, than the majority of the Germanic peoples.

For studying primitive Germanic conditions, institutions and customs, we have, first of all, contemporaneous statements in Greek and Latin literature. The Romans began to take a keen interest in the Germans more than a century before Christ because they had become dangerous neighbors. Cæsar gives us some information, partly based on direct contact, partly on more or less fantastic travellers' tales. The *Germania* of Tacitus is based on fuller and more accurate information. In the main the details he gives us regarding German conditions and customs are strikingly confirmed by modern comparative study of the legends and early laws of the different Germanic peoples. His generalizations about the Germans are, however, to be read in the light of the obvious purpose with which his book was written. Like many of his contemporaries, Tacitus was deeply grieved by the decadence of Roman morals. He was also an opponent of the imperial régime under which he was living; he was an unreconstructed republican. His *Germania* seems to have been written primarily as a satirical protest against Roman corruption and submission to monarchic rule. For his purposes, he uses the noble German as modern satirists in civilized countries have used the noble red man. Tacitus is largely responsible for the idea, first developed by modern German historians, and to some extent accepted by English writers in the last century, that the liberties of modern Europe have their starting point in the German forests. Later Roman writers, secular and ecclesiastical, give us a less attractive picture of the Germans. It should be remembered that, when Tacitus wrote, the Roman frontier was securely held, and he could well afford to praise German independence and the simplicity and purity of German life at the cost of the Romans because, after all, Rome was still the unquestioned mistress of the world, in the fullness of her power, and a Roman could afford to be magnanimous. After his time the German peril steadily increased. Later Roman writers view the Germans very much as Americans on the frontier viewed the American Indians.

The most valuable sources for the reconstruction of early German law are the earliest written laws of the continental Germans, including of course the Scandinavians and the Anglo-Saxons. Where, in spite of long separation, we find among these different peoples similar institutions, we may assume that they are probably ancient. The earlier the separation, the more valuable this evidence. The testimony of language is here of great value. The name of a legal institution is in a sense its birth certificate. Where the same words are used to designate similar institutions among branches of the Germanic family that had separated before the dawn of history, the assumption of the essentially primitive character of the institution is especially justifiable.

Modern German writers, on the basis of particularly close resemblances in speech and in institutions, divide the Germanic races into two groups: that of the East Germans, including the Scandinavians, the Goths and the Vandals; and that of the West Germans, including the Germans, the Dutch and the German invaders of Britain. The earliest home of the East Germans is placed in Scandinavia and on the lower Vistula. That of the West Germans is placed on the coasts of the Baltic and North Seas, in the valleys of the Elbe and the Oder and the adjacent plains.

The greater part of the territory now occupied by German-speaking peoples in central Europe was occupied at the dawn of history by Celts. In the second century before Christ we find the West Germans pressing south and west upon the Celts and even upon the Romans. In the years 102 and 101 before Christ, Cimbrians and Teutons drove into Italy. Repelled by the Romans, they swept the Celts out of central Europe into Gaul. In the time of Julius Cæsar the Germans were pressing into Gaul. Cæsar checked their advance, subjected the Germans who had settled west of the Rhine to Roman control and began a counter attack east of the Rhine.

In the time of Augustus the Roman frontier was pushed to the Elbe. In the battle of the Teutoburg forest, A.D. 9, a serious defeat was inflicted upon the Romans. This was avenged by a punitive raid, but no further attempt was made by the Romans to hold permanent control of any considerable territory east of the Rhine. Until the fifth century the boundary between the Roman world and the barbarian followed the lines of the Rhine and the Danube, but included the territory between the upper courses of these rivers. The Roman province of Lower Germany lay entirely west of the Rhine; while that of Upper Germany was mainly west of the Rhine.

SECTION 2

Economic Conditions and Social Classes

At the beginning of the Christian Era the German tribes in eastern Europe seem still to have been nomadic. Their settlements were temporary: exhaustion of soil or pressure of enemies was constantly driving a part or the whole of a tribe to migration. In central Europe, however, where German movements west or south were barred by the Romans, we find more permanent settlements. Even here, however, the economic basis of life was largely cattle-herding. Cattle furnished the chief food of the people (Cæsar ascribed their great stature partly to the fact that they ate much more meat than the Mediterranean peoples and partly to the fact that the young people grew up unrestrained by any sort of discipline) and cattle represented their chief wealth. The oldest words for wealth and property refer to wealth in cattle. Cattle formed the standard of value. Fines were paid in so many head of cattle. Agriculture was a secondary matter. In the earliest laws of the Franks, we find few rules regarding agricultural implements and household utensils, but a wealth of rules regarding cattle and implements of the chase. There was apparently no permanent distinction between grazing and agricultural land. Patches of grazing land were fenced in and tilled for a year and then thrown open again to the herds of cattle. Under these circumstances, there was of course no reason why any individual Germans or German families should desire permanent possession of agricultural land — a matter to be kept in mind when we have to consider the subject of early titles to land.

Further evidence of the minor importance of early German agriculture is found in the fact that in the different branches of the German family we find no common word for autumn. The early Germans seem to have had three seasons only, spring, summer and winter. There was no autumn, because culture of fruit and vines was not developed, nor was any crop sown except in spring. The Germans reckoned years by winters and weeks by nights (in modern English still *sennight* and *fortnight*).

There was little trade beyond simple barter, except as the Germans came in contact with Greek and Roman merchants.

Writing seems to have been used primarily for religious purposes only. In drawing lots, for example, runic letters were scratched on beechen staves, while charms were muttered ("runic" from *raunen*, to mutter; the modern German word for a letter, *buchstabe*, means beechen staff). Runic characters were perhaps used also in branding cattle and marking utensils. The development of a written German language was very slow. We shall see that down to the ninth century all the German laws were written in Latin; and in the thirteenth century the *Sachsenspiegel*, a notable statement of Saxon laws, was written first in Latin and only subsequently put into German.

In the earliest social classification, we find above the class of ordinary or common freemen, who make up the bulk of the population, a limited noble class; and below the common freemen, a body of half freemen. Below these there are slaves.

The old Germanic nobility seems to be closely connected with the development of monarchy. It is always from the class of nobles, and usually from a particular noble family, that kings or local princes are chosen. In some cases all the nobles in a tribe seem to belong to one family and to be kin of the elected ruler. The composition (*wergeld*) paid for killing a noble was usually larger than that paid for killing a common freeman. Tacitus tells us also that while the Germans were for the most part monogamous, a noble usually had several wives, *propter nobilitatem*.

The half-free class perhaps represents earlier inhabitants or the descendants of earlier inhabitants of territory conquered by the Germans, who had not reduced them to slavery but simply to peonage. Conquerors have no more interest in slaying agricultural laborers than in killing cattle. This half-free class was steadily reinforced by manumission of slaves. As among the Romans, the manumitted slaves were not placed on an equality with those who were born free. They remained dependent members of the household, acting commonly as domestic servants, but also, as private property in land develops, they were sometimes placed in charge of outlying farms, bound in such cases to the soil as domestic servants were bound to the house.

In the economic interpretation of history, dependence of one class upon another is usually explained on economic grounds alone. In early society, however, there is another ground on which a manumitted slave must necessarily remain dependent upon his former master. In early society the individual has to rely for protection of life and property upon the support of his kinsmen. The kinship group forms a protective association and in early society discharges many of the functions which afterwards pass to the tribal or city state. The slave, who is not a person but a thing, who cannot have a wife in the eye of the law or be recognized as father of his children, has, in the eye of the law, no kin. Hence the manumitted slave, being a member of no kinship group, must rely for protection upon his former master and his master's kin. This seems to be the basis in the ancient Mediterranean world also of the relation of protection and allegiance between patrons and clients, the client class being mainly composed of manumitted slaves or freedmen.

The chief advantage that comes from manumission is that the services due from the freedman are limited, or, as the Germans expressed it, measured. To slave labor no limits are set except by the arbitrary will of the master. The freedman, moreover, may be permitted to work for others than his former master, and, if he earns money or acquires goods through such service, these earnings are his and with them he may possibly buy fuller freedom. He may marry, with the consent always of the former master, and he is legally father of the children born of his wife.

In the historic period, we find evidence that a half freedman may become full free, evidence that even a slave may from the outset be granted full freedom. The test of full enfranchisement is that the freedman is no longer bound to house or land. He can go where he will. This was symbolized in the early Lombard form of manumission. The slave is taken to crossroads and there manumitted in the presence of witnesses, and wanders into the world by whatever road he pleases. He has renounced protection, and takes his chances.

A different and interesting form of establishing full freedom is found at an early period among the Swedes. Here the former slave or freedman becomes full free by becoming through adoption a member of his master's kinship group. He offers, at a ceremonial banquet, ale to his master's kinsmen, and through participation in drinking, kinship is held to be established. We have many evidences that in early society the partaking of common food or of a common drink is regarded as establishing kinship.

Other forms of manumission which make the former slave or freedman full free appear with the strengthening of princely or royal power. Manumission in the presence of a king or prince or duke makes the man full free. In these cases, however, he looks to the king or prince for protection and owes in return a special personal allegiance.

In republican Iceland the grant of full freedom was formally made in the *folkmoot* or popular assembly. Among some of the continental Germans, if a freedman receives from his former master a spear and shield in the popular assembly, he becomes thereby full free. All these last methods of manumission came with the growing power of the tribal state and the possibility of obtaining protection not solely through the support of kinsmen but through the state and through courts of justice.

Manumission of a slave, says Tacitus, does not put him on an equality with those born free. He plays no rôle in the family or in the state except in those tribes where there is a strong kingship. Here he sometimes achieves a position higher than that of the freemen or even of the nobles; but among other tribes "the inequality of their freedmen is an evidence of the liberty of the people." (*Germania*, c. 25.) At Rome there was in fact a disposition of the emperors to employ their freedmen for important political services and this constituted a grievance in the eyes of Romans of the old families. Later sources show the accuracy of this statement of Tacitus. Where a strong monarchic authority is developed, the freedmen of the king frequently attain important positions.

The slave, as already noted, is a thing, not a person. In the earliest Germanic laws he is constantly compared to an animal. If he is killed, no *wergeld* is paid to his master, but damages based on value, as in the case of animals. The master has the power of life and death over the slave. The slave acquires not for himself but for his master. As already noted, he can contract no marriage, and his relations with any slave woman are dissoluble at the pleasure of the master.

For his torts the master is responsible. The slave himself cannot be put out of the peace — that is, outlawed — for he has no share in the peace. "The slave would be glad to break the peace," says a Swedish law book, "if that would put him out of it."

The actual position of slaves was, as always in slaveholding communities, better than the legal position. Brought up in the house of the master and employed in domestic service, his position was almost that of a subordinate member of the family.

Slavery, as among other peoples, is established by capture in war; by sale of one's self, or one's wife, or children; by inability to pay debt, particularly to pay damages or fines. As among other slaveholding peoples, slavery is inherited from the mother. In the German phrase, the calf follows the cow.

SECTION 3

Military and Political Organization

Among the Germanic peoples, as in other branches of the Indo-European family, notably among the Romans, the military and political organizations are closely connected. The army is the people. Its leaders are normally rulers in peace as they are leaders in war. The Germanic army was divided into thousands and hundreds. In the hundreds kinsmen fight side by side. When a German tribe passes out of the nomadic stage, in which we find many of the East Germans in the early centuries of the Christian Era, settlement is made by thousands and by hundreds. Here again the kinship group holds together, and the earliest villages appear to consist of bodies of kinsmen.

In the great plains of eastern Europe the nomadic or seminomadic hordes were in closer touch with each other, and the tribes seem to have been larger than were the tribes settled in central Europe which are described by Cæsar and by Tacitus. These smaller tribes not only occupy distinct sections of the country but have little to do with one another. Tacitus describes them as separated by mutual fear and by mountains. Where they were not separated by natural boundaries, like mountains or virgin forests, it was customary for each tribe to lay waste a broad stretch of borderland in order that it might not attract members of neighboring tribes.

The Romans speak of a tribe as a *civitas*. They tell us that each tribe was divided into *pagi*. The usual German word for this division was *gau*. Brunner regards the *pagus* as the district settled by the military thousand. Cæsar tells us that each *pagus* of the Swabians furnished one thousand fighting men. These thousand-groups seem largely independent in their action. When Arminius stirred up his tribe against the Romans, one *pagus*, with an uncle of Arminius at its head, remained neutral. Some historians believe that the *pagus* represents a tribe originally independent. Others, like Brunner, regard it as simply a settled thousand.

These thousands are divided again into hundreds. This division, which seems primarily to have been military, was utilized also for judicial purposes. It does not seem, however, to have been originally a definite territorial district. Among many branches of the Germanic family there were no hundreds. Among the Anglo-Saxons the existence of hundreds is not demonstrated before the reign of Edgar (959-75). The head of the hundred seems to have been originally simply its military commander. When Tacitus tells us that at the side of the prince administering justice there is always one or another body of a hundred (*centeni singuli*), this, according to Brunner, means simply that, as the prince rides circuit holding local courts, he summons one hundred after another.

These, then, are the political units: tribe, *gau* (or thousand), and hundred. Villages or groups of villages (*markgenossenschaften*) are economic, not political, units.

Most of the tribes described by Cæsar had no kings; they were ruled by princes, each at the head of a single *pagus*. Tacitus tells us that some of the tribes have kings while others, which he calls republican, are ruled by a number of princes. As the smaller West Germanic tribes were welded together into larger confederations, which ultimately became permanent unions, kings appeared at the head of these larger groups. At the end of the fifth century all these larger unions have kings except the Saxons and the Frisians.

Later Roman writers, like Ammianus, indicate that in

the tribes ruled by kings there were still always princes ruling smaller districts, who are described as *reguli* and *subreguli*. There seems in fact to have been little difference between the princes and the earliest kings except in the extent of their rule.

Some of the words used to designate a king also mean people. The idea which results in the use of the same word for king and people finds illustration in the fact that tribes sometimes bear the name of the royal house, while in others the royal house bears the name of the tribe. The word "king" itself is a derivative from the word "kin." In fact, as among other branches of the Indo-European family, while kingship is not distinctly hereditary but elective, the king is usually chosen from a particular family. Among the Germans the local princes were also elected, and here again usually from a particular princely family.

The difference between a king and a prince is rather one of degree than of kind. Both are military leaders. Both have retinues (*comitatus*). Both receive gifts of honor from the people, which are voluntary but customary. At the outset everywhere the peace is not the king's peace or the prince's peace, but the peace of the people. The notion of the king's peace is gradually developed and at first is something connected with but distinct from the people's peace. It seems rather to supplement the people's peace. It is an old dispute whether the chief root of kingship is religious or military, whether the king is primarily the leader in war or the representative of his people over against the gods. As far as we can see, these two functions are usually connected. In the tribes that have no kings but only local princes, a single prince is chosen in case of war to lead the tribe (*herzog*, *dux*). His authority lasts only during the war, but successful conduct of one or more wars may lead to his recognition as king. Among the kingless tribes, the tribe is represented in religious matters by a tribal priest, a sort of sacral king. But where there is a king, he seems also to be tribal priest.

Where the kingly office had been recently evolved, we sometimes find side by side with the king a tribal priest who continues to represent the sacral unity of the tribe. But such a division of supreme religious and political authority is unusual among the Germanic peoples. In Iceland there was for a time no central authority but that of the priests. Here, however, the priests gained political authority and became magistrates. Among the Scandinavians it was one of the regular functions of the king to make sacrifices to the gods on behalf of the tribe. We find accordingly that the Swedes, while still heathen, deposed a king who had become a Christian and chose another, that sacrifices might be made.

In the kingless tribes the prince in whose district a tribal meeting is held presides over the meeting, but the other princes form a sort of council in which matters of concern are discussed before they are submitted to the people. In the tribes having kings, the king of course presides over the tribal assembly, but the princes apparently still constitute a council with which the king consults before making any proposal to the people.

When, particularly in the third and fourth centuries, single tribes already having kings were merged into larger unions, these lesser kings in some cases maintained their positions as a sort of underkings; in other cases they seemed to be regarded simply as members of a higher nobility. The earls of Scandinavia and of Anglo-Saxon England seem to have been mediatized kings or princes.

In every German tribe large or small, we find tribal assemblies, *folkmoots*. For these the most common and widespread name is *ding* or *thing*. The tribal assembly met at certain fixed times in the open in a place consecrated to the gods. It is a religious as well as a political assembly. It is also a gathering or review of the tribal army. All the freemen attended armed. (Compare *comitia centuriata*.) In this assembly young men who have reached military age are formally equipped with arms and by the fact of this arming become members both of the army and of the assembly. When the Batavians fell under Roman rule it was one of their chief grievances that they were not permitted to meet except under Roman supervision and without arms. (Tacitus, *History*, 4, 64.)

The fact that the *folkmoot* represents the tribal unity enables us to see when a league or confederation of tribes passes over into a larger tribal organization. On the other hand, the appearance of separate assemblies indicates a division of a large tribe into smaller units. In the earlier seminomadic stage, when a tribe was growing inconveniently large, a portion of the tribe would swarm out like surplus bees from the hive and form a new tribe.

Upon its face the tribal assembly seemed to exercise very important functions. It elects kings, or in the kingless tribes temporary war-lords. It declares war and concludes peace. To it is submitted every important measure of tribal policy — that is, it possesses legislative authority. It is also a court, particularly in criminal cases. It is only in the tribal assembly that a free man can be put out of the peace. In all these matters, however, the power of the *folkmoot* is simply a power to assent to a proposal made by the king or by the presiding prince, or to refuse its assent. It seems to have exercised no initiative. The method of expressing assent or dissent is significant. Assent to any proposal is given by the weapon clash (*wapentake*); dissent is expressed by groaning. When you consider how impossible it would be for a presiding officer to measure the volume of these totally different noises, particularly if, as seems to have been the case, there was no call for ayes and noes and in case of a difference of opinion weapon clash and groans would be simultaneous, it is obvious that there was as yet no notion of majority rule. There is a clear assumption that the whole assembly, or virtually the whole assembly, will act in unison, and there must have been an assumption that it would normally assent to any proposal presented to it. Such an assumption is in accordance with all that we know of early society. In bodies essentially homogenous and living under identical conditions, the reaction to any situation or event is commonly practically unanimous. If a proposal made by a king with the support of the council of princes was in any case met by a general groan, it seems probable that the king and his retainers would at once have taken to the woods. It would have been a revolution. Such revolutions might in fact occur. We have already seen that the Scandinavians deposed a king because he had become a Chistian while they were still heathens. We know also that they and other early Germanic tribes sometimes deposed and even sacrificed their kings because they were beaten in war, and sometimes because the crops had failed and there was a famine.

As already indicated, the *folkmoot* was a religious as well as a political assembly. Tacitus tells us (*Germania*, c. 11) that it was opened by a religious act. "Silence is commanded by the priests," who have on this occasion power of coercion. Assemblies were held either at the period of the new moon or of the full moon. As a military organization the assembly met under the auspices of the Germanic god of war, *Tiu*, and because his day was Tuesday, it of course met on that day of the week. In modern Dutch the word for Tuesday is *dingsdag* — that is, "assembly day."

Of importance in the military organization of the tribe

and also of political importance were the retinues of kings and princes, the *comitatus*. The *comitatus* is described by Tacitus, and his description is confirmed in ancient Germanic poetry. Among the later sources one of the most important is the Anglo-Saxon poem of Beowulf. It is characteristic of the earliest retinues that the retainers are taken into the household of the king or prince. They eat, drink, and sleep in the lord's hall. The lord's wife, we are told, looks after their personal needs. Saxo Grammaticus tells us that King Frotho was besought by his retainers to take a wife that there might be someone to mend their old clothes and to make them new ones.

The *comitatus* obviously had a certain fundamental connection with the ancient Germanic custom by which any freeman, in order to obtain support or protection, might enter the household of another freeman and there render domestic service without loss of personal liberty. As long as economic conditions were simple and the kinship organization strong, the practice can hardly have been frequent. It was perhaps only the man without kin who would thus seek protection. From one point of view, the entry of a freeman or even of a noble into the retinue of a king or prince established a similar authority and protection; but the purpose of such entry was different. Freemen and even nobles entered the household of a king or prince to obtain more frequent military occupation than service in the popular army would afford. In the loose organization of the early German tribe, we find that single princes may lead their retainers, and others who volunteer, into the service of a neighboring tribe engaged in war, the rest of their tribe remaining in a state of peace. Thus service in the retinue of a warlike prince took his retainers out of the everyday life of the tribe and gave them greater prospect of excitement, fame and honor. The retinue might include men only half free, manumitted by the lord from slavery, but it seems to have consisted more largely of freemen. In the *comitatus* of a king there was always a preponderantly noble element. Noble birth and illustrious deeds on the part of a father might secure for a boy admission to the king's household at a very early age. For such boys of course the *comitatus* is a sort of cadet school. Such boys pass out of a household authority of their fathers into the *mund* or guardianship of their lord. Over them and also over the adult members of a retinue the lord has disciplinary authority. As in every case where a man lives as a dependent in the household of his superior, the lord is responsible to third parties for the acts of his retainer unless he places the alleged wrongdoer before the popular court. On the other hand, it is his duty to protect the rights of his retainers and to secure either vengeance or composition when they are wronged. In Anglo-Saxon and Swedish laws, if a retainer is slain, besides the *wergeld* or composition paid to the kin of the slain man a special fine is paid to the lord. Among the Franks, the lord has the right to raise feud or sue for composition when his man is slain, and in the early Frank laws the *wergeld* of a king's retainer is higher than that of a common freeman.

Membership in the retinue is not necessarily lifelong. When a youthful member of the retinue has completed his military education, he frequently returns to his native place, marries and settles down. He may return to take a place in the estate of a father when the father dies. If of princely family, he may leave the retinue at the call of his people to assume the princely dignity of a deceased father or uncle.

In the household of a king or prince, older and more experienced members of the retinue are regularly charged with various household offices.

The different sides of the relation between lord and retainer are indicated by the very words used in various branches of the Germanic race to designate a retainer. Some of these words mean the follower. In this word is contained the notion of service. In the Anglo-Saxon, *folgeras* means servants who dwell in the master's house as opposed to servants set out on his land. Among the Scandinavians free domestic servants in ordinary households and the retainers of the king are alike designated as hearth men or house carls. Other words run back to the *trust* root. Among the Franks the king's retainers were the *antrustiones*. Other words mean simply friends, still others mean kinsfolk, entry into the house of the lord being regarded apparently as a sort of adoption.

In war the retainers served not on foot like the common freemen, but on horseback. In battle they may be used as *aides de camp*, but their main duty is to serve as the lord's bodyguard. If the lord is slain in battle, it is regarded as dishonorable that they should survive him; if he is captured they should share his captivity.

As long as the retainers lived in the household of the lord their number cannot have been very great. Ammianus tells us that when the king of the Allemanni was captured in the battle of Strasbourg his *comites*, two hundred in number, surrendered to share his fate. In Norway in the eleventh century we learn that a king had a hundred and twenty retainers. His successor doubled the number, but this roused murmurs among the people and gave him an ill name.

The historic importance of the *comitatus* was at one time exaggerated. Some historians have assumed that the incursions that overthrew the West Roman Empire were raids of kings and their retainers. In the reaction against these theories there has been a tendency to underrate the importance of the *comitatus*. On its peaceful side, it was the source of the later European system of court offices, including those offices which carried with them the direction of various departments of public administration. In particular such offices as seneschal and marshal clearly run back to household duties assigned to retainers. On the military side the *comitatus* was of great importance in the development of the feudal system. It is the starting point of that personal relation between the lord and the vassal which characterizes all feudal tenures, the relation of protection and allegiance. This relation is clearly expressed in the Anglo-Saxon oath of fidelity. The retainer swears that he will be true and faithful to his lord, love all that the lord loves and shun all that he shuns, nor will do anything that is grievous to him. But all this is sworn under the express condition that the lord will maintain his follower according to the latter's deserts and "do all that he pledged himself to do when I put myself under him and took his will for mine." Brunner holds that the feudal right of the Anglo-Saxon lord to the horse, weapons and money of a deceased follower was originally simply the right of the lord to take back what he had given.

The real as distinguished from the personal side of the feudal relation begins when a retainer is set out of the lord's house on land bestowed upon him, with the understanding that he shall continue to render service in case of need.

SECTION 4

Crimes

Early law is essentially a law of crimes and of torts. At the outset many offenses regarded later as crimes are viewed simply as torts, and the protection of the family relations and of property rights is given by actions of tort. Actions *in rem* and on contract are of later development.

The development of the law of torts and of crimes antedates the establishment of courts and of judicial procedure. Action on tort represents primarily the reaction of the individual against a wrong, the desire to take vengeance. The reaction of the community against conduct which is felt to menace the welfare of all gives us the starting point for the development of the law of crimes. In early society this reaction may not be caused so much by any single act as by general conduct; it seems like a reaction against a variation from type which is felt to be highly objectionable. Among the North American Indians, for example, we find nothing like the trial of an offender by a court. The nearest approach to this is found among the Eskimos. Here we are told that the older members of the tribe will sometimes discuss informally the question whether the character and conduct of a particular member of the tribe is not such as to make it desirable that he shall be put out of the way. If this question is answered in the affirmative, the objectionable person is invited to go off on a seal hunt, from which he never returns. The beginning of criminal law is to be found in the immediate and instinctive reaction of the community against an objectionable act; the offender is lynched or chased out of the group.

In early society death or outlawry is not infrequently based on the notion that the offense is one that will bring down upon the whole community the wrath of the gods unless this be averted by the sacrifice or expulsion of the guilty party. It is apparently largely through priestly influence that the field of criminal law is first extended to cover offenses which are primarily offenses against individuals but which tend to undermine the social order. In other words, it seems to be through priestly influence that offenses previously regarded as torts first came to be regarded as crimes. Many forms of punishment for crime are identical with forms of religious sacrifice.

In early German law the distinction between tort and crime is that the tort creates a relation of hostility between the offender and the kinship group of the person injured. The offender is out of the peace as far as that group is concerned. Crime, however, puts the offender at once out of the peace of the tribe. Where the offense is clear, he may be slain by any member of the tribe. If a person primarily injured or his kinsman immediately slays the criminal, the slayer is regarded as acting for the whole tribe. It is not a case of vengeance for private wrong but of vengeance taken in behalf of the whole community.

Even in the historical period, the criminal taken in the act may at once be slain. If he escapes he becomes an outlaw. The outlaw may not dwell among men. His home is in the woods. The Scandinavians call such an outlaw a "wood-walker." A law of the Frank King Chilperich describes the outlaw as a man who walks through the woods, and as late as 1187 in the *Landfriede* of the Emperor Frederick I, it is said that the lord or vassal or kinsman of an outlaw is not indeed bound to deliver him up to punishment, but he must not harbor him. He must send him *in sylvam*.

In many of the Germanic tongues the outlaw is called a wolf. In Anglo-Saxon England the man who by his act has put himself out of the peace or has been put out of the peace by the decision of a court is said to wear a wolf's head. Such expressions of course mean that, like the wolf, the criminal is an enemy of human kind and may, like the wolf, be slain by anyone who meets him. In Germany in the middle ages a man banished was said to have the freedom of beasts or of birds (*biesterfrei* or *vogelfrei*).

The werewolf of old Germanic legend, the thing that walks in the woods in the guise of a wolf but with something of human semblance, is connected by German legal historians with outlawry.

Outlawry affects not only the person but the property. This does not fall to the criminal's heirs but to the tribe or to the king; or else it is divided in fixed proportions between the heirs on one hand and the tribe or king on the other. The complainant who secures sentence of outlawry against the wrongdoer through judicial procedure often receives the composition due to him for his private wrong, or a share of the outlaw's estate.

Significant reminiscences of early lynch law are found among the Saxons, Frisians and Franks, and apparently also in Scandinavia. When a man has been outlawed as a result of criminal procedure, he may at once be pursued "with flame and fire," "with fire and brands," etc. If he escapes, his house is torn down or burned down. This right of popular execution of judgment is both attested and confirmed for the Saxons in a Frank capitulary of 797. Similar usages survived much later in Flanders, in Holland and in Norway. In city laws of Holland at a late period in the middle ages, sentence of outlawry by the judges was accompanied by the symbolic act of waving three times a burning torch.

In early German law we find traces also of sacral punishment or sacrifice of the criminal to the gods. Tacitus tells us that the Germans in his time imposed and executed the death penalty for certain grave offenses. Some of these offenses are primarily political. Traitors and deserters are hanged; cowards and skulkers are buried alive in bogs. Tacitus tells us also that the latter penalty was imposed upon persons guilty of unnatural vices, and later German evidence indicates that while the Germans were still heathens those who profaned holy places of the tribe were drowned, and those who were guilty of sorcery (black as distinguished from white magic) were burned alive. In all these cases the comparative study of early institutions indicates that the form of punishment was originally sacral. Hanging, burning, burying alive appear to have been modes of sacrificing criminals to the superior or inferior gods. Among the Scandinavians, where heathen usages lingered longest, some criminals had their backs broken on the stone altar where victims were regularly offered to the gods. Others were plunged into a sacred swamp where other than human victims were sacrificed to the gods. There are traces of such sacrificial punishment among the Frisians.

Sacral punishment fell naturally into the hands of the priests. It is significant that among the Germans the execution of an enemy captured in war or of a criminal was preceded by an appeal to the gods, by augury, by drawing of lots or by some other ordeal to ascertain whether they desired the sacrifice. As regards captives in war, this is attested to by Cæsar (*Gallic War*, 1-53). There is later German evidence of similar customs. As late as the beginning of the 9th century a law of one branch of the Franks, the Chamavi, declares: "If a thief has been convicted of certain thefts, let it go to the judgment — that is, to ordeal. If he is burned — that is, if he fails to stand the ordeal of fire —

let them deliver him to death. If he is not burned, let it be permitted to his lord (*seniori*) to pay his fine and free him from death." Here the ordeal is clearly no test of guilt. It has been decided that certain thefts have been committed. The ordeal is used to ascertain the will of God as to whether he shall be hanged or only fined. This is an old heathen usage in a Christian coloring.

With the conversion of the continental Germans to Christianity, traces of religious or sacral punishment were largely obliterated. Brunner finds it significant that the church in many cases strove to secure composition as a substitute for the death penalty. It is believed that this was not the result so much of instincts of humanity — the church apparently made no effort at Rome to interfere with the numerous and often cruel death penalties inflicted in the later empire — but rather a result of the obvious connection between the forms in which the death penalty was being executed and forms of sacrifice to heathen gods.

The list of recognized crimes in early German law was a brief one. In addition to those already noted, we find only treason, arson and secret slaying. Open slaying with no attempt at concealment was not a crime but a tort.

Of forms of prosecution for crime in the popular court, I shall speak in a later section.

SECTION 5

Torts

Where wrong done to an individual is not regarded as an injury to the entire tribe, the wrongdoer is out of the peace only as regards the wronged party and his kin. The situation created by such wrongful deed is feud (Anglo-Saxon *fæhth*, Latin *faida*). The root meaning of the word is "hatred." Feud is legally sanctioned hostility. The recognition of feud by the law is found in the fact that revenge taken in lawful feud is not a breach of the peace. It is not a wrongful deed. It furnishes no basis for any claim for fine or punishment. The man slain in lawful feud is not to be avenged nor has composition to be paid for his slaying.

It is the wrongful deed itself that puts the wrongdoer out of the peace as regards the injured party. No judicial determination of wrong is needed, unless subsequently to prove that the slayer was justified in taking vengeance.

The taking of vengeance, the prosecution of the feud, is the right of the injured party and of his male kinsmen — his sword-kin. It is their right to seek satisfaction. The satisfaction sought is vengeance, the most primitive reaction against wrong. Vengeance can be taken at the very instant when the right of feud arises — that is, at the very instant that the wrong is done.

The wrongful deed does not sever the bond between the wrongdoer and his kin. Unless they voluntarily thrust him out, they are bound to defend him. Hence the old German feud is regularly a clan feud and its prosecution involves a little war between the two bodies of kinsfolk, the result of which the rest of the tribe watches in perfect neutrality.

As late as 1439 the *schöffen* (criminal judges) of Namur declared in a judgment: "If the kin of the slain man will and can avenge him, good luck to them, for with this matter we *schöffen* have nothing to do." The vengeance of the injured group does not necessarily direct itself primarily against the wrongdoer. It may even be that he is less menaced than some of his kin. In Norway the relatives of a slain man were in the habit of picking out and slaying, if they could, the best man of the hostile group. In the peasant feuds of Holstein, as late as the fourteenth century, we are told that he whose father, brother or cousin has been slain does not attempt to slay the slayer but the father, brother or cousin of the offender, as the case may be, in order that vengeance may precisely correspond to the wrong.

No declaration or proclamation of feud is legally necessary; but if the wrongdoer were not slain in the act or overtaken and slain in flight, it was customary for the kin of the wronged party to meet, resolve to prosecute feud and take steps to initiate it. In later laws we find that the nearest kinsman of the slain man formally and solemnly summons the different branches of the kinship group to take vengeance. In some cases the corpse is carried about and literally laid at their doors. The group prepares to prosecute feud as a tribe might prepare for war. They elect one of their number a leader of the feud. In the laws of some of the Netherlands cities as late as the fifteenth century we find settled rules as to which relative has the first claim to "captain" the feud. The law of Namur speaks of this leadership as chieftainship of the war. Of great antiquity was the custom that a slain man was not buried until his death had been avenged. As late as the thirteenth century the Frisians were in the habit of hanging the body of the murdered man in his house until he was avenged.

Manslaughter in the way of feud must be publicly proclaimed, or at least it must be made perfectly clear in some way that the slaying was an act of feud. Revenge kept secret is a wrongful deed. Among the Franks the head of a man slain in feud was set up on a pole, or his body was hung on a gallows or exhibited publicly on a bier. In later laws of the Netherlands the avenger must leave on the breast of the man he has slain the weapon with which he slew him.

It was of course in the discretion of the injured party instead of prosecuting feud to accept composition. Originally composition for different private wrongs was not fixed by law. It was a matter of agreement. When the two kinship groups have agreed upon the substitution of composition for feud by the payment of so many head of cattle, or later of so much money, there is a solemn contract of atonement. The injured group formally renounce all further prosecution of vengeance. Their representatives swear to the representatives of the other group an oath of peace.

Because a feud between opposing groups might easily result, like a modern vendetta, in wiping out one or the other group, and since this would lessen the fighting force of the entire tribe, there was naturally a very early tendency to encourage composition. In the historic period we find that by law the right of feud has disappeared as regards all minor offenses. We find also that by custom the sum to be paid in composition for any offence has become fixed, and the early tribal laws consist largely of tariffs of fines or compositions to be paid for various specific torts.

In cases of grave wrong, in cases of "blood or honor" like manslaughter or the abduction of women, it was not easy to persuade the injured group to accept composition. It was regarded as distinctly disgraceful in such cases to sell revenge for money. Among the Scandinavians we find an ingenious device for avoiding this point of honor. Before accepting composition and concluding a treaty of peace, the injured group insists that the wrongdoer and his kinsmen shall take an oath that they if similarly wronged would have accepted a similar composition. This was called the "equality oath." A similar oath, though with a different name, existed on the island of Rügen. Here the wrongdoer and his kinsmen must swear "that they so much would take if it had happened to them."

In the historic period, in the period of the earliest written German laws, we find that in cases of blood and honor it is still within the free choice of the injured group to prosecute feud or accept composition. If they decide to accept composition, it is not in the power of the wrongdoer and his kin to refuse composition and permit feud to take its course. They have no such election. If they refuse to pay the customary composition, the injured group can sue for it in the popular court, and if the wrongdoer and his kin do not satisfy judgment they may be put out of the peace of the people. The only choice open to the wrongdoer, accordingly, is between composition and outlawry. In all cases where the wronged party has his option between feud and composition, and has the right of claiming composition in the popular court, the amount of the composition is legally fixed. The *wergeld*, the penalty paid for manslaughter or abduction, is simply one special form of composition. Other and lower fines or rates of composition are established for lesser offenses.

Composition, as already indicated, was originally paid in cattle. Tacitus (*Germania*, c. 12) says it was paid in a number of horses or cattle.

Besides the composition obtained by suit in court or included in such composition, there was a definite smaller sum to be paid to the people or to the prince or king, which was called "peace money," in the Anglo-Saxon *wite*, and in Danish England "lawbreach." In some of the written laws this sum is included in and forms a part of one general fine, the greater proportion going to the injured party, the smaller to the court. In other written laws the smaller fine is paid independently. Brunner thinks that the former system, the inclusion of the peace money in the composition, is the older system. Tacitus tells us that part of the fine (*mulcta*) went to the *civitas* or to the king. Brunner regards this as a price paid to the plaintiff for the assistance given by the court in enforcing his right, a sort of commission for service rendered, and that it was accordingly first paid by the plaintiff out of the composition he had received. To regard this peace money as costs imposed upon the defendant to be collected later from his property is a later point of view.

SECTION 6

Courts and Procedure

The early Germanic courts are those of the tribe and of the hundred. Each consists of the whole body of freemen, in the one case all the freemen of the tribe, in the other all the freemen of the hundred.

The tribal assembly at least, and probably the assembly of the hundred also, is in the earliest period a sacral as well as a political and judicial gathering. It is opened by staking off the ground, fencing it in with ropes and proclaiming a sacral peace within the limits thus defined. The Icelandic word for the peace of the court is *thinghelgi*, hallowing, and in the old Norse the ropes stretched about the court are called "holy bands." Tacitus tells us that at the opening of the court, silence was enjoined by the priests. In later sources, in the German tribal laws of the next period, it is always the presiding judge or magistrate who opens the court and proclaims peace. Very general, however, even in the next period, was the custom that the magistrate first addresses to the assembly, or to one or more representative members of the assembly, three questions: first, whether it is the time and place for the meeting; second, whether the court is rightly marked off; and third, whether he shall proclaim peace. The answers, like all answers of the assembly, were called judgments; and these particular answers were called *fronurteile* — that is, "holy judgments." A very old formula for proclaiming silence, which occurs in Scandinavian, Frisian, Frank and Saxon sources, is: "I bid listening and forbid unlistening." This proclamation is the direct ancestor of the Norman cry still used in our courts: "Oyez."

Brunner thinks that in the earliest period the ceremonial questions just noted were addressed by the king or hundred-man to the priests, and that when these questions were properly answered the priest proclaimed the peace.

An essential attribute of judicial power in the later periods is the *bann*, the right to command and forbid. Etymologically, *bann* comes from a root signifying loud speech. It may have meant at first the order issued by the leader in war; later an administrative command or ordinance. Hence it covers the official proclamation of peace in the court, and then it comes to mean the peace itself. In the older Frank sources, *bann* appears in the Latin as *sermo*, and *sermo regis* is the king's peace. *Extra sermonem regis ponere* means to put out of the peace. Another Latin or rather Latinized German word is *forisbannire*, from which comes our word "banish."

In later sources, especially in tribal laws, there are three kinds of *things* or courts: first, genuine or regular courts (*echte dinge*), which met at customary times and which the freemen were bound to attend without special summons; second, courts specially commanded (*bot dinge*); third, prorogued assemblies (*afterdinge* or *nachdinge*) — that is, assemblies held immediately or shortly after the regular meeting, to complete unfinished business.

The tribal assembly acting as a court had exclusive jurisdiction in certain matters, and concurrent jurisdiction with the courts of the hundred in other matters. The court in which the great majority of controversies came to settlement was the court of the hundred. Even the hundred was not yet a territorial division; it was a military division, a body of freemen, and in administering justice the prince of the *gau* seems to have held court at different times in different parts of the territory, one hundred after another meeting for judicial purposes. Under this system the court held in each hundred might be described as a "*gau* court"; but it seems that except in this sense there was no *gau* court. A much mooted question is the relation of the king, prince or presiding judge to the assembly and their respective functions in the administration of justice. The Roman accounts are not very clear, and when we get clear Germanic evidence in the next period, the position and powers of presiding judges or chairmen differ widely in different tribes. In the older period, according to Cæsar and Tacitus, the princes *jus dicunt, jura reddunt*. This, however, does not necessarily mean that the princes decided cases. At the time of Cæsar and Tacitus the Roman magistrate heard the pleadings, but the case went for decision to a jury, normally a single juror; but jurisdiction was ascribed to the magistrate. In the period of the written Germanic laws, the chairman of the German court has nothing to do with finding judgment; this is found by the assembly. Tacitus himself recognizes the coöperation of the assembly by declaring that the hundred acts as *consilium* to the prince and gives him its *auctoritas*.

In the earliest written tribal laws we find that the judgment is really found, or at least proposed, by one or more persons designated as "wise men" or "law speakers," and that their proposal is regularly ratified by the assembled freemen. It is the wise men who give the "word," but the assembly gives the "full word."

Among the Bavarians and Swabians an official law speaker or judgment finder (*esago, urteilo*) sits by the presiding magistrate. He proposes a judgment. If this is accepted by the other law speakers, it is submitted to the assembly and becomes valid through their assent. This procedure was followed as late as the ninth century. In every case in which judgment proposed by the law speaker is approved, he receives one-ninth of any fine imposed upon the defendant. A similar official was found among the Allemanni. In later texts this official law speaker is called the *judex*. The Frisians also have a law speaker (*asega, judex*) who is not the chairman or presiding magistrate. Unlike his Bavarian colleague, he is the sole proposer of a judgment, no other wise man being asked to approve it. He finds a judgment at the request or order of the presiding magistrate and he, like the Bavarian law speaker, has a share of any fine imposed. His judgment also requires the assent of the assembly. He seems to have been chosen by the people from some prominent and distinguished family.

In the laws of the continental Saxons it is the people of the vicinage or of the *gau* (*convicini, pagenses*) who find the doom or judgment.

It has been asserted that among the Anglo-Saxons the chairman or presiding magistrate finds the judgment, but the weight of evidence is to the contrary. Documents attest and laws seem to presuppose a judgment by the assembled freemen.

Among the Scandinavians and Icelanders there is an official law speaker who not only, as among the continental Germans, suggests or proposes judgments to be ratified by the popular court, but who also from time to time gives public instruction to the people concerning their law — we might almost say, delivers law lectures to them. In the Icelandic court he proposes a judgment only when asked to do so by the presiding magistrate. In Norway, however, he proposes all judgments; and in Sweden he develops into a sole and final judgment-finder.

Turning back from these varied institutions of the fifth and following centuries to the old German court, it would appear that in the earliest German court the chairman commonly asked one or more of the freemen recognized as wise in the law to propose a judgment, which is then submitted to the assembled freemen. It seems clear that from the outset the assent of the assembly (*umstand*) is the judgment and that all that precedes is proposal. The oldest form of assent seems to be, as in the case of other proposals made to the freemen, the spear clash.

Procedure in the early German court is either a suit in tort, for fine or composition, or a criminal action in which the complainant demands that the defendant be outlawed. Tort cases were usually brought before the hundred court; criminal cases were always brought before the tribal court, since only in the tribal assembly can a freeman be put out of the peace. In either case the defendant or accused is personally summoned by the complainant, accompanied probably by some of his kinsmen, and like all early proceedings, summons is made in traditional and fixed words. It is disputed and is in fact doubtful whether it was necessary for the man summoned to agree to appear in court. In Iceland, however, there is some evidence that plaintiff and defendant each summoned the other three times. These reciprocal summonses constituted a sort of voluntary submission to the jurisdiction of the court. It is, however, disputed whether any such form was in general use in the earliest periods. In historic times the defendant, when properly summoned, was bound to appear, and if he failed to appear, could be put out of the peace. In earlier times, it is probable that a refusal or failure of the defendant to appear would be taken as admission that he was in the wrong and would justify self-help on the part of the plaintiff and his kinsmen by feud. It is always to be remembered that in early society the redress of manifest wrongs is sought by self-help without appeal to any court. Courts, in fact, seem to have been instituted mainly for the purpose of clearing up unclear or doubtful cases. Later, with the weakening of the kinship bond, the court becomes the protector of the weak against the strong.

In judicial procedure the complaint, which is a demand either for composition of tort or for outlawry, is formulated in set and traditional words by the complainant, who appears with a *secta* or following composed of his kinsmen. The answer to the complaint, which must be an absolute denial of the claim, or, as the phrase ran in England as late as the Norman period, "a downright nay," must also be made in set and traditional words. During the recital of the complaint the plaintiff holds in his hand a staff and therefore, in some dialects, the complaint is called a "bestaving" or a "staff saying."

The judgment or doom, according to all the German tribal laws, follows immediately after the denial of claim by the defendant. The judgment proposed and accepted by the assembly is not a decision of the controversy but merely a decision as to how the controversy is to be decided.

In order to understand these early judgments, we must put ourselves in the frame of mind which is characteristic of early society in all cases where one man says one thing and another the opposite. In such cases God only knows the truth. There is no notion of ascertaining the truth by testimony of witnesses. These also may be expected to make contradictory statements. In any case accidental witnesses have nothing to do with the settlement of the controversy. As the truth is known to God only, the settlement of controversy is attained either by some process by which God may show the right, such as the ordeal, or by forcing one of the parties to the controversy to tell the truth by appealing to his fear of divine wrath if he persists in falsehood. One of the parties must swear to the truth of his statement. In early Germanic law such an oath may be fortified by the oath of friends, originally always of kinsmen, that the oath taken by the litigant is "pure and free from perjury." This is "oath-help" or compurgation. This oath-help may be based on some knowledge of the facts or on the general confidence which the oath-helpers have in the truthfulness of their principal. In early society there is no inquiry as to the grounds on which oath-help is given. In early German society a man's kinsmen seem to be bound to give him oath-help, just as they are bound to support him in feud, unless they rid themselves of this obligation by expelling him from the kinship group. This they may conceivably do in order themselves to avoid the wrath of the gods if they have no confidence in the truth of his assertion or denial. Oath-help, accordingly, is a sort of primitive testimony of good character.

In cases of tort — that is, in cases where the claim is for fine or composition — the controversy is usually settled by imposing upon one of the parties the taking of an oath to the truth of his assertion or denial, with a possible requirement of oath-help. Oath and oath-help seem to have been regarded rather from the point of view of right of proof than from that of burden of proof. One or the other of the litigants is assumed to be nearer to the proof and is to prove his claim or his denial by oath or by oath and oath-help.

Since the object of early procedure is to impose upon the parties a mode of settlement where they cannot agree upon any settlement, we find that in some cases where a judgment is proposed, that one party shall prove his case by oath and oath-help, the other party may himself propose to prove his case with the support of a larger number of oath-helpers. It is proposed, for example, to the assembly by a wise man or by the wise men that one of the parties shall swear "self seventh" — that is, with six oath-helpers. In such a case the other party may offer to prove his case "self thirteenth" —

that is, with twelve oath-helpers. In case of such a higher bid, the right of proof is transferred to the higher bidder, unless the other party will himself raise his bid to equal that of his adversary. Evidence of such overbidding is, however, found in later sources, and it is disputed whether this institution was really primitive.

In such cases of suit for composition the form of judgment would be either that the plaintiff must swear alone or with a certain number of oath-helpers in order to win his case, or that the defendant must swear alone or with a certain number of oath-helpers, or pay the customary fine or composition.

In criminal cases, where the demand of the complainant is that the defendant be outlawed, the mode of proof is by ordeal — that is, by direct appeal to the judgment of God. Among the Germans, as among other peoples in the earliest stages of legal development, there were various forms of ordeal. Among the Germanic peoples the customary ordeal was by battle. We find also ordeals of fire, such as walking blindfolded over heated ploughshares, and ordeals by water. The latter may be ordeals of hot water or of cold water. A common form of the ordeal by hot water was that the individual who is to prove his innocence by ordeal must extract a ring or other small object from the bottom of a kettle of boiling water. In the ordeal of cold water the accused person is thrown with bound hands and feet into a river or pond. This latter form of ordeal is found among many peoples. Among the Babylonians a person thrown into the water is guilty if he sinks, innocent if he floats. Among the Germans, oddly enough, the opposite rule prevailed. The person who floated was held to be guilty, on the theory that the pure element will not receive the impure. If, therefore, an accused person sank, it must have required prompt action on the part of his friends to prevent him from proving his innocence by the sacrifice of his life.

It is easy to dismiss all ordeals as purely irrational. It should be remembered, however, that at a period when everybody believed that God knew the right and, if properly appealed to, would show the right by one or the other of these ordeals, an innocent person may really have had a better chance of demonstrating his innocence than a person who knew his assertions to be false and believed that this was known to the gods. In wager of battle the combatant who knows his cause to be just may well fight with greater assurance and therefore with a better chance of success than his antagonist who is conscious of wrong. In the ordeals of fire and of hot water it was not assumed that an innocent person would not be burned nor scalded. Immediately after the ordeal, however, the injured foot or arm was bound up, with proper prayers or incantations, and after a certain fixed period of time the bandages were removed and the wounds inspected. If they were in process of normal healing the individual was innocent, the truth of his statement was demonstrated. If the wounds were found to be suppurating, he was guilty. We know enough today of the influence of mental conditions upon bodily processes to realize that a conviction of innocence or of guilt might have some effect upon the healing of the wounds.

Among the early Germans it seems that freemen were commonly directed to settle their controversy by combat. For the interests of the tribe a substitution of combat between two persons was a distinct advantage over the settlement of controversy by a feud between clans or bodies of kinsmen. Ordeals of fire and water do not seem to have been imposed upon freemen but only upon slaves.

When it has been proposed that a controversy shall be terminated by oath or by oath and oath-help of one of the parties (and in cases of tort the defendant seems usually to have been regarded as nearer to the proof), or when in criminal cases an ordeal by battle or otherwise has been proposed, and when the proposal, whatever its nature, has been accepted by the spear clash of the assembled freemen, procedure in court is substantially ended. All that remains is that the defendant must promise to bring the required proof, and it seems frequently, if not usually, to have been necessary for him to give sureties who made themselves responsible for his subsequent appearance to prove his case. The actual decision of the case, whether by oath or by ordeal, is a matter that concerns the parties alone. The object of judicial procedure, as already noted, was to secure the settlement of the controversy by deciding how it should be settled. In subsequent extra-judicial proceedings, if the plaintiff has been ordered to prove his case and fails to do so, the dispute is terminated because he has lost his case. If, on the other hand, the defendant fails to appear or fails to prove his case, he is clearly in the wrong. He must pay the composition demanded or he is *ipso facto* outlawed (for example, by defeat in battle).

It should be noted, however, that parties are not bound to settle their controversies in the manner prescribed by the judgment of the court if they are able to agree upon any other settlement. The community is interested only in getting a settlement. It should be noted further that, among some of the Germanic peoples, where the decision was to be made by oath or oath-help, and where the party upon whom this proof had been imposed, had brought his proof, it was possible for the antagonist to swear that the oath just sworn was perjured. If the proof was brought with oath-help, the antagonist must bring an equal number of oath-helpers to swear that both the oath of the principal and that of his oath-helpers were perjured. Where oath, or oath with oath-help, was thus challenged, it appears to have been necessary to have resort to the ordeal of battle by conflict between the two parties or between the two parties and their oath-helpers.

What may be called the final judgment attained outside of court was regularly executed by the primitive process of self-help. If it was decided in a case of tort that the defendant owed fine or composition, the right of the judgment creditor would be enforced either by arrest of the debtor or by distraint upon his goods. Resistance to such an arrest or distraint would be a breach of the peace and might subject the debtor to outlawry. In some cases, especially in later procedure, the judgment debtor had to give sureties for satisfaction of judgment. And in default of satisfaction these sureties would be responsible and liable to arrest or distraint of goods.

In criminal procedure the accused who has been proven guilty is *ipso facto* outlawed. His antagonist or any member of the tribe may slay him; if he escapes, he becomes, as we have seen, a wood-walker. We have seen also that in many cases his house is burned.

In later medieval developments we find that answer to summons is regularly enforced by outlawry in case of failure to appear. In several cases such outlawry may not become immediately operative. The delinquent may purge himself of outlawry by subsequent voluntary appearance. In later periods, again, non-satisfaction of judgment in cases of tort or in other civil cases may be followed by outlawry, from which a judgment debtor may free himself by satisfaction of judgment. In the Frank Empire there was later developed an administrative process by which a ban might be imposed not upon the judgment debtor himself but upon his property; his property was put out of the peace and might therefore be seized and sold in satisfaction of judgment.

SECTION 7

Forms of Legal Acts

In every stage of legal development, legal relations are established to a large extent by acts of parties, and private rights are protected and enforced by action or suit. In early law, when pleadings are formal, forms of action indicate what private rights are judicially enforceable and determine their extent. In early law, again, all acts that are to produce legal results are formal, and the forms in which parties must act determine the existence and the extent of private rights.

In modern law we draw a sharp distinction between rights over persons and rights over things. Rights over persons are always limited positively or by the association of duties with the rights. In early law, however, relations in which the rights and duties of the parties are reciprocal seem scarcely to exist. The normal legal relation is simply power on the one side and subjection on the other. Sir Henry Maine has described the development of law as a development from status to contract. Jhering includes this in a broader generalization: The evolution of law is from a system of one-sided powers to a system of legal relations with reciprocal rights and duties.

The early lack of distinction between power over persons and over things is indicated by the fact that alike in the earliest Roman and the earliest Germanic law there seems to have been but a single word to indicate legal power, and in both systems the meaning and root of the word are identical: *manus* or *mund* signifies the hand, a natural symbol of power. The German word is not the modern German *mund*, which is masculine in gender and means the mouth; it is an older feminine word, *die mund*. We find this feminine *mund* in an ancient German rhyme still quoted: "The morning hour has gold in the hand" (*in der mund*). We find this old word also in compounds, such as *vormund*, the guardian.

In Roman law the broader earlier meaning of *manus* is indicated by numerous compounds — for example, *mancipium*, which in classical Latin meant a slave. In the historic period, however, the significance of *manus* was limited to the power of the husband over the wife. In early Germanic law *mund* is power over free persons and carries with it the idea of protection as well as authority. The word for power over things is *seizin*, Latinized into *saisina*. Another German word is *gewer*. That different words are used in different branches of the Germanic family to designate power over things indicates the later emergence of this distinction.

In early German as well as in early Roman law, the symbol of power is the spear. In both systems later a wand or rod is substituted for the spear. In early German law the symbol of power over things is the hand itself or, as some of the German legal historians assert, the gloved or gauntleted hand. It seems doubtful whether a glove or gauntlet is really a primitive thing.

In early society, where it is of a supreme importance that rights should be made clear by the very form of their establishment, not only is there a set form of words for every transaction, but there is regularly a symbolic act. The nature of the right established is to be made clear to the eye as well as to the ear. In dealing with early German acts of various sorts, we shall find that the spear or rod plays a great rôle. In addition to the glove or gauntlet, we find another symbol, the turf and twig. We shall also find symbolic movements and gestures. It is an old German saying that all legal acts are performed with hand and mouth.

SECTION 8

Family Relations

The relation of husband and wife is established, as among other early peoples, either by capture of the woman or by her sale to the husband by her family. Whether the early Germans had also a religious marriage we do not know. The early conversion of the continental Germans to Christianity would naturally have swept away any heathen forms. There is, however, no evidence of a religious marriage among those tribes which in historic times were still heathen. Marriage by sale in the historic period consists first of an agreement on the part of the bridegroom to pay the customary price, consisting originally of a number of cattle, later of so many *solidi*, and on the part of the father or guardian to deliver the woman to her husband. Originally these arrangements are made by the respective kinship groups. As Tacitus tells us, *intersunt parentes et propinqui*. The consent of the woman is not required.

Capture of a woman from another and independent tribe would, of course, establish not the relationship of husband and wife but that of master and slave. Capture within the tribe of a woman belonging to another group is, of course, a tort, but one that may be healed by composition. If the abductor offers and the woman's family accepts composition, the relation of husband and wife is thereby established. The composition is the same as for homicide; it is customary *wergeld*. The price paid for a bride properly purchased seems to have been identical. From this fact and from a custom widely diffused and traceable in Scandinavia in modern times — a custom by which a peaceful and prearranged marriage is accomplished by a mock pursuit and seizure of the bride — some writers have conjectured that the capture marriage was originally universal and that the marriage by sale was of later development. Recent writers on early magic maintain, however, that pursuit and capture merely represent certain early superstitions. In any case, there seems no reason to doubt that marriage by sale may be quite as old as marriage by capture.

Tacitus tells us that in a German marriage the bride brings to the bridegroom something in the way of arms — *aliquid armorum*. This he explains as due to the warlike habits of the people. As we have seen, however, the spear is the symbol of power over free persons, and the delivery of the spear to the bridegroom by the woman's father or guardian indicates transfer of power.

In the marriage by sale, a portion, usually half, of the price is contributed by the kinsmen of the bridegroom, and the price itself is divided between the father and the woman's kin, precisely as in the case of composition of tort.

In connection with the delivery of the bride, we find in some branches of the Germanic family forms that are symbolic of adoption. For example, the wife is taken upon the husband's knee, a form also used in the adoption of a child. You will remember that in early Roman law the legal position of a wife — for example, as regards rights of inheritance — was identical with that of a daughter.

Without the payment of price or *wergeld*, there is no regular marriage. Unless and until the price is paid, the woman remains in the *mund* of her father and kinsmen. At a fairly early period the price comes to be regarded as a provision for widowhood, to be held in trust for that contingency. In other words, it becomes a settlement upon the wife. At a still later period this settlement or provision for widowhood may be made without actual transfer of money or property. In the English law such a provision for widowhood is eventually made by giving the wife a lien on the husband's real property. The English dower right thus represents the last form of the price paid for the wife in marriage by sale.

It was originally customary, or it became customary at a very early period, for the husband to make some gift directly to the wife upon the morning following the marriage (*morgengabe*, Latinized *morganatica*). Where a woman is not purchased from her kin, perhaps because she is of servile origin, a freedwoman, who has no kin, or because she is of inferior social position (we are told that Saxon nobles did not intermarry with the common free class), the morning gift is still made. This is the origin, of course, of the morganatic marriage. Ultimately, probably under the influence of Christianity, the woman becomes a wife; but neither she nor her children obtain the higher legal status of the husband.

The German marriage was commonly a marriage to one wife and no more, but since, as already noted, princes and nobles were in the habit of taking a number of wives, *propter nobilitatem* as Tacitus expresses it, the Germans can hardly be called a monogamous people. Among polygamous peoples today it is regularly only the wealthier class that can afford to support a number of wives.

In the German marriage, as we have seen, the woman is not a contracting party but an object of sale. A Kentish law of Ethelbert reads: "When a girl is bought, it is a sale if there is no fraud about it. If there is fraud, let him bring her back and take his money again." Another law, of Ethelred's, reads: "If a freeman lies with the wife of a freeman, let him pay him *wergeld* and let him get the other with his own money another wife and bring her home to him." The notion that the early Germans showed any special honor for women seems based entirely on the fact that there were, as among other early peoples, priestesses, who were, of course, subjects of religious veneration.

The power of the husband over the wife was almost as great as over his children. He has the right to kill her or to chase her out of the house — that is, to divorce her — but only for grave offenses. He may sell her in case of extreme poverty. These limitations upon the husband's power, as compared with his power over his children, were doubtless due to the fact that her kinsmen, although she is no longer a member of their group, were presumably ready to protect her extra-legally against gross abuse. It is here, probably, that we have the decisive factor in the advancement of the wife from the position of a chattel to that of a free person, subject only to a limited authority on the part of the husband.

The power of the father over children was greater than the power of the husband over the wife. In the earliest period children were not in the *mund* but in the *gewer* or *seizin* of the father. The father has the choice of accepting and rearing the newborn child or, as among other early peoples, the right of rejecting and exposing the infant. If he accepts the child, he at the same time gives it a name. This ceremony, which customarily took place "within nine nights," was accomplished in historic times with the sprinkling of the child's head with water. The father has the right to kill a child or sell a child by way of punishment.

The head of the house represents wife and children in all matters, including judicial procedure, and he is personally responsible for their torts.

By marriage a daughter goes out of her father's *seizin* into the *mund* of her husband. The sons also go out of the father's power, not by marriage, if the wife is brought into the father's house, but whenever they establish separate households. The German son is emancipated when he has "his own hearth and smoke." He also goes out of his father's power by being transferred to a new adopted parent or by being taken into the retinue of a prince or king.

The attainment of majority or full age on the part of a son is signalized by bringing him into the assembly and there arming him. This, of course, does not emancipate him from the father's authority, but it makes him a member of the army and the assembly.

Among the Germans as among all other peoples, kinship is determined by the family organization. When, upon marriage, the wife enters the husband's household, she becomes also a member of his kinship group, and the children are born members of that group. Wherever, on the other hand, as among many early peoples and some modern races, the husband goes into the wife's original household, he also becomes a member of her kinship group, and the children are born members of that group. In such case, of course, we have what is called *mutterrecht* or the metronymic system. Among the Germans there are some slight traces of such a system. In any case, the Germans in the earliest historic period are living distinctly under father right, not mother right, and relationship is reckoned through the male line.

It has already been pointed out that in early German society the kinship group, or *sib* (to use an old German word which has survived in English), played a very important rôle. It was to one's kinsmen that one looked primarily for protection. As we have seen, they support him both in feud and in judicial procedure. We have already seen that marriage is arranged between *sibs* rather than between households. In the earliest laws we find also that the *sib* has guardianship over widows and children. If these duties are primarily delegated to a special guardian, he is chosen by the *sib* and acts under their supervision and control. This is especially clear in the Anglo-Saxon laws. A West Saxon law of Ine (about 700) declares that the fatherless child is to be supported and cared for by the mother but is to be brought up under the supervision of the *mægth* or kinship group. The kinsmen, as it is expressed, are to have the "chief seat." They must also give the mother six shillings, a cow in summer and an ox in winter. There are similar provisions in a Kentish law of the seventh century and in early Scandinavian laws. Among the continental Germans the practice of appointing the nearest kinsman of the dead husband early hardens into a right of the next of kin to assume the duties and rights of guardianship.

The *sib* has disciplinary power over its members. The *sib* has the right of expelling a member from the group. An Anglo-Saxon law of Edmund II presupposes the right of kinsmen to forsake "a homicide." They then escape all consequences of his act. They are neither involved in feud nor responsible for the payment of composition, but they must give him neither food nor shelter.

If a wrongdoer be outlawed by the tribal assembly or put himself out of the law by his own act, he of course loses at the same time his connection with his kinship group.

Conversely, a stranger might be taken into the *sib* by adoption. This is especially clear in Scandinavian law. In Sweden, as already noted, adoption into the group was a form of full manumission from slavery. In Norwegian law it was a method of legitimizing a child born of a slave mother.

In some of the earlier German laws kinship seems to be reckoned through the female as well as the male line. This cannot have been originally the case. When the protection of an individual or the taking of vengeance for his death rested upon his kinsmen, it was clearly impossible that kinship could be computed at the same time through the male and the female lines. Suppose, for example, that my cousin on the father's side has killed my cousin on my mother's side, it is clearly impossible that I should hunt with the hounds and run with the hare; in case of a feud I must belong to one group or the other, and the same is true if it comes to giving and receiving composition.

In those feuds that appear during even the later middle ages, notably in the Netherlands, it is nevertheless clear that when a wrong is to be avenged by the kinsmen, men connected through the female line with the person slain or otherwise wronged, as well as those connected through the male line, are called to the feud. This can be explained only on the ground that place of residence has modified the constitution of the kinship group. Those who live in the same place, whether connected through the male or the female line, form the body of kin for all important purposes, certainly for the purpose of feud and composition. Blood relations in either line who reside in another community have gone out of the group.

SECTION 9

Movable Property

Individual right in movable property is much more ancient than individual rights in land. The right in movable property is not, however, in early law a fully developed right *in rem* by virtue of which the owner can follow up his goods and take them out of the hands of any third person; the right is rather a legally protected right of possession, which is lost if the possessor voluntarily parts with possession. The right was termed *seizin* or *gewer*.

The protection of *seizin* in movables, like the protection of early private rights in general, is by action of theft. In early German law, as in early Roman law, the conception of theft is extended to cover lost, strayed and missing things, as well as things stolen. In early Roman law, the householder who misses cattle or any personal property and goes in search of it is entitled to search a neighbor's house and if the object is found the neighbor is constructively a thief and not only loses the movable but pays a penalty. If, however, he has obtained the thing in question from some third person, he has an action to recover from that third person the penalty that he has paid; and so there may follow a series of suits until the man who cannot show from whom he received the property bears the ultimate burden of penalty. In early German law we have a similar procedure, known as the *anefang*, which Maitland calls "the cattle action," but which is by no means limited to search for missing cattle. The only difference between the German and the Roman procedure is that the person in whose possession the missing property is found is not himself liable to any penalty if he can say from whom he obtained the thing. The *anefang* proceeds against the person designated and continues until a person is found in whose hands the thing had been and who cannot tell from whom he got it.

Any such procedure is excluded where the possessor of personal property has voluntarily put it out of his hands — for example, by any sort of bailment. In all such cases *seizin* has passed, and the man who has parted with it has no right except against his bailee. This is the meaning of the old German rule *hand wahre hand* — that is, the later possession is the only protection of the earlier.

In the German *anefang* we have the direct ancestor of the English action of trover. In English law, even in the Norman period, a bailor has no claim against a person who has obtained in good faith the object bailed from the bailee. The Roman rule, according to which the owner of movable property can take it wherever he finds it, came into the English law in the fifteenth century (Maitland). It is a curious fact that the Germanic rule, which perhaps should rather be called the primitive rule, has not only held its own in modern Germany but has been accepted by most countries of continental Europe. In France in the eighteenth century, it was the recognized rule in all the northern *coutumes* that "as regards movables, possession amounts to title." An exception was then made in case of stolen and lost things, which might be taken out of the hands of any possessor, even a *bona fide* purchaser for value. In southern and eastern France, on the other hand, the law of movables was Roman. When at the beginning of the nineteenth century the law of France was unified by the Code Napoleon, the codifiers adopted the north French rules; and largely as a result of imitation, the Code Napoleon serving as a model for other and later codes, the primitive Germanic rule has found its way into countries like Italy and Spain. It is certainly an odd thing that we should find in this matter the Roman theory embodied in English law and the Germanic theory in continental European law.

Succession to movable property, in case of death, was fully established in early German law not merely as regards direct descendants, but also in favor of collaterals. We find in many Germanic laws a distinction between war gear, which passes primarily to sword kin, and house gear, which goes primarily to spindle kin.

SECTION 10

Real Property

Inasmuch as rights come into existence only where interests already exist which claim protection, we should not expect *a priori* to find individual or even household rights in real property developed at a time when the economic basis of the social life is hunting and fishing, or even when the pastoral economy has been developed. Tribal grazing lands, like tribal hunting grounds, may be satisfactorily utilized in common by all members of the community.

When anything like intensive cultivation of soil begins, an interest in permanent possession and use of land of course existed in lands kept perpetually fertile by inundation. Where, on the other hand, the soil was soon exhausted and where artificial fertilization and rotation of crops are as yet unknown, it is not in the interest of the individual to sow or plant permanently any particular field or fields. That is the economic stage in which we find the Germanic peoples of central Europe at the time of Cæsar and of Tacitus. In his *Gallic War* (6, 22), Cæsar tells us that among the Germans "no one has any definite quantity of land nor any boundaries of his own, but the magistrates and princes assign year by year to the clans and groups of kinsmen who assemble for the purpose so much land and in such a place as seems good to them, and in each following year they force changes of holdings." In another passage (4, 1) he tells us that among the Swabians "there is no private or separate land nor is it permitted anyone to remain longer than a year on one piece of land for the sake of tilling it."

When these writers speak of these changes of holding as forced and of permanent holding as not permitted, they are writing from the point of view of a society in which private right in land has long been recognized.

In Cæsar's time the territory of each tribe, as we have seen, was divided into *gaue* (*pagi*), within each of which there were various bodies more or less of kin — *gentes et cognationes*. Cæsar says nothing of any division within the clan or group of kinsmen, and it is probable that each such group tilled in common the land assigned to it, dividing only the crops.

Separate tillage and appropriation of the yield developed with varying degrees of slowness in different Germanic territories, and separate possession and tillage produced in time individual or at least household *seizin*. At the time of Tacitus the fenced enclosure of a household which contains the house, barn, etc., is in private *seizin*. It is the arable land which is still periodically assigned for tillage. In the *Germania* (c. 26) Tacitus writes, "The open land is occupied by all interchangeably and in proportion to the number of cultivators. This open land they divide among themselves in proportion to their dignity. The great amount of land available makes the division a simple matter; they change the fields (*arva*) annually, and what remains is pasture." This system was maintained as long as the greater part of the communal or village land was used for grazing purposes and only a smaller part for growing crops. At this period still the constant abandonment of exhausted arable land and the tilling of other patches that had lain fallow and had been used as grazing land were distinct advantages for everybody concerned. But when agriculture began to predominate over grazing and the greater part of the cleared land about the villages was used for agricultural purposes, when manuring began to be resorted to, also rotation of crops, interest in permanent control of arable land developed and separate *seizin* appeared.

All that has just been said is said of those districts where the necessity of constant defense against hostile neighbors forced the people into village settlements for more efficient protection. In mountainous districts where there was less danger of hostile incursion, separate household settlements — separate farms, as we should say — were of course held by single households or groups of kinsmen at a much earlier period than in the great plains of central Europe.

In the period of the written laws, the periodical assignments of arable land described by Cæsar and Tacitus have disappeared. In many cases tracts of land seem to be held by *sibs*, or kinship groups, rather than by households; but household ownership not only of house and lot but of arable land generally prevails. In the villages grazing and forest land seems still to have been in common use. It should be noted at the same time that such arrangements persisting through the middle ages and in modern times appear to have been determined by the manorial organization and are not necessarily, as was formally assumed, direct survivals of those more primitive arrangements which existed before the feudal system was developed.

In transfer or conveyance of land, we find in early German law an interesting use of symbolic forms. Very ancient as a symbol of land transferred is the turf and twig. Pliny tells us in his *Natural History* (22, 4) that where a German tribe is conquered and subjected to the rule of the victors "the sod is the supreme symbol of victory." In the conveyance of land held in private *seizin* we find frequently that a sod is delivered or thrown into the lap of the conveyee. In some cases a glove or gauntlet is stripped from the hand of the conveyor and placed upon the hand of the conveyee. We find also that the parties and their friends or witnesses walked about the boundaries of the property transferred and that the ceremony terminates with a symbolic self-ejectment of the conveyor by leaping over the fence or hedge about the land.

Succession to rights in land is very limited in the earliest written German laws. In accordance with the older idea that land is divided in proportion to the number of cultivators, we find that succession to land is limited to males. In the earliest texts of Salic law, land goes to the sons, but in default of sons it reverts to the community. In later texts we find a right of succession given to brothers, and later to male collaterals. This development antedates the general establishment of feudal tenures, and in these earlier German laws there is no trace of primogeniture.

SECTION 11

Contract

Personal obligation based on contract is everywhere later in its development than rights in tangible property. In early society it does not seem that there was any recognized method of compelling a man to keep a promise except by the simultaneous establishment of some economic or religious sanction. Economic security is found in the handing over of a pledge. The promisee has then the right of holding the pledge until the promise is fulfilled; he surrenders the pledge in exchange for fulfillment; but there is not yet any idea that pledge is something collateral to obligation. There is really not yet any idea of direct personal obligation on the part of the promisor.

Religious security for the fulfillment of a promise is obtained when the promisor swears or vows fulfillment of his promise. Here again there is at the outset no idea of direct obligation to the promisee. The obligation is to the gods; as far as the promisor is concerned, we have what we should today call a contract in favor of the third person.

The earliest contracts, when legal contract can be said to appear, are of course formal. The promisor is bound not so much by his promise or consent as by the form. When we study the roots of early formal contracts we do not find that any of them clearly run back to the giving of a pledge, except where the pledge given consists in the body of the promisor. When in early times a promisor, in exchange for some benefit received or promised, must give a pledge and has nothing to pledge except his own person, he pledges or mortgages that. This self-mortgage, which may be made in various forms, is an important root of early formal contracts, as for example the *nexum* of early Roman law. In early German law the promisor or debtor mortgages himself by handing over his spear to the creditor. That puts him legally in the *mund* or power of the creditor, and in case of his default the creditor forecloses upon his security by seizing the person of his debtor and holding him, perhaps not as a slave but as a dependent servant. This is what in the German is described as *schuldknechtschaft*, or servitude for debt. Here the right of the creditor has become emphatically a right *in personam*.

This is the origin of the chief formal contract of early German law, the so-called *wed* contract; or in the Latinized form *wadiatio*. The spear may shrink into a staff, the staff into a straw, but it is always in virtue of something passing from the promisor to the promisee that the promisor is bound.

Very ancient, apparently, among the Germanic peoples is the notion that a promisor may be effectively bound by pledging not his body but his honor. The pledge amounts to something because it is something on which the creditor can foreclose. This he does by proclaiming publicly to anyone and to everyone that his debtor has lost his honor. But for the pledge of honor, such a statement would be an insult justifying prompt vengeance. Where, however, honor has been pledged to the creditor and forfeited by the debtor's default, the latter has no redress. In taking his honor the creditor was simply taking what he had a right to take.

Among the heathen Germans there seem to have been formal contracts derived from the religious root. We are told that among the heathen Saxons there was a binding oath sworn with crooked fingers. Very common, as among other early peoples, was the imprecation of divine vengeance upon the promisor if he fails to fulfill his promise. Among the

Germans we find a so-called "cattle oath" by which, if the debtor defaults, a murrain or disease is to descend upon his cattle. Another form of oath was that sworn upon the weapon, which amounted to an invocation of death to be inflicted by divine agency (and perhaps with the very weapon on which the oath is taken), upon the oath breaker. Most of these religious contracts disappeared with the conversion of the Germans to Christianity. The sword oath survived because it was susceptible of a Christian interpretation: the oath upon the sword hilt is regarded as an oath upon the cross.

The sort of contract with which we are today most familiar, the contract in which the promisor is bound by consideration, is everywhere of late development. In bailments, for example, where a person has received something for a time only and has expressly or impliedly agreed to return the thing or its equivalent when the purpose of the bailment has been accomplished, the promisor is not originally bound in contract. Retention of the thing or failure to do what he promised to do when the thing was received is a tort. In the case of the bailment the wrong may be brought into the group of thefts, which of course involves an extension of the conception of theft. Among the Germanic races, however, the failure of the bailee to do what he undertook to do seems rather to have been regarded as a breach of faith for which vengeance may be taken or, at a later period, composition demanded.

It is probable that this point of view dominated the law of bailments long before we obtain any clear evidence of its recognition. The first evidence is derived from the forms used in judicial procedure among the Franks when the defendant is to give surety that he will bring the proof which he has been directed to bring and will pay composition if he fails to bring such proof. The form is as follows: the defendant or promisor hands his spear to the plaintiff and the plaintiff hands his spear over to the surety. In the first half of this transaction we have simply a wed contract. The promisor has given to the promisee power to seize him in case of default. In the second part of the transaction we see that this power over the promisor has been given to the surety so that the surety may compel the promisor to keep his promise. On what ground, however, is the surety bound to the promisee — that is, in this case, to the plaintiff? The very word used to describe this whole transaction gives us the answer. It is described as *fides facta*, faith established. The existence of this transaction in the fifth century seems to be attested. Later we find that, in some cases at least, the defendant can be his own surety. In this case he first delivers his spear to the plaintiff and this spear is then returned to him; but instead of taking it back with his right hand, he takes it with his left. That means that the plaintiff, in addition to his original claim, has now a claim over the defendant to keep faith, and may take summary proceedings in case of breach of faith.

It is difficult to distinguish this Germanic notion of breach of faith from the notion of breach of trust. I think we have here one of the earliest indications that the conception of the trust was developing in Germanic law.

In examining primitive forms of establishing an enforceable agreement, we constantly find that something is passing from one party to the other. In all such cases it is important to see whether the passing of a thing or of a symbol binds the giver or the recipient. If it binds the giver, we may assume that the transaction grows out of self-mortgage. If it binds the recipient, we have the consideration contract if not already developed, yet in process of development.

German writers tell us that in sales the custom of giving something to bind the bargain — a small coin, for example, or even a drink — is very ancient. This does not mean that the consideration contract is already developed. The transaction is a sale in which the thing sold is actually delivered. Primitive sales, like the still more primitive transaction of barter, are executed agreements, and contain originally nothing of the executory contract.

SECTION 12

The Spirit of Early Germanic Law

To the early Germans law presents itself in the main as a method of preserving the peace. Peace is often used as equivalent to law: to put a man out of the peace is to make him an outlaw.

Law, as is usual in early society, is deemed to be of divine origin. The Frisians, for example, believed that a god had communicated its rules to a first law speaker. It was closely interwoven with the national religion and had a distinctly sacral character; but as already noted, the early conversion of the West Germans to Christianity obliterated so much of the heathen forms as to leave but scanty traces of its originally sacral nature.

Among the various branches of the Germanic family we find different words used to designate law. One set of words, such as the North German *ewa* and the Anglo-Saxon *â*, from which we have *ever* or *aye*, indicate that which has always been there. Another set of words come from the Indo-European root *lag* and signify that which has been laid down or imposed. A third group of words mean "wisdom," Anglo-Saxon *witod*. I do not think it fanciful to say that we have here certain conceptions which play a rôle even at the present time. The notion that the English common law has always existed, at least in its nebulous essence of which judicial decisions represent the occasional precipitations — the notion, in other words, that judicial decisions do not make but simply declare law — represents the orthodox view of our common or judge-made law. In many languages — in the Latin, for example — there is a tendency to narrow the meaning of words derived from the *lag* or *leg* root to enacted or statutory law; but our English word *law* is still used in the wider as well as in the narrower sense.

The word most widely used today by the Germans to describe law in general, *recht*, was not used in this sense except at a rather late period, a fact which perhaps indicates that the purpose of early law and the function of early courts was rather to prevent or terminate controversies than to do justice — an idea already contained in the identification of law with peace. In early German law, as in other systems of early law, equity is completely subordinated to certainty.

Early German law, like all early law, is primarily unwritten custom. It is, of course, in every case the law of the tribe or folk which it rules, and attaches to every member of the tribe by virtue of his membership. It is thus personal, not territorial, law.

The statement of legal rules is, of course, not abstract; the rules are extremely concrete. Early German rules of law are clothed in simple language and often, to facilitate their transmission, in poetic and sometimes in almost humorous form. Early German rules sound like proverbs and, like early German poetry, are frequently alliterative.

Like all early law, Germanic law is a very strict law. The individual is mercilessly subjected to the established rules of law as he is subjected to the whole body of established custom. The general rule binds without discrimination — that is, without equity. There is no escape from the constraint of customary law except by outlawry. Everything that one does or says is interpreted by the customary and traditional view of acts and of words: what the individual intends is of no consequence. It is the act, without regard to the intent, that determines crime or innocence; and in all dealings or transactions a definite result flows from the forms employed.

The conditions of life being in the main simple, and the

habits and feelings of the people being similar, the individual is not oppressed by, is in fact hardly conscious of, the pressure of iron custom. It is like the pressure of the atmosphere, which we do not feel because internal and external pressure are equal.

Brunner somewhere says that what characterizes early German society is not the freedom of the individual but the equality of all free members of the community. This equality is, of course, maintained at the cost of individual liberty. We have here nothing peculiar to early German life; all that has been said is true of all uncivilized or half civilized society.

We see something of the same difference in modern times if we contrast country life with the life of large cities. Wherever conditions of life are relatively simple and people are all very much of the same sort, the local tradition of morals and of manners rules the village or countryside with an iron hand. The individual who disregards tradition is looked at askance. In large cities, on the other hand, where all sorts of people are herded together, there is not and cannot be any such uniformity in the standard of morals or of manners, and there is consequently, as is often noted today, more individual freedom of conduct. Imagine all these differences multiplied tenfold or a hundredfold, imagine real penalties substituted for social disapproval, and you will get some conception of the unfreedom that prevailed in early communities.

BOOK II
INTERPENETRATION OF ROMAN AND GERMANIC LAWS

SECTION 13

Relations between the Germans and the Romans

During the first four centuries of the Christian Era the line which the Roman Empire held against the Germanic tribes was more than once seriously menaced. About the middle of the second century the Goths who inhabited the plains in northeastern Europe about the lower reaches of the Vistula began to move southward toward the Danube, driving or carrying with them a number of different German tribes. Marcomanni, Vandals, and Goths drive over the Danube and are repelled by the Roman legions only after fourteen years of conflict. This the Romans called the Marcomannic War (166-80). Thrown back across the Danube, some of these tribes, including the Vandals, pressed westward toward the Rhine, while the Goths streamed down toward the Black Sea.

During the next two centuries there was more or less constant border warfare between Romans and Germans, but the line of the Rhine and Danube was fairly well held until the close of the fourth century, when repeated incursions of the Huns keep central Europe in turmoil and drive various German tribes against the Roman lines. In the fifth century practically all the provinces of the West Roman Empire fell into the hands of the barbarians.

During the four centuries in which Romans and Germans faced each other across the Rhine and the Danube, important changes occurred both in the German and in the Roman world — changes which largely resulted from the situation. Those Germans who were in closest contact with the Roman world learned much of military science and, in periods of peace, learned something in the way of agriculture — they learned to store and use manure and to vary the crops grown on the same plots of land. There was some trading, and Roman coins, *solidi*, became the measure of value. Many tribes were converted to Christianity. At this time the Roman world was still torn by theological disputes concerning the doctrine of the Trinity, and the Nicene creed had not definitely triumphed over the Arian heresy. The missionaries who carried Christianity across the Rhine and the Danube appear to have been Arians; it was the Arian form of Christianity that was accepted by the German converts.

During these centuries we find the smaller German tribes of central Europe entering into larger unions which at first are often temporary leagues but become in time new and larger tribes. This seems to have been due largely to military necessity. The movement was facilitated, however, by the fact that the tracts of forests which at the time of Cæsar and of Tacitus separated many of the tribes were steadily invaded by clearings. As the Germans were dammed up against the Roman frontier and were increasing rapidly in numbers, agriculture rather than herding became the economic basis of life, and new land was constantly needed for agricultural purposes. In many cases the smaller tribes thus brought into closer contact with one another seem to have had a certain community of dialects and of customs and were presumably closely akin in origin.

Beginning with the third century, we find six of these larger unions taking form.

The Swabian tribes unite under the name of Allemanni. They are in more or less constant and obstinate conflict with the Romans; they drive the Burgundians into Gaul and ultimately occupy a considerable part of the province which the Romans called Upper Germany.

Some decades later we find the tribes along the lower Rhine united under the name of Franks. The name means "free" and seems to have been adopted by them to distinguish themselves from their kinsmen to the west who were under Roman rule. In the second half of the fourth century the more important branch of the Franks, the Salian Franks, are in occupation of the lands to the east of the lower courses of the Rhine.

The Saxons, a word which means swordsmen, we first hear of in the second century. They were then on the right bank of the lower Elbe. Toward the end of the third century the name is greatly extended; there are Saxons as far south as the Harz mountains. In the time of Diocletian they were known as dangerous pirates. At the time of Charlemagne Saxons occupy pretty much all the northern and northeastern parts of the territory then held by Germans.

Between the Saxons and the Franks on the coast of the North Sea, we find Frisians. Those living in the delta of the Rhine, subject at first to the Romans, become free before the end of the third century.

In the heart of Germany at the end of the fourth century, we find a number of different tribes united in one Thuringian group.

From a mixture and fusion of those German tribes who were driven back across the Danube in the Marcomannic War and who then swept westward, emerged the Bavarians. At the beginning of the sixth century they are occupying pretty much the Bavaria of today. Their older home retained and still keeps their name, for Bohemia means the home of the Baii.

Of these six unions formed between the third and the close of the fifth century, four, all of them except the Frisians and Saxons, have kings. At first there seem to have been several kings in each of these larger tribes, but later, in every case, there is but a single royal house.

During these same centuries important changes were taking place in the Roman Empire. Military necessity made the new monarchy established by Augustus increasingly military in its character, and produced an increasing centralization of administration throughout the empire.

During these centuries there was also a constantly increasing Germanic element in the empire. Before Gaul was conquered by Cæsar, German tribes had penetrated Gallic territory and effected extensive settlements in northeastern and eastern Gaul. In the time of Augustus and until the close of the third century the Romans held the delta of the Rhine, inhabited by Batavi and Frisians. Some points on the eastern bank of the lower Rhine and the triangle between the upper Rhine and the Danube were under Roman control. Numbers of Germans thus held under Roman control were Romanized, received Roman citizenship, and became capable not only of serving in the Roman legions but also of obtaining important positions in both the Roman military and civil services.

A further infusion of Germanic blood into Gaul and also into Italy and the Danubian provinces resulted from the capture of a great number of hostile Germans in the constant border wars. Great numbers of these were settled in Roman territory as *coloni* or serfs. In the earlier empire, as in the republic, *colonus* always indicated the free tenant; it is only in the later empire that the *colonus* is regularly a serf. It is certain, however, that many Germans, and in the later empire large bodies of Germans, were allotted to great Roman landowners or settled on the imperial domains as serfs, particularly along the borders of the empire. These importations recruited the weakening agricultural forces of the Roman Empire and ultimately its military forces as well.

After the close of the third century we find in Gaul entire districts of *leti*. This, of course, is the Germanic name of the half freemen, and these *leti* are clearly Germans and their descendants. They are bound to the soil like other *coloni*, but they stand in many respects on a higher plane. They have an organization of their own under the supervision and control of imperial prefects, and they appear to live among themselves according to their own tribal customs. These districts, accordingly, strongly suggest what in this country we call Indian reservations. The names given to bodies of troops later recruited from among these *leti* indicate that in most cases they were Franks.

In the second half of the fourth century we find similar arrangements in Italy; we find bodies of Sarmatians and also of Germans from the Danube settled under the control of Roman prefects and known as Gentiles — that is, tribesmen.

The old Roman custom of assigning land on the frontiers to veterans was modified after the reign of Alexander Severus by making the inheritance of these lands conditional on rendering military service. In the later empire the borderlands are all occupied by such military settlements. The legions are settled on the land and till it. They form border armies and their sons inherit their rights and duties. These are the *milites limitanei* or *castellani*. This latter word indicates the fact that the Roman frontier was protected by a chain of forts.

Closely connected with this infiltration of German blood, but in part independent of it, a Germanizing of the whole Roman army was taking place.

There were Germans in the army that Pompey led against Mithridates in Asia Minor at Pharsalus; there were Germans fighting on Cæsar's side against Pompey. Aliens could not be taken into the legions, but Roman military commanders had the power of conferring Roman citizenship.

All the Germans settled within the Roman lines were subject to conscription, but until they received Roman citizenship they fought as auxiliaries, not in the legions.

Another important barbarian element in the Roman army was the Illyrian. The rivalry between the armies of the Rhine and of the Danube, which appears in numerous cases of contested succession to the imperial dignity, was largely a race rivalry between Germans and Illyrians. With the fall of the Claudian dynasty the Illyrians won the upper hand, and in the third century there were several Illyrian emperors, some of them the strongest rulers in the history of the empire. With Constantine, however, the Germans were again in the ascendency.

It was largely through the influence of a king of the Allemanni serving with the Roman army in Britain that the British legions proclaimed Constantine emperor. Germans helped him to defeat his rivals Maxentius and the Illyrian Licinius. These Germans, caring nothing for the older Roman state religion, readily supported the new imperial religion. After Constantine it is clear that there were many Germans in the legions. The auxiliary troops were now recruited entirely from captives in war — that is, from among peoples outside of the empire.

The bodyguard of Augustus (*custodes corporis*) consisted mainly of Germans. This German guard was dissolved after the defeat of Varus but was later reorganized. In the Prætorian Guard, an army division that was always kept near the capital, there were at the outset no Germans. In the later empire, however, the Prætorian Guard has disappeared and has been replaced by a force known as *gentiles et scrutarii* — that is, tribesmen and shield bearers. In this body there was a strong Germanic element. In the latest period of the empire we find Germans among the *protectores* who constitute the immediate imperial bodyguard, and service in this guard led in many cases to the highest offices in the state.

From the fourth to the sixth century, *barbarus* is the technical name for soldier. The military treasury is occasionally termed *fiscus barbaricus*. We find German customs creeping into the army. Roman armies are fighting in wedges and not in ranks. In proclaiming emperors — for example, in proclaiming Julian the Apostate and Valentinian I — the soldiers raise their candidate on a shield. In the year 377 a Roman army opens battle against Visigoths with a shield song.

At the close of the fourth century and the beginning of the fifth, whole tribes of hostile Germans were permitted to settle within the limits of the Roman Empire on condition that they would defend these borders against the other tribes of Germans behind them. This arrangement was made with the Ostrogoths on the Danube and with the Burgundians on the upper Rhine. This, of course, was the beginning of the end.

In the last century of the West Roman Empire we find some Germans in possession of the highest offices. For example, we find among the celebrated military leaders and statesmen Merobaudus and Arbogast who by their names were Franks; Stilicho, identified as a Vandal; the Swabian Ricimer; the Burgundian Gundobad, and the Goth Aspar.

It was a revolt of mercenary soldiers of Rome that dethroned the last of the West Roman emperors in the year 476. Their leader, Odoacer, proclaimed himself king of Italy. At this time German kings were already in possession of many of the West Roman provinces.

SECTION 14

Germanic Kingdoms Established on Roman Soil

The so-called migrations of the peoples, a movement which ended in the overthrow of the West Roman Empire, was started at the close of the fourth century by the movement of the Huns from Asia into central Europe. The Goths, who were settled on the lower Danube and the coasts of the Black Sea, were attacked in the middle of the fourth century by the Huns. A large number of these Goths, who appear later as the Ostrogoths, were subdued by the Huns and accepted Hunnish rule. The rest of the tribe, the Visigoths, crossed the Danube and destroyed a Roman army at Adrianople in the year 378. Theodosius made peace with them and assigned them territory south of the Danube on condition that they would hold the line of the Danube against all other invaders.

In the year 406 a horde of Vandals and Swabians broke into southern Gaul. In the year 409 they crossed the Pyrenees and made themselves masters of the greater part of Spain, the Swabians occupying and ruling for several generations northwestern Spain. Not long after this, Alaric, king of the Visigoths, led an army into Italy and sacked Rome. His successor, Athaulf or Adolphus, entered into alliance with the West Roman emperor and led his Goths into Gaul and Spain. He drove the Vandals, in the year 429, out of Spain into Africa. In the year 435 the Vandals made peace with Rome and agreed to pay tribute to the West Roman emperor. A new war soon broke out, and in the year 442 a treaty between King Genserich and the Emperor Valentinian divided north Africa. After this time the Vandal kingdom was independent of Rome and paid no tribute. In later wars Genserich conquered the rest of north Africa.

The Burgundians, who in the third century were settled about the river Main, and who at first lived in friendly relations with the Romans, fighting with them against the Allemanni, were permitted early in the fifth century to extend their settlements west of the Rhine, on condition, of course, of continuing to defend Gaul against other invaders. In the year 435 we find them in conflict with Romans and badly defeated by Aëtius, the Roman governor of the province. In the following year the Burgundians were disastrously defeated by the Huns. The remnants of the tribe were allowed by the Romans to settle in Savoy. Later, recuperating from these defeats, the Burgundians moved westward into Gaul and established the Kingdom of the Burgundians.

The Ostrogoths, who in the fourth century had been subjected by the Huns, remained for a time the allies and followers of these Asiatic invaders. In the middle of the fifth century we find them fighting on the side of the Huns against Romans and Visigoths. After the death of Attila they broke loose from the Huns and settled, with the consent of the Romans, in Pannonia. Some of them pressed westward into Gaul and joined the Visigoths. A great body of the Ostrogoths invaded Italy under the leadership of King Theodoric in the year 489 and overthrew Odoacer, who had ruled as king of Italy for only thirteen years. The Empire of the Ostrogoths was for a time the greatest power in central and western Europe. It included the Danubian provinces, the greater part of Italy, the southern Alpine slopes, a portion of southwestern Germany and southeastern Gaul.

At the end of the fifth century, accordingly, all the provinces of the West Roman and some portions of the East Roman Empire were in the hands of Germanic conquerors. Angles, Saxons, and Jutes had taken possession of a large part of Britain; the Franks had conquered Gaul as far as the Seine; the Burgundians held part of eastern Gaul; the Visigoths held most of southern Gaul and the greater part of Spain; the Vandals were in possession of Africa; and the Ostrogoths, as we have seen, were in possession of all the other provinces that had been ruled directly from Rome. The emperors at Constantinople were in control only of the greater part of the Balkan peninsula and of Asia Minor.

In the first half of the sixth century the Franks expelled the Visigoths from Gaul and subjected the Burgundians to their rule. The armies of Justinian overthrew the Ostrogoths and the Vandals, so that for a time Italy and the Danubian provinces and north Africa were reunited to the Roman Empire.

Before the close of the sixth century, however, northern Italy and Rome fell under the rule of new invaders, the Langobards. At the time of Christ this tribe was settled on the lower reaches of the river Elbe and fought with Arminius against the legions of Augustus. In the latter half of the fourth century they moved southward; in the sixth century they occupied Pannonia and then, as we have seen, the greater part of Italy. North Africa, however, continued to be ruled from Constantinople until it fell into the hands of the Mohammedans in the seventh century.

The earlier conquests of Roman territory were made by tribes that had long been in contact with the Roman world and knew much of Roman military methods and something of Roman methods of government. The kingdoms which they established were in theory still parts of the Roman Empire. When there was no longer an emperor in Rome they held their territories, nominally at least, from the emperor at

Constantinople. This theory is most distinctly visible in the case of the Burgundians and the Ostrogoths. As ruler of Italy Theodoric always insisted that he and the emperor at Constantinople were joint rulers of one Roman Empire (*unum corpus*). He even asked the emperor to confirm some of his appointments. King Odoacer had not attempted to disturb the general scheme of governmental administration; Theodoric was particularly careful to respect it. He employed all the established forms. He addressed the senate as "conscript fathers." His realm is essentially Roman and his Goths are Roman soldiers.

Nearly all the German kings bore the Roman title of *magister militum*. They claimed the rank of "patricians," and in Burgundian inscriptions of the years 466 and 473 the East Roman Emperor Leo is expressly termed "our Lord" (*dominus noster*). In the following century King Sigismund in a letter to the East Roman Emperor Anastasius describes the Burgundians as imperial soldiers.

This theory had important results as regards the attitude of the German conquerors toward their Roman subjects. These, if free, kept their freedom, lived among themselves by their own law and retained at least a portion of their land. Some land, at least, the Germans needed and took, but in taking land they followed the practices observed by the Romans in quartering troops upon civilian proprietors.

It should be remembered that in the later Roman Empire nearly all the land that was not held by the emperor, by municipalities or by ecclesiastical establishments, was held by a comparatively small number of great landowners. When Roman soldiers were quartered in any part of the open country each soldier had assigned him one-third of the proprietor's house or villa. The owner had the right to reserve one-third, and the soldier had his choice between the remaining two-thirds. Such a quartering, or rather thirding, was euphemistically described as "hospitality"; the soldier is always a *hospes*, and sometimes the same term is applied to the householder.

The Roman soldier, however, had no claim upon his host for sustenance. He received rations, or ration money, from the military administration. In most instances there were military storehouses supplied by contributions of meat, grain, etc., exacted from the Roman civilians, from which the soldiers received their rations.

Under the German conquerors, this complicated system of military administration soon disappeared. The German soldier had to get his sustenance directly from the land. Accordingly each German requires not only a third of the house but a third of the land belonging to the Roman upon whom he is quartered. With the third of the land he receives the same proportion of the serfs or slaves who till the land. The portion ceded to the German is described as a lot or *sors:* the original owner and the German invader are *consortes*. Apparently the Germans themselves drew lots to see upon what proprietor each should be settled. The Roman terms *hospitalitas* and *hospes* were in many cases still employed.

In many cases the Germans did not remain content with this original division. By the end of the fifth century the Burgundian guest has usually two-thirds of the arable land, with the serfs who till it. The Visigoths may at first have taken only one-third of the land, but in the earliest texts of their written laws, we find that they have two-thirds.

The Langobards were at first quartered on the Roman proprietors. In the year 574 a revolt occurred, the king was slain, and for ten years the people lived under thirty-five dukes. During this decade many Romans were slain and their land occupied. Moreover, where the Roman kept his land or a part of his land, the Langobard quartered upon him demanded one-third of the yield. The Germanic guest was therefore really a proprietor and the original owner his factor, one might almost say his serf. When these arrangements had been completed, the Langobards chose a new king, and the dukes turned over to him half of their holdings. At the same time the relations of the Langobards to the Romans were adjusted somewhat more evenly, and the Romans were protected against further violent dispossession.

To people living at the time, even to the Romans who were thus brought under Germanic rule, the revolution established by these Germanic conquests must have seemed far less radical than it does to us. In the first stages of the revolution especially, it may well have seemed to contemporaries that no very great changes had occurred. The provincials are living under German kings, but these kings call themselves officials of the empire, and in many cases before the Germanic invasions the provincials had lived under Roman governors who were Germans. The armies were German, but the Roman armies had been largely German. The soldiers quartered upon the Roman proprietors have taken portions of their land, but the portion which remains in the hands of the Roman proprietor no longer has to make contributions to any military storehouse. The duty of contributing a considerable part of the produce of the land had been released in consideration of the surrender of a part of the land itself.

It should be noted that this method of settlement scattered through the Roman population a smaller number of German invaders. Thrown thus into intimate contact, the absorption of the Teutonic by the Roman element and the acceptance by the German conquerors of the language of the conquered population was only a question of time. The fusion of the races was at first retarded by the difference of creed. The Burgundians, the Visigoths, the Suevi who mantained their rule in northwestern Spain, the Vandals, the Ostrogoths, and the Lombards were already converted to Christianity when they forced their way into the Roman world, but their creed was heretical. They were still Arian Christians. This seems to have been one of the chief grounds of hostility to the invaders. It is a rather significant fact that each of these Arian kingdoms was overthrown or reduced to narrower limits by orthodox armies. The kingdoms of the Ostrogoths and of the Vandals were overthrown by the armies of the orthodox Justinian. The Visigoths were driven out of Gaul and across the Pyrenees, and the Burgundians were conquered by Frankish kings who had accepted the orthodox Christian creed. The Lombards accepted the orthodox creed before the end of the seventh century, but here the establishment of the secular authority of the bishop of Rome brought about a political conflict between the Romans and the Lombards. It was in this conflict that the Franks appeared as allies of Rome, and Charlemagne seized the iron crown of Lombardy.

When the recently converted Frank King Clovis drove the Arian Visigoths out of Gaul, the Gallician clergy everywhere greeted him as a servant and agent of God; and we may assume that elsewhere the feeling of the orthodox Latin population and the support of the clergy had something to do with the defeat of the heretical armies.

Ultimately all the Germanic rulers of Roman territory accepted the orthodox Christian creed, and the greatest barrier to the fusion of the races by intermarriage disappeared.

SECTION 15

Ostrogothic, Langobard and Burgundian Legislation

We have noted that Theodoric, king of the Ostrogoths, held with peculiar consistency to the theory that his kingdom was a part of the Roman Empire and that his Gothic followers were merely soldiers of that empire. Early in the sixth century, between the years 511 and 515, he issued a code of laws described as an edict (of which today we have no manuscript, but which has come down to us in the form of the first printed edition, which itself, of course, must have been based upon the manuscript since lost). In the introduction to his edict he states that it is issued in order that barbarians and Romans alike may know what rules they are to observe. The edict, which consists of only 155 articles, deals with those violations of law which were most frequent and aims to secure prompt prosecution and punishment of offenders. He makes, indeed, no attempt to establish a common law for Goths and Romans; in each case the rule binding the Goths is based on Gothic custom, and that binding the Romans, on Roman laws. In the edict, however, there is more Roman law than Gothic. Further legislation was promulgated by his successor Athalric, who reigned from 526 to 534. The edict of Theodoric was put in force not only in Italy but also in the other districts that belonged to the Ostrogothic Empire. It lost its authority in Italy when the Ostrogothic rule was overthrown by the armies of Justinian and the law books of Justinian were introduced. These law books, however, were largely superseded in northern Italy by Langobard legislation and, in so far as they were used at all, remained in force only in central and southern Italy.

Of Langobard or Lombard law, the earliest written statement was made in 643 under the auspices of King Rothari. It is one of the numerous statements of German custom, of the so-called *leges barbarorum*, that took form between the end of the fifth century and the ninth century. It is the most remarkable of all these early compilations; in many respects it is the best piece of work; it is arranged on a definite plan and the single rules are distinctly and clearly formulated. This earliest Lombard code shows little trace of Roman or of ecclesiastical influence. The Lombards were still heretics. There are no special rules regarding the Romans. Here as elsewhere, the Romans were subjected to the Lombard law in all controversies between them and the Lombards, but were governed as among themselves by Roman law.

To this original code later supplements were added. Of greatest importance were the laws issued during the reign of King Liutprand (713-35). Here we find some striking changes. The Lombards were now orthodox Christians and ecclesiastical influence is evident. The language is more diffuse; prologues explaining the purpose of new laws appear; and in these prologues there are frequent quotations from the Bible. Manumission in the church is recognized. Penalties are imposed on heathen practices. Testamenting by dispositions for the welfare of the testator's soul are favored. Marriage with the widow of a cousin is prohibited because the Pope, "who in all the world is head of God's churches and priests," has required this prohibition. Even in this legislation, however, not much Roman private law is discernible. It is, however, declared that it lies in the free choice of contracting parties whether they shall observe Roman or Lombard forms.

Further "chapters" are added by later Lombard kings in 746 and in 755. All these additions are stated to have been made in regular Lombard diets on the advice of royal officials and with the assent of the people. Here, as in Visigothic Spain and in the Carolingian Empire, we see that an assembly of magnates is taking the place of the whole German assembly of all the freemen, and that the assent of the people is becoming a purely formal ceremony.

After the conquest of Lombardy by the Franks, Lombard law continued to develop on its own lines with little trace of Frank influence.

The Lombard law is closely related to the laws of the ancient Saxons and to those of the Anglo-Saxons. Characteristic rules and expressions are common to these three groups. The next closest relation is to Scandinavian law. All this confirms the tradition that the Langobards came from the north. The tenacity with which they held to Germanic customs seems to have been part of their obstinate resistance to Roman and to Frank influences. They were a very conservative people. We shall see later that during the middle ages Lombard practice and theory and Lombard compilations of law had a very considerable influence upon medieval European law.

A compilation of Burgundian law was made apparently before the close of the fifth century under the auspices of King Gundobad, who reigned 474-516. For centuries the *Lex Gundobada* remained in force; in the Carolingian Empire, those who lived by it were known as *Gundobadi*. In general this law was to be applied in all disputes between Burgundians and Romans but not in controversies between Romans. Only a few of the later laws were expressly stated to be binding upon all the subjects of the king. This compilation shows a very considerable influence of Roman ideas. There is far more Roman law in it than in the first compilation of Lombard law, which appeared a century and a half later.

After the conquest of Burgundy by the Franks (532) this code remained in force. It was attacked by the church — notably by Bishop Agobard of Lyons — partly because the church desired uniform secular law as well as uniform ecclesiastical law, and partly, as the bishop argued, because Gundobad himself was a heretic. It remained, however, the personal law of all inhabitants of the district, except men of other German tribes and Romans, as late as the eleventh century.

At about the time at which this first compilation of Burgundian law was made, a compilation of Roman law was issued for the use of the Roman population. It was undoubtedly made by local Roman lawyers and was based in the main on some of the handbooks of Roman law most in use and to a considerable extent on the code of Theodosius. A similar and better compilation was made, as we shall see later, early in the sixth century, in Aquitaine under the authority of the West Gothic king Alaric. In the Empire of the Franks no such compilation was made and this so-called Breviary of Alaric was chiefly used in the application of Roman law, and it appears to have superseded the Burgundian compilation even in Burgundy. In some cases the Burgundian compilation was treated by scribes as a sort of supplement to the Breviary of Alaric, and inasmuch as the last passage in the Breviary of Alaric was an extract from Papinian, the citation of his name (corrupted into Papian) was supposed to cover the whole Burgundian compilation, which accordingly was described through the middle ages and until its real character was reëstablished in modern times, as the *Liber Papiani.*

SECTION 16

The Visigothic Kingdom: Historical Data

The original population of the Spanish peninsula, so far as the ancients knew, was that which they called Iberian. The Iberians seem not to have belonged to the Indo-European language group. The Basques apparently represent a survival of this Iberian element. About 500 B.C. came a great Celtic immigration. On the southern coasts of Spain Phœnician trading posts, said to have been established before 1100 B.C., grew into cities. Of these Gades, the modern Cadiz, was the most important. As early as the sixth century before Christ, Greek colonies also were established in Spain. Of these the most important was Emporiæ, the modern Ampurias.

In the later part of the third century before Christ, the Carthaginians brought all southern and southeastern Spain under their control. At the close of the second war with Rome they ceded all this territory to the Romans, and for more than six centuries (202 B.C. to 409 A.D.) Spain was a part of the Roman Empire. Central and northwestern Spain, however, were not wholly subdued by the Romans until the time of Augustus.

Before the establishment of Roman authority the Iberian-Celtic population lived in tribal relations, with pastoral-agricultural economy. Under the Roman rule cities sprang up in the interior as well as on the coasts, and the municipal organization of local government — the Hellenic-Latin type of political organization — was extended through the greater part of Spain. The native speech was gradually supplanted by Latin and the native customs were replaced by Roman law. To the Roman world Spain gave writers, jurists and emperors. Christianity gained an early footing in the coast cities, and at the close of the second century of the Christian Era all that part of Spain that had been thoroughly Romanized appears to have become Christian.

Early in the fifth century, as we have already seen, Spain fell under Germanic rule — at first, under the rule of the Vandals and Suevi. In 429 the Visigoths drove the Vandals out of Spain and into Africa. The kingdom established by the Suevi in the northwest maintained, however, a separate existence until 585 when it was overthrown by the Visigoths. From this time the Visigothic kingdom included the whole peninsula except the extreme south, which was occupied by the forces of the East Roman emperor in 534. In the course of ninety years of conflict the Visigoths expelled the Byzantines first from their inland possessions and then in 624 from the coast cities. Early in the eighth century the Visigothic king was overthrown by the Moors.

As already noted, the Visigoths, like the other Germanic tribes who were familiar with Roman usages, quartered or thirded themselves upon the Roman landowners. Aside from this partial expropriation, the Roman provincials retained their possessions and, if they were personally free, their freedom also. They lived for more than a century and a half by their own law, and it does not appear that in the earlier period of Gothic rule the Roman municipal organization was disturbed. The Goths, like other Germans, had little liking for city life.

Here, as in the other Germanic kingdoms established on Roman soil, the fusion of the two races was long delayed by differences of creed. The Gothic law itself at first forbade marriages between Goths and Romans. Before the close of the sixth century, however, the Goths accepted the orthodox Catholic creed, and a law passed in the middle of the following century legalized Gothic-Roman intermarriages.

In Gothic Spain, as in other kingdoms established by the Germans on Roman soil, the municipal type of local government was replaced by the county system. Dukes or counts were appointed by the Gothic king to govern the various provinces and cities. These officers at the outset held office for five years only, unless reappointed. At the close of the Gothic period, however, these offices were held for life. These local officials and the officials of the palace who conducted the central administration were the secular magnates. When the Goths abjured Arianism, the Catholic prelates also were treated as magnates.

The Visigothic kings were elected by the magnates. The traditional right of every freeman to participate in the election survived only in a custom by which the new king after election was presented to the people of the city in which the election had been held and was acclaimed by the crowd.

A considerable number of the Visigothic kings came to the throne by successful sedition, sometimes by conspiracy and murder of their predecessors, sometimes through open revolt. In all such cases, however, the form of subsequent election was scrupulously observed.

A maxim of ecclesiastical origin, adopted in 653 by the eighth council of Toledo and ultimately embodied in the Visigothic code, stated that the king was king so long as he did right, but when he did wrong was no longer king. However defensible as a political theory, as a legal rule this maxim was nothing less than an incentive to sedition. Its enunciation by the prelates in council was possibly due to the fact that they regarded themselves as the most competent judges of right and wrong.

When the Visigothic kings became orthodox Christians,

they became also, in form at least, heads of the Spanish church, but in fact the church became the dominant power in the kingdom.

National councils of the Spanish church were held at brief intervals and usually in Toledo. In the seventh century there were fifteen such councils. They were convoked by the king and he presented a schedule of business, presided over the deliberations and sanctioned the resolutions adopted. These resolutions or canons went far beyond the field of ecclesiastical legislation and covered a large part of the field which we should call constitutional. They dealt, for example, with the office and prerogatives of the king, the mode of his election and the law of treason. They distinguished crown property from the private property of the king. It was a church council that established in 638 a rule that dukes and counts should be deprived of their offices only for cause and after a hearing. This of course gave the dukes and counts a life tenure.

To the eighth council of Toledo, held in the year 653, the secular magnates were summoned, and from this time they sat with the prelates with the right of voting, at least upon matters not distinctly ecclesiastical. Here then we have a parliament of the sort established almost everywhere through the middle ages; but here the ecclesiastical magnates were far more numerous than the secular. In the eighth council, for example, there were seventy-four ecclesiastics and sixteen secular magnates. In summoning his secular officials to attend this eighth council, the first to which they were invited, the king declares that they are summoned in order that they may become imbued with the principles according to which they should administer their charges.

This parliament, if we may so call it, is the regular legislature of the kingdom. As in the election of a king, so in the matter of legislation, the earlier rights of the whole body of freemen were at least ceremonially recognized. Measures of particular importance, adopted by the council, were proclaimed to the people assembled before the doors of the church, and the people shouted their approval.

To the predominance of the ecclesiastical hierarchy, some historians, and among them some Spanish writers, attribute the fall of the Visigothic monarchy. It was, they say, because the power of the state was undermined by priestly rule that it fell before the first shock of the Moorish invasion. The majority of Catholic historians, however, and apparently with justice, attribute the weakness of the state to the elective character of the monarchy, the increasing independence and ambition of the magnates, secular as well as spiritual, and the resultant civil discords.

SECTION 17

Visigothic Legislation

Until the middle of the seventh century the Goths lived by Gothic law and the Romans by Roman law. In controversies between Goths and Romans Gothic law was applied. We find, accordingly, as in Burgundy, a double current of legislation. While on the one hand Gothic customs are set forth and developed in the form of royal laws, on the other hand a compilation of Roman law was made under royal authority for the use of the Roman subjects of the Gothic kings.

Alaric II (484–507), the last Gothic king who ruled both in Southern Gaul and in Spain, caused to be made for the use of his Roman subjects a compilation of Roman law. It was prepared by a committee of provincial Roman lawyers and was submitted to and accepted by an assembly of bishops and other provincial notables in Gascony in the year 506. Dahn plausibly suggests that it was made in view of the impending conflict with the Franks which broke out in the following year and resulted in the expulsion of the Visigoths from Gaul. The provincials, as we have seen, were in sympathy with the orthodox Frank king as against their heterodox Gothic ruler, and this compilation, tending to secure for them the effective observance of their own law, was very possibly intended to reconcile them to the Visigothic rule.

The original manuscript of this code was placed in the royal archives at Toulouse and all copies sent out were attested to by the royal referendary (chancellor) Anianus. For this reason the code came to be called the Breviary of Anianus, and it is still so described by the majority of Spanish legal historians. In other European countries it is known as the Breviary of Alaric or the Roman Law of the Visigoths. It had no short official title. In his attests Anianus describes it as a "codex selected from the laws of the Theodosian code, from legal decisions and from various books." This is a fairly accurate description.

Outside of Spain the Breviary of Alaric was largely used as a source of Roman law wherever the Roman provincials were still living according to their own laws. It was so used in Gaul, since no compilation of Roman law was made under the authority of the French kings, and it seems to have been frequently used, whenever Roman law was wanted, in all parts of the Frank Empire except Italy.

It was well known in England also, and down to the twelfth century it was the chief and almost the only source from which Roman law was drawn in western Europe. Nearly all references to Roman law in French, German or English literature down to the twelfth century and nearly all bits of Roman law inserted in the law books of the period can be traced back to this Visigothic compilation.

With its suppression in Spain its rules were by no means discarded, for many of its provisions passed over into the general law of the Visigothic kingdom.

Even before the compilation of Alaric's Roman law book the existence of the two systems of law had led to an effort to set forth the customary law of the Goths. A code of Visigothic law was published in the reign of King Eurich (466-84), the conqueror of Spain.

In the National Library at Paris there is a palimpsest containing a portion of these old Gothic laws. There are strong reasons for believing that they are part of Eurich's fifth-century code in its original form. This is Brunner's view; and if this be true, this Paris palimpsest is the oldest existing manuscript of German legislation.

These ancient laws are substantially statements of old Gothic custom with some newer rules regarding the relations between the Goths and the Romans. There are, however, not a few rules of Roman origin.

This code, like all the early written laws of the Germans, is in Latin; and in many cases the form of statement suggests that provincial Roman lawyers aided in framing it.

In the seventh century begins a new era in Visigothic legislation. The laws issued in the reign of Chindasvind (641-52) bind Goths and Romans alike. His son Reccesvind, who reigned until 672, carried the work of establishing a common law for both races to its conclusion. It was in his reign that intermarriage between Goths and Romans was legalized. It was he who forbade the application of Roman or other foreign law. He revised and republished the ancient Gothic laws and those issued by his father and himself. Before the close of his reign he caused this whole maze of legislation to be adjusted on a new and more systematic plan suggested by that on which the Theodosian code was arranged. His code is divided into twelve books and subdivided into titles. In each title come first a series of laws described as ancient (*lex antiqua* or *lex antiqua noviter amendata*) and among these we find many of the same laws that are found in the Paris palimpsest. After these ancient laws come laws issued by his father and by himself. About seven-tenths of the laws are ancient; of the rest, about half are his father's and half his own.

Reccesvind forbade under heavy fine the production in courts of justice of any other laws than those contained in his revised code. If any older copies of Visigothic laws were produced, the judge was to seize and destroy them.

This code was subjected to later revisions. A final revision was made by Egrica (687-701) who inserted some laws of his own and restored some laws omitted by Erwig.

As compared with the earliest statements of historic law, the legislation of Reccesvind and of his successors is more verbose and less clear. More and more Roman law, civil and canon, finds its way into the code. In the attempt to establish common law for the two races concessions were made to the Romans; and as the Goths became more civilized, Roman rules suited them in many instances better than their own cruder customs. In the code of Reccesvind there are many rules taken from the Breviary of Alaric or borrowed from the law books of Justinian, which had been introduced in southern Spain during the Byzantine occupation (534-624). In consequence of the increasing influence of the church, not a little canon law was gradually incorporated into the secular legislation. It seems clear that all the later revisions of the code were made by ecclesiastics; and it is certain that they were submitted to the national councils, which, as we have seen, contained more prelates than barons. Ecclesiastical influence is everywhere revealed: most obviously perhaps in the law of marriage, in the punishment of sexual offences, in the laws against the Jews, and in lengthy preambles, which precede the various titles and sometimes introduce single laws, and which seek with frequent quotations from Holy Writ to justify their provisions.

In the end — that is, at the beginning of the eighth century — the Visigothic code had become distinctly ecclesiastical in its form and Roman rather than Gothic in its substance. Leaving out of consideration rules which may have been derived either from Gothic or from Roman civil or canon law and confining our comparison to the distinctively Gothic and distinctively Roman elements, we find the Roman preponderant. The most Germanic part of the code is matrimonial property law. As Tacitus remarks of the Germans in his time, the wife does not bring dowery to her husband; on the contrary, the husband gives dower to the wife. There is no separation of goods during marriage nor any control by the wife of her share of the property, but a community of goods under the husband's administration.

In the law of torts and crimes, we find a curious combination of Germanic and Roman penalties. Murder — that is, homicide with malice aforethought — is punished with death. In case of conspiracy to murder, however, the death penalty is inflicted only upon the person who committed the murder; those who instigated or abetted the deed pay composition (*wergeld*) to the wife and next of kin. For all injuries to the person short of death, we find definite compositions varying with the degree of injury. There are fixed compositions, for example, to be paid for mutilations of the hand — the largest for cutting off the whole hand, the next for cutting off the thumb, the smallest for cutting off the little finger.

The courts were organized on Roman rather than Germanic lines. In the local courts there is no recognition of any participation of assembled freemen in the finding of judgments; and the fact that the presiding royal official sat with advisers skilled in the law indicates that he rendered judgment. From the courts of first instance in city and country, appeals ran to the courts of the counts, and from these to the king's court. In the king's court the king renders decision, again with the advice of councillors. In both cases it is to be noted that advice given to count or king is not binding upon him; he has the power to decide and responsibility for the decision. This rule is distinctly Roman, and these councillors accordingly were not Germanic judgment-finders.

The ecclesiastical influence which appears to have determined this organization showed itself particularly in that the prelates had the right and the duty of watching over the administration of justice and denouncing any defects which they might observe.

Judicial procedure also was Romanized. The Germanic methods of proof, oath, oath-help and ordeal were not recognized. Evidence was given not only by ceremonial witnesses but also by accidental witnesses, and documentary evidence played an important part. Torture was freely used in criminal proceedings, as in the late Roman Empire. Penalties were severe and often cruel. Germanic, on the other hand, is the penalty of *decalvatio*, which some earlier historians interpreted to mean scalping, but which in fact consisted only in cutting off the hair, which to the early Germanic mind signified a total loss of honor. Germanic also, or rather simply primitive, was the provision made in certain cases for delivery of the wrongdoer to the wronged party for retaliation.

The Visigothic code was of course not a complete exposition of the legal rules by which the people of Spain were governed. No code ever is complete, not even a twentieth-century code. The Visigothic kings, or the churchmen who worked under their authority, were, however, anxious that the code should be made complete, and they anticipated the scheme advocated by Jeremy Bentham in that they directed the judges, whenever a case should arise not covered by the written laws, to refer it to the king in order that he might not only settle the special controversy but consider whether supplementary legislation were needed. (*Lex Vis.* II, 1, 11.)

It is uncertain how far the rules laid down in the Visigothic code were actually enforced and prevailed in practice. The Visigothic kingdom was frequently torn by civil discord and was at times almost in a state of anarchy. After its destruction by the Moors, we find in the northern Spanish kingdoms of the middle ages institutions characteristically Teutonic and unrecognized in the Visigothic code. For example: feud and extrajudicial composition; proof in judicial proceedings by compurgation and by ordeal. When the customary law observed in these new kingdoms begins to take written form, we find that concubinage (*barragania*) has legal recognition, even where there is also a lawful wife, that there may be investigation of paternity of children, and that sons born of a concubine, or whose paternity has been established, have rights of succession. These later rules, as has been shown by the Austrian historian Ficker, have analogies in Scandinavian law and were probably Gothic. In consequence of the prompt reversion of the Spanish people to more primitive customs and rules, some legal historians infer that the Visigothic code was never fully enforced and that its rules represent the aspirations of churchmen to get their moral ideals on the statute book — a tendency that is not confined to ecclesiastics and is sometimes observed even in modern legislation.

In the eighth and following centuries, after the conquests of the Moors, the Visigothic code was sometimes cited in the Latin as the Law or Laws of the Goths, or the Book of the Goths, sometimes as the Book of Laws or the Book of Judgments or the Book of Judges. *Forum judicum (Gothorum)* is a title found as early as the year 932, and in the eleventh and following centuries this is the most common designation of the code. In the vernacular it became *Fuero juzgo*. This latter title is still commonly used by Spanish legal historians.

The Visigothic code was first translated into the vernacular at the instance of Ferdinand III of Castile and Leon (1229-34) and was given as local law or Fuero to the town of Cordova. Of printed Latin editions the oldest appeared at Paris in 1579. A text published by Villadiego at Madrid in 1600 was regarded as authoritative until a new edition was prepared under the auspices of the Spanish Academy and published in 1815.

SECTION 18

The Frank Empire: Historical Data

In the fourth century we find Franks of the Salian branch south and west of the lower Meuse and extending their occupation up the valley of the Scheldt. They recognized the authority of the Roman Empire, particularly that of the Roman officials in Gaul. In the fifth century they crossed the Scheldt, and by the middle of the century they had occupied northeastern Gaul as far as the Somme. Up to this point the movement was a popular one induced mainly by land hunger. They settled the country as they pressed forward. In this occupation there was no partition of land between Franks and provincials; the provincial proprietors were simply ousted.

Of a different character were the conquests of King Clovis (481–511). In these we find distinct royal initiative and the purpose to establish royal authority. In the year 486 Clovis conquered northern Gaul as far as the Seine. Later in his reign he subdued the country between the Seine and the Loire. In the year 496 he conquered the Allemanni and annexed a portion of their territory. The rest of the tribe sought and received the protection of the Ostrogoths, whose empire at the time extended as far as the Provence.

The conversion of Clovis to Christianity of the orthodox type brought the most important and capable organization in the decadent Roman world, the Latin church, to his support. Welcomed by the Gallican clergy as a servant and agent of God, he attacked the heretical Visigoths, and between the years 507 and 510 wrested from them the territory between the Loire and the Pyrenees. Under the sons of Clovis the Thuringians were conquered (531) and the Burgundian kingdom was overthrown (532). The conflict between the Ostrogoths and the East Roman Empire, which ended in the overthrow of the Ostrogothic monarchy, enabled the Franks to annex southeastern Gaul and to extend their authority in what is today southwestern Germany. Before the end of the sixth century the Bavarians were also brought under Frank authority.

An important difference between the empire established by the Franks and those established by the Ostrogoths, Visigoths, and Vandals was that instead of pushing into purely Romanic territory and ultimately losing themselves there, the Franks alternately extended their rule into Roman and into German territory. This remained true as late as the time of Charlemagne, who annexed the Langobard kingdoms in Italy and wrested northeastern Spain from the Moors, but who at the same time subjected the Saxons to Frank authority and pushed the frontier of his realm farther east.

Under weaker successors the great territorial magnates, originally and in theory crown officers, became more and more independent. In accordance with Frank theory, which regarded the royal power as property and recognized equal claims of all sons to succession, there were frequent divisions of the realm. In every case the different parts of the realm were later reunited, but sometimes only by means of civil war. In these wars the magnates were able to sell support in return for concessions, and the power of the kings was steadily weakened. In almost every division there was a tendency for at least a temporary separation of Roman from Teutonic territories, like that which finally came in the ninth century. The dissolution of the realm was postponed when the powerful house of Amalfings, better known from their most illustrious representative as that of the Carolingians, brought into their hands as mayors of the palace the actual control of the whole realm, which was later legalized by the deposition of the last Merovingian king and the assumption of the royal title by Pepin. The Carolingian rulers established a much stronger central government than the Merovingians had ever attempted to develop. They undertook to reform and modify local institutions and customs which the Merovingians had not disturbed. They began to create a body of uniform imperial law. Their relation to the church became much closer. Pepin obtained a papal sanction for his usurpation of the royal power, and he in turn forced the subjects of the Frank Empire who were still heathen to embrace Christianity. The Carolingians granted to the church greater influence upon the life of the people, making it to a considerable extent a coördinate branch of government. They protected the Pope against his adversaries in Italy, the Langobards.

The Frank Empire reached the height of its power under Charlemagne (768–814). He conquered Lombardy and assumed the title of "King of the Franks and Langobards" (774). He forced the Saxons and the East Frisians under Frank supremacy and into the Christian church. He brought the Bavarians and other German tribes, which had formed small subkingdoms in the empire with their old dynasties, under the direct authority of the crown. He pushed the frontier of the empire eastward by successful war against the Avars, and farther to the southwest by victorious conflict with the Moors and the annexation of Catalonia.

The position which Charlemagne had obtained as ruler of nearly all the Christian world except that which belonged to the East Roman Empire, as ruler of nearly all the Christian world that recognized the supreme authority of the Bishop of Rome, and the protectorate which he exercised over the church led to his coronation at Rome, Christmas

800, as emperor. Here we have not only a revival of ideas that had played a rôle during the establishment of Germanic kingdoms on Roman soil, and especially of the idea that in some sort all governmental power was derived from the Roman Empire, but we have also a new and distinctly ecclesiastical idea. As protector of Catholic Christendom, the emperor is to secure and defend the ecclesiastical unity of the western world. In this world there is to be one supreme secular and one supreme ecclesiastical head.

This involved a conflict between the imperial idea and older Frank ideas and customs, a conflict in particular between the indivisibility of imperial authority and the divisibility of royal authority. The imperial idea could triumph only if a strong feeling of unity could be established among all the peoples of the empire. In fact this feeling existed only among the higher clergy and the Frank nobility. The more rapid centralization of power which began after the coronation of Charlemagne intensified particularistic feeling among the different German tribes and strengthened centrifugal tendencies. The compromise planned by Louis the Pious — namely, a division of royal power among his sons, with recognition of a superior authority of the eldest son as emperor — led to a conflict which resulted in the division of the empire in 843.

Weakened by internal dissension, the empire proved unable to protect its frontiers. The eastern Franks successfully resisted the attacks of the Slavs, but the rulers of the western part of the empire were less successful in resisting the Moors in Spain and in protecting their coasts against the attacks of Scandinavian pirates. In the year 885, largely on account of the inroads of the Northmen, the empire was reunited under Charles III, "the Fat." His incompetency resulted in the election of his nephew Arnulf as king of the East Franconian tribes. In the year 888 Charles abdicated and the final division of the empire took place. There were at first five kingdoms: a West Frank and an East Frank kingdom — the starting points of the future France and Germany — and three middle kingdoms, the Lower Burgundian, the Upper Burgundian, and the Italian. In the course of the middle ages Italy and Burgundy were temporarily brought under the authority of the Holy Roman Empire of the German nation, but the separation between West Franconia and East Franconia, between France and Germany, remained permanent.

The Frank Empire thus represents a transitional stage in the development of Europe which was followed by the gradual creation of national states. But this empire gave medieval and modern Europe certain common points of departure: it created certain common ideas of civilization and of law which have not yet lost their force in western and central Europe. In particular the notion of the ecclesiastical unity of western Europe survived until the Reformation. The notion of a community of Christian nations lasted even longer and profoundly influenced the development of international law. The theory that all power was somehow derived from the old Roman Empire, the theory of "continuous empire," helped to secure a general reception of Roman law at the close of the middle ages.

SECTION 19

The Frank Empire: Economic and Social Conditions

In Gaul at the period of the Frank conquest there was practically no middle class. The land was held chiefly by the emperor or by municipalities, by the church and by a small and powerful secular aristocracy. In the fourth and fifth centuries the small landholders had surrendered their independence to obtain protection: they had become tenants or serfs. Here, as in other parts of the Roman Empire, the *coloni*, who were originally free tenant farmers, had become serfs. Free tenants of leased land were still to be found, but the greater part of the land was tilled by serfs or slaves.

In the German portion of the empire, we find at the outset a greater economic equality. Separate ownership of arable land generally prevailed. In the villages a degree of communal control of the mode of cultivation still existed. Alienation of land was impeded at first by the recognition of certain residuary or eventual rights of all the villagers, and later by the recognition of rights of the family. All through the middle ages we find the notion of family right in land expressing itself in various ways, particularly in family rights of preëmption in case of sale and even a right of repurchase within a term of years.

During the Frank period, however, there was a steadily increasing inequality of possession in the German territories. The kings were from the outset great landholders. The notion that forest and waste land belongs to the people disappears, and it is held that all such land that is not within the limits of the village or in the possession of individuals belongs to the king.

The dukes of many of the German tribes held also large tracts of land.

Great tracts of land passed into the hands of the church, partly by gifts from individuals. The zeal for endowing the church with gifts for the good of the donor's soul reached its highest point at the time of Charles the Great. In many cases we find that the donor retains a life interest but bestows the reversion after death, the remainder, upon the church. An imperial ordinance of 811 censures certain methods employed by ecclesiastics to obtain gifts of land.

There were other forces working for inequality.

Large estates were building up, or estates already large were becoming larger, through the clearing of forest land. Where such clearings were made within the recognized territory of a village, the result was either an increase in the possessions of each household or the creation of a new village with equal rights on the part of all the free inhabitants. Where clearings were made in the king's forests, on the other hand, all the land cleared belonged to the new occupant, subject to the payment of a moderate fee or rent to the crown, even though no permission to clear had been previously obtained. Where such permission had been granted, the new occupant obtains complete and unincumbered ownership. Such clearings were most easily made by individuals who could command a considerable amount of labor power — by nobles, that is, who already had large holdings and many dependents.

The establishment of rights of inheritance to land, first in the case of sons, later in the case of collaterals, operated of course in some cases to divide *hufen* — that is, estates sufficing only for the maintenance of a single family — into portions inadequate for such maintenance. In other cases, of course, inheritance concentrated many holdings in single hands.

Fines and compositions, in many cases, operated to impoverish the small landholders. The *wergeld* in ordinary cases amounted to 160 *solidi*, and with the peace money or fine paid to the court, to 200 *solidi*. Among the Franks the *wergeld* rose in some cases — for example, in the case of the slaying of a retainer of the king — to 1800 *solidi*. What this meant is indicated by the fact that the price of an ox varied from 1 to 3 *solidi* and that the value of the ordinary *hufe*, or small family holding, appears to have been about 200 *solidi*. In many cases the payment of large fines would have been impossible but for the duty of the wrongdoer's kinsmen to pay at least half of the fine. This rule, however, not only impoverished the wrongdoer but weighed very heavily upon the whole kinship group.

The duty of the common freeman to attend all courts held within the hundred or within the county, to attend special sessions as well as regular sessions, obviously interfered with the cultivation of small holdings and constituted a serious burden upon the small freeholders. There is evidence that some local officers of the crown called frequent sessions of court in order to impose fines for non-attendance.

A still more serious burden upon the small freeholder was imposed by duties of military service. Since the German army was substantially an army of foot soldiers and military duty was exacted of every freeman, the burden of military service, particularly in the case of frontier wars, became ultimately unendurable.

Gradually, and especially in the reign of Charlemagne, the judicial and military duties imposed upon the small landholders were considerably lessened, but until this relief was granted many small freeholders seem to have been forced into surrender of their holdings to magnates, receiving in return the position of free tenants or, in some cases, of serfs, together with protection by the landlord. Where the tenure carried with it rights of protection the tenant was no longer regarded as fully free. In the ninth century royal commissioners reported that many freemen had been forced into dependence in consequence of misuse of official authority on the part of local officers of government. It seems that the counts who held royal lands only as an appanage of their office and during their continuance in office were endeavoring to build up independent personal holdings.

During the period under review the *sib*, or kinship group, which played so important a rôle in early Germanic life, was being deprived of what may be called its public powers by the state and of its private law powers by the increasing importance and autonomy of the narrower family, the household. What may be called public law powers are passing not only to the state but to magnates. In proportion to the weakening of the kinship group, relations of protection and allegiance between persons not of kin — relations such as we find largely developed in the feudal system — were steadily increasing. A lord or *seigneur* gives more effective protection than the *sib*. An illustration of the diminishing importance of the *sib* is found in the matter of guardianship. The right and duty of the kinship group to protect widows and orphans is being replaced partly by the gradual transfer of this right and duty to the next of kin and partly by development of a superior guardianship on the part of the state. Charlemagne in particular insists upon his duty and right to defend widows, orphans, and other helpless people and calls upon his commissioners (*missi*) to give such protection. The rights of the *sib* are still largely recognized in the matter of assent to marriage. A strong tendency appears to promote marriage within the kinship group in order to keep the property of the group intact. This meant a tendency to objectionable inbreeding and met with strong opposition on the part of the church.

In studying the social organization of the period we have in the *wergelder* a quantitative measurement of the valuation of the various social classes, and we find changes in the position of a class or of a portion of a class gradually revealing themselves in changes of *wergeld*. There are different valuations not only as regards the Germanic social classes but also as regards different races. The *wergeld* of the Roman was at the outset only half that of the free German. Whether Jews were treated as Romans is disputed. Brunner thinks this was true as regards the Jews settled in Gaul and in other Roman provinces. Other Jews were regarded as a distinct race, and in the written laws they have no *wergeld*. They buy the protection of the king, and Louis I imposed a very large fine for the slaying of a king's Jew. It is, however, fine, not *wergeld;* the whole sum goes to the royal treasury.

The number of slaves in the empire was greatly increased. There were of course many slaves in Gaul before the German conquests, and not a few free Romans became slaves as a result of capture in battle by the invading Germans. In Gaul in the Merovingian period, slaves formed an important item both in inland and import trade. At the beginning of the ninth century, as a result of warfare against the Slavs in the east, numerous captives were brought into the empire, and in addition to the old German words for slave, *knecht, schalk*, the new word *slav* appeared and found its way into nearly all the west European languages.

During this period the legal position of slaves was improving. They gained, first among the Franks and in south Germany, later among the Saxons and Frisians, a limited legal capacity. The fine paid for killing a slave ranged in the earlier laws from 12 to 15 *solidi*. This is gradually tripled and in some cases brought up to half the *wergeld* of the half freemen, so that it looks more like a small *wergeld* than like a fine. At the beginning of the ninth century it is called *wergeld* or *leudis;* and while the whole sum in most of the laws is still paid to the master, we find (appearing in some of the laws — for example, among the Lombards) a claim of the slave's widow and children to a part of this composition.

There is a greater improvement of status among certain classes of slaves. In the later Roman Empire, particularly in Gaul, many agricultural slaves were placed in charge of special holdings of land and their actual position came to be that of serfs rather than slaves. They pay rent in money or in kind and are usually not disturbed in their possession as long as the rent is paid; and when the land is sold they usually go with the land like the *coloni.* These were the *servi inquilini.* We find a similar development in the German territories: the housed slaves (*servi casati*) rise into the position of serfs, and in the early ninth century they are regarded not as chattels but as real property. In the royal domains the fiscal slaves have practical security of tenure, and this tenure is becoming heritable. It is also becoming alienable: they may sell their holdings. We find a similar improvement among the slaves of the church. It was perhaps first on the church lands that slaves were put in charge of separate farms with a definite rent and with fixed or limited services to be rendered.

In the class of household slaves — *famuli, pueri, vassi, vasalli* (Celtic *gwas*) — the improvement of position as indicated by the *wergeld* came earlier and was greater. It was here that the valuation first rose to 50 *solidi.* Among the Franks the cost of killing a household slave, including the peace money, rose to 75 *solidi.* The household slaves of the king, (*ministeriales*) played an important rôle in the Frank Empire. They were appointed in some cases to public office. With the development of the feudal cavalry, as will be noted later, not only did many of the king's household slaves but also many of the slaves of the magnates rise into the position of knights.

In the half-free class (*liti*), which included manumitted slaves, there was on the whole no general increase of *wergeld*. It varied in the different laws (from one-third to two-thirds of the *wergeld* of the freeman) but was usually one-half — that is, 100 *solidi*. There was a gradual improvement, however, in both their economic and their legal status. The services to be rendered seem to have been lessened. In judicial procedure they need no longer be represented by their lord. They could appear in court and take oaths. If land on which they have been established is sold, they go with it. Their position is the same as that of the *coloni* in the Roman parts of the Frank Empire. As long as the free Roman had only half the *wergeld* of the free German — that is, 100 *solidi* — the *colonus* in Gaul had a *wergeld* of only 50 *solidi*. In later laws, however, the *wergeld* of the Roman *colonus* rises to 100 *solidi*.

The half-free class was greatly increased during this period by manumission. The new forms of manumission introduced by the church — manumission in *ecclesia* and by testament — obtained general recognition; but, in accordance with German ideas, such manumission does not make the former slave full free. In the case of manumission in the church or by testament, the church authorities claim and exercise a right of protection over their former slaves. Forms of manumission by which the former slave or half freeman may become full free were still recognized, the most commonly employed being manumission by the penny (*per denarium*) in the presence of the king or in the presence of the duke of the Bavarians, who in the earlier Frankish period retained this and other vestiges of royal right. The penny freeman (*denariales*) were valued at 200 *solidi*, but this was fine, not *wergeld;* it all went to the king.

During this period the old Germanic tribal nobility still existed, but a new noble class was developing, whose nobility was based on service to the king. Among the Franks, according to the earliest historical evidence, the only class standing above the common freeman was composed of members of the royal family. It seems probable that an older and a larger noble class had been crushed by the development of a strong monarchy. Among the other German tribes, we find the older hereditary Germanic nobility. The noble has a higher *wergeld*, which varies from 300 *solidi* among the central Frisians to 1200 *solidi* among the Saxons. Among the Saxons, nobles were more distinctly a separate caste than among the German tribes. They did not intermarry with the common free class. They became reconciled to the rule of the Frankish monarch more rapidly than the rest of the Saxon people. They took no part in any revolt against the Frank Empire after the death of Louis the Pious. As early as the year 782 some of the Saxon nobles were made royal counts. The medieval Saxon nobility was partly based on the old tribal nobility and partly on the new nobility of royal service.

The new official nobility was developed first and most strongly among the Franks. Royal service gave a higher *wergeld*. The counts, the *missi* and the retainers of the king had in each case three times the *wergeld* of the common freeman. This new nobility was at first not a true class: it was open from below and was not hereditary. At the close of the Frank period, however, when royal offices and their endowments of land were tending to become hereditary, the new service nobility was fairly started.

After the dissolution of the Frank Empire, the old tribal nobility gradually disappeared everywhere except among the Frisians, where the distinction between ethelings, common freemen and half freemen was recognized as late as the fifteenth century. The higher nobility of medieval Europe was derived from the official nobility developed in the Frank period.

In Gaul before the Germanic conquests there was something amounting to a noble class, having its economic basis in extensive territorial possessions, and a certain official basis in service rendered to the empire. These were the *nobiles* or *honorati*. In the kingdom of the Burgundians they were put upon the same footing with the old Burgundian nobility. The Franks, however, recognized no legal superiority of this class in Gaul. The *wergeld* of the Roman magnate, like that of other free Romans, was only 100 *solidi*. By royal service, however, or by the attainment of ecclesiastical dignity, the Roman might obtain a higher *wergeld*. The sole basis of the later French nobility seems, accordingly, to have been service to the kings of the Franks.

During this period the common free class was disintegrating. Some members of the class were rising through service, the majority were sinking as a result of economic dependence. Where freeholds were converted into leaseholds, the former owner, as long as he kept his place in the local courts and in the army, does not seem to have suffered any loss of legal status. He had generally the same *wergeld* as the other freemen who had remained freeholders. The payment of rent did not affect his position as long as the payment was simply economic rent. Where, however, the former freeman who had surrendered his land to a lord is not only paying economic rent but is also paying for protection (*schutzzins*), he is sinking into serfdom. The conversion of former freeholders into serfs was closely connected with the development of the manorial jurisdiction in the immunity, a matter to be treated later when we consider the development of the feudal system.

SECTION 20

The Frank Empire: Legal Development

In the Frank Empire there was an extraordinary diversity of legal systems. Not only do the members of each German tribe live by their own law, but the Romans, the conquered provincials, are also entitled to live by their law. This principle, as we have seen, was recognized in the other kingdoms established on Roman territory as far as the relations between the Romans themselves were concerned; but when a controversy arose between a Burgundian, a Lombard, or a Visigoth and a Roman, it was not the Roman but the German tribal law that was applied. In the Frank Empire a different principle was established. It was recognized that the claim of the Roman to live by Roman law had the same force and validity as the right of a Frank or Bavarian to live by Frank or Bavarian law. It seems probable that this new principle was first recognized as regards the other German tribes that were brought under Frank rule, and was based on a desire to secure to the Franks everywhere in the empire the protection of their own tribal laws. The equality of the various tribal laws having once been established, the principle was extended to include the Roman law. The general principle was that Germans and Romans alike lived by the law of their birth.

The Roman law of the provincials was a greatly simplified form of Roman law. The so-called "vulgar" Roman law of the provinces was based rather on the practical needs of an economic life that had become far simpler than that of the early Roman Empire than on legal tradition or logic. This vulgar Roman law was related to the older imperial law very much as the spoken Latin was related to the written classical tongue.

The personal law (*lex originis*) was determined by descent. Legitimate children lived by the father's law, illegitimate children by the mother's, the wife by that of her husband. The widow regularly remained under the husband's law as she remained under the guardianship of her husband's kin. In Italy, however, in the ninth century an ordinance of Lothair I established the opposite principle that upon the death of the husband the widow's birth law reverted.

The personal law of the freedman was determined to some extent by the form of manumission. Those manumitted by the penny in the presence of the king lived by the personal law of the king — that is, by Frank law. Those manumitted by testament, by charter, or in the church lived by the Roman law. In other cases a freedman lived by the law of the former master. In the later Lombard law this last rule was extended to all freedmen.

Not all the clergy lived, at the outset, under Roman law. In the Frank Empire this was the case only so long as the clergy was wholly or mainly Roman by birth. In the earliest Frank law, for example, the *wergeld* of a priest, like that of other free Romans, was only 100 *solidi*. Later, however, when men of German birth became priests they retained the *wergeld* of their birth. Throughout the Frank Empire the later rule was that each clergyman, from deacon to bishop, lived by the law of his birth. A different idea seems to have prevailed in Lombardy. In the eleventh century at least, Lombard jurists regarded the subjection of all the clergy to the Roman law as an ancient, well-settled rule.

The alien — the person, that is, who was born outside of the empire of the Franks — was regarded, as he was generally regarded in the early law everywhere, as having no law, as being out of the law. As in other systems of early law, he may be protected by guest right or hospitality, becoming a member of the host's household. He may also buy protection without becoming the member of any household. At a later period he may obtain protection through treaty with his nation.

Among the various Germanic peoples there seems to have developed early a notion that the alien who enjoyed no other protection was entitled to the protection of the king. From this there developed later a practically exclusive right of the king to protect aliens, and the sale of such protection became, in medieval Europe, an important source of royal revenue. If the foreigner was slain, the Anglo-Saxon king shared the *wergeld* with the kin of the slain man. Among the Franks the alien who had bought royal protection lived by the king's law — that is, by Frank law — and his *wergeld* went wholly to the king. Among the Franks the king succeeded to all the property of the alien who had died within the realm. In Lombardy the king was heir to the alien only if the alien left no sons. In these royal rights derived from the right of protection, we have, of course, the starting point for the *jus albinagii* or *droit d'aubaine* of the middle ages.

For the various German tribes and for the Romans it came to be recognized, as we have seen, that every man had the right to live by his own law. In the Frank Empire this meant frequent conflict of laws. There was no complete territorial separation between Romans and Germans or between the different German tribes. Salian Franks settled as landholders all over the empire. In certain parts of the empire, notably in Burgundy and in north Italy, the population was so mixed that it was hardly possible to speak of any dominant territorial law. Agobard, the Bishop of Lyons, wrote: "It often happens that five men walk or sit together of whom no one has a law in common with another." In north Italy there was even greater confusion. Here were men living under Roman law, Langobard law, Frank law, Allemannic and other German tribal laws. According to charters or deeds drawn between 850 and 1000 the majority of the great landowners in north Italy were Franks and Allemanni.

When representatives of the two races met in transactions, in suits, etc., it was, of course, necessary to find some solution for these conflicts of law. To a considerable extent such solutions were found, and the rules developed in the Frank Empire form the starting point of modern European international private law. These rules cannot properly be called rules of international private or criminal law because, as we have seen, aliens — that is, men living outside the Frank Empire — had no rights in that empire. The rules developed were applied only to men living under Frank rule.

Some of the principal rules established are as follows:

(1) *Wergeld* was determined by the birth law of the person slain. So also all compositions for less serious personal injuries.

(2) In distinctly criminal cases, on the other hand, where it is a question not of the composition to be paid to the injured person but of the sum with which the wrongdoer can escape physical punishment, the fine goes to the court. The pecuniary penalty is determined by the birth law of the wrongdoer.

After the year 800 a new principle makes its appearance — namely, the application of the law of the place where the offense was committed. This of course meant the law most generally used in the locality, and is an indication of the emergence of local custom as against personal law.

(3) In civil actions the rights and obligations of the defendant are based on his birth law: so, for example, the term within which he may answer his right of proof and the form of oath and compurgation.

(4) In contracts, each party to bind himself must observe the forms of his birth law. Conveyances must be made in the form required by the law of the conveyor. This rule was at first applied to deeds conveying land. In the course of the period a tendency was developed to recognize the law of the first documentary grantor as the law governing all subsequent conveyances.

(5) In betrothal and marriage the bridegroom binds himself according to the form of his birth law. In the delivery of the woman which completed the marriage, the forms of her father's or guardian's law had to be observed.

The church resisted the application of two systems of law in the matter of marriage. In a case where a Frank forsook a Saxon wife because he had married her according to Saxon and not Frank form, the synod of Tribur declared, in the year 895, that a marriage was valid if either system of law, that of the man or that of the woman, was observed. This seems to be the first recognition of the alternative system so largely recognized today in the field of contract. Today, of course, the choice is usually between the law of the place where the contract is concluded and the law of the place of performance.

In marriage at the present time between persons of different religious faith, we find, not indeed as a matter of law but as a matter of custom, a survival of the older Germanic idea that each party should be married according to the forms of his or her confession, which means two religious ceremonies.

(6) Questions of guardianship were determined by the tribal law of the ward.

(7) Inheritance was governed by the tribal law of the deceased.

During the Frank period there were in operation forces making for unity of law or at least for the lessening of the diversity of laws.

One of these forces was imitation or the borrowing of law. The laws and customs of the different German tribes were from the outset more or less similar, the resemblances outweighing the divergences, and when they were first reduced to written form an earlier compilation in one tribe was often used in drawing up the later statement of a different tribal law.

Before these earliest compilations were made, Roman law had exercised some influence on Germanic customs and Germanic customs upon Roman law wherever the two races had been living in close touch one with the other. As we have already seen, the German tribes that were in earliest and closest contact with the Roman world — the Burgundians and the Visigoths — adopted many Roman ideas and institutions. On the other hand, Germanic institutions filtered into the Romanic portions of the empire. Toward the close of the Frank period we find documents by which Romans in Burgundy and Italy professing to act "according to my Roman law" are doing thoroughly un-Roman things. The Austrian writer, Ficker, one of the leading authorities on medieval Italian law, maintains that in Lombardy living by Roman law ultimately meant only that the persons professing Roman law were observing a few rules derived from the Roman law.

The strongest force working for unity in the empire was that of the Franks, by reason of their dominant position. To some extent Frank ideas influenced the customs of other races, to some extent they modified the written formulation of their customs. The decisions of the king's court, which in theory was controlled neither by Frank law nor by any other tribal law, were still very naturally controlled by Frank points of view. In the local courts, where one or another system of tribal law governed all proceedings, the fact that Frank officials, or at least officials who had been educated at the royal court, presided over and largely controlled both procedure and decisions had much to do with the diffusion of Frank ideas and institutions.

In the Merovingian period the influence of Frank ideas and views upon the various tribal laws was largely unpremeditated. In the Carolingian period there was an obvious desire to unify the law. In the reign of Louis the Pious the influence of the clergy was exercised in favor of uniformity. Bishop Agobard proposed that the law of the Franks be extended over the entire empire so that the realm might be ruled by one law as by one king. No such far-reaching attempt was made, but the suggestion was characteristic of the spirit of the time.

At the close of the Frank period considerable progress had been made toward minimizing divergences and unifying the law. At the end of the period the tribal laws showed no inconsiderable divergence, and even such institutions as were borrowed from the Franks underwent local modifications.

By far the most important factor making for unity of law was the development of royal law. This development proceeded along three lines — governmental custom, judicial decision, and legislation.

By virtue of their administrative power the royal officials were able to enforce a new rule without formally declaring it, and if the enforcement was constant, governmental practice became a source of law, at least coördinate with the development of law in the popular courts and with the other processes by which royal law was developing.

In the Frank monarchy an independent central legislative power was exercised by the issue of royal ordinances. Nothing quite like the Frank ordinance power is demonstrable among other Germanic tribes. It was the early development of royal power among the Franks, the establishment of a royal court, the maintenance of the peace as the "king's peace" and the appointment of royal representatives to all important judicial posts that put the kings in a position to enforce their ordinances without popular coöperation. As far as a royal ordinance introduced new rules, these were enforced not by judgments of the people or of their judgment-finders in the local courts but by executive power.

We have accordingly among the Franks a development of written law partly through action of popular assemblies, which accept a proposed new rule, and partly through royal ordinances.

Royal ordinances may be related to folk law in one of three different ways. They may supplement tribal law; they may be applied concurrently with tribal law; they may contradict and override popular law.

A very important difference between tribal and royal law is that the former, as we have seen, is personal while the latter is territorial. Ordinances were sometimes made applicable to the entire realm, sometimes to a special district. A still more important difference is that the tribal law was primitive and strict; the royal law progressive and increasingly equitable. Royal law, whether developed through ordinances or through the decisions of the royal courts, was in this period the chief method of legal reform. Toward the close of the period under review it becomes usual to submit important ordinances to the assent of the secular and spiritual magnates of the empire. The same thing had happened, as we have seen, in the kingdom of the Visigoths. We have here the beginning of the medieval system of legislation in assizes and parliaments.

In so far as royal innovations were introduced into the various systems of tribal law, either by express or tacit acceptance of local assemblies, these persisted as local custom after the dissolution of the empire. Where, on the other hand, royal law remained outside of tribal law, and was dependent for its enforcement on the royal administration, it disappeared to a large extent with the disappearance of the central authority.

SECTION 21

The Frank Empire: The Written Laws

Much more law was put into writing between the years 450 and 850 than in the following four centuries — from 850 to 1250.

We have noted already that some brief compilations of Roman law were made in Germanic kingdoms for the use of the Roman provincials. We have also seen that the contact with the Roman world led to attempts to set forth tribal customs in written form. We have seen that the Visigoths, the Burgundians, and the Langobards put their customs into the form of written law within half or three-quarters of a century after they settled on Roman soil. Turning now to the Franks and the other German tribes which came ultimately under Frank rule, we note that in the Merovingian period the tribes settled in the western and southern portions of really German territory first followed this example. In this period were formulated the laws of the Salian Franks, of the Ripuarian Franks, of the Allemanni or Swabians and, at the close of the period, of the Bavarians.

It was not until the Carolingian period that this movement spread into central and northern Germany. In this period the laws of the Frisians, of the Saxons, of the Chamavian Franks and of the Thuringians (*Angli et Werini*) were formulated. These later compilations are briefer and less interesting than those made in the Merovingian period. It would seem that these collections were regarded as less important than those made in southern and western Germany. And it seems to be clear that they were less used in the finding of judgments in the tribal courts. This is indicated by the numbers of manuscripts that have come down to us. Of the Salic law there are in existence more than sixty manuscripts; of the Allemannic or Swabian law nearly fifty, or the Ripuarian more than thirty, and of the Bavarian law thirty. On the other hand, of the Saxon law we have but two manuscripts, of the law of the Chamavi two manuscripts, of the law of the Angli and Werini one manuscript only.

Finally in the case of certain tribes in the heart of Germany, in the case of the East Franks, the Hessians and the southern Thuringians, no compilations were made.

In the middle ages these collections of tribal laws were described as *leges barbarorum*. In the manuscripts they are described sometimes as *leges*, sometimes as pacts or edicts, and in some cases the Latinized German word *ewa* is used.

In their form these different compilations are sometimes purely statements of existing custom, of the "wisdoms" handed down by tradition; in other cases the form approaches that of legislation, the rules being stated as constitutions or statutes issued by the king. Whatever form is observed, they are all in the main statements of custom; what appears as legislation is merely declaratory.

Where the form is legislative the coöperation of the people is often noted. In the Salic law the initiative is attributed to the people. In the law of the Allemanni it is declared that the magnates have united with the duke and the rest of the people in framing the law. The Langobard edict of King Rothari was approved by the judgment of the people in the ancient form of the spear clash. King Gundobad of Burgundy states that the collection is made "by the common consent of all."

The notion that all legislation is compact or agreement reveals itself in the frequent use of the word *pactus* instead of *lex*. In *Lex Salica* many sections begin "*Hoc convenit ob-*

servari." We find a similar phrase at the beginning of the law of the Allemanni.

Whether the form employed suggests legislation or a digest of ancient decisions, the wise men, the *sapientes*, are everywhere active. They either propose the form of the rules or, being questioned, give expert answers regarding the existing customs. In many cases they are described as legislators.

All these laws were written in Latin. It does not seem to have been thought possible to write German. In this respect Anglo-Saxon England was far more progressive than continental Germany. We may imagine that the earliest of these continental compilations took form in something like the following fashion. The king or duke addresses a series of questions to the wise men; they give their answer; each of these answers is accepted by the assembly; and somebody who understands the tribal dialect and can write Latin — a priest or a provincial Roman lawyer — translates the approved answer into Latin.

Throughout the period under review the influence of the monarchy on the formal declaration of tribal laws was steadily increasing. Some of the later collections made in the Carolingian period were obviously due not to any demand on the part of the tribes whose law was written down but to the desire of the king or of his court officials to carry on and complete the work of codification — to get a full set, so to speak, of tribal customs.

The real influence exercised by the kings in the Carolingian period created legends as to similar activity on the part of the Merovingians. These legends put into shape by the clergy were often prefixed, in the manuscripts that have come down to us, to the older texts of the Merovingian period. These so-called "prologues," which regularly state that the whole *lex* was drawn up on the initiative of such and such a king, frequently contain statements that are quite irreconcilable with what we know of the date of the original compilations.

Regarding the activity of Charlemagne our information is more trustworthy. He is said to have contemplated the reduction to writing of the customs of all the tribes that in his time had no written *leges*. It is asserted by some monkish historians that this plan was acutally carried out, which is not true. The compilations made in his time, however, seem to have been due to his initiative. He also took care that better and more uniform texts of some of the older Frankish laws were prepared and distributed. The court of Charlemagne was a center of learning; and the "amended laws" issued in his time were put into better Latin than that found in earlier texts.

To the different tribal laws new matter was constantly added. In the code of the Langobards, as we have seen, new legislation was added with the name in each case of the king who had proposed it, as was done in many cases in the compilations of Anglo-Saxon dooms or laws. In the other laws of the continental Germans new provisions were either put at the end of the older text without any distinct heading or they were inserted in the body of the old text in whatever way seemed fittest. It was not merely new laws — that is, new rules formally approved — that were thus inserted, but new wisdoms or expert opinions accepted in judgments rendered in the administration of the law. When the new law or judgment seemed more important or of broader application than the older rule it was sometimes put first, so that the order of sections in single parts of these compilations is no conclusive evidence of their date.

Much of this work of enlargement was unofficial. In the Empire of the Franks we have no such successive official revisions as were made in the kingdom of the Visigoths.

In no case is the written law of any tribe a complete statement of the rules actually observed. Those things were set down which seemed to need formal statement. Fundamental rules of law were often omitted because they seemed so self-evident as not to need statement. Rules of an arbitrary character — for example, the amount of the fine or composition to be paid for different offenses — were of course set down, as were the rules of judicial and of extra-judicial procedure for the enforcement of rights.

How far these compilations were really used in the administration of justice in the popular courts is uncertain. There was of course a tendency to have recourse to the written law, and in the laws themselves and in royal ordinances the duty of judgment-finders to follow the written law and of royal officials to see that this is done are frequently emphasized. It is probable, however, that in northern Germany the local judgment-finders commonly based their decisions on their impressions regarding the law and that the written laws were little used except by the royal counts and their deputies. Among the Frisians, Saxons, and Thuringians the extremely small number of manuscripts that have come down to us indicates that the written compilations were never very generally diffused.

Of these German *leges* perhaps the most noted, certainly that which has been most studied, is the *Lex Salica*. Its date is disputed, but it is generally believed to have taken form in the time of Clovis (481–511).

It contained, of course, many traditional wisdoms of earlier date living in men's memories, and many additions were made later. The oldest of these is a special law of King Clovis, the latest is a wisdom sanctioned by Louis the Pious about 819. The different parts of the law, accordingly, cover a range of more than three centuries.

Of the numerous manuscripts that have come down to us

none dates back of 750. Some of these manuscripts obviously give much older texts than others. German legal historians divide the manuscripts into four so-called families. The last of these, which is represented by five-seventh of the manuscripts, is the amended law or revision made in the time of Charlemagne. In the texts of the oldest group there are no distinctly heathen rules, and but few rules which indicate Christian influence. The second family or group shows a greater influence of Christian ideas, in particular prohibitions of marriage on account of affinity and provisions against sacrilege. In the texts of the second and third groups we find the so-called *malberg* gloss. The text is glossed or interpreted in these manuscripts by inserting certain German words and phrases relating to procedure. It is called the *malberg* gloss because these insertions regularly began *in malbergo*, which means in the court or in the judicial assembly. Even in those texts which are clearly the oldest there are so many obviously later interpolations that the reconstruction of the fundamental text as it existed at the close of the fifth century gives no little room for critical ingenuity.

An edition published in England by Hessels in 1880 gives in parallel columns ten different texts.

The *Lex Ripuaria* is largely modelled on the Salic law but exhibits interesting variations. The date of its original compilation is uncertain; it is placed by different authorities either before the middle of the sixth century or shortly before its close. What appears to be the oldest part is a collection of traditional rules, but it includes some provisions that look like legislation. Interwoven with the original text is royal legislation from the time of King Dagobert (628–79) down to that of Charlemagne. Reconstruction of the oldest part is more difficult than in the case of the Salic law because all the manuscripts which we have are based on a revised Carolingian edition of the eighth century.

Of Swabian tribal law there were two early compilations. The older is the *Pactus Alemannorum* compiled at the end of the sixth or in the first half of the seventh century. Fragments only of this Pact have come down to us. At the beginning of the eighth century a second compilation was made described as the *Lex Alemannorum*. It was made on the initiative of Duke Lantfrid (709-30) and received the assent of the people. In 730 Lantfrid was conquered and slain by King Lothair, the king of the Franks, and the duchy was brought under direct control of the Carolingians. Under their influence changes and additions were made.

The written law of the Bavarians first took shape between the years 744 and 748. In this compilation use was made of the oldest written law of the Visigoths and of the *Lex Alemannorum*. The opening sections, which deal with ecclesiastical and governmental matters, indicate coöperation of bishops and Frank officials. Subsequently additions were in the main kept separate and not interwoven with the older text.

The law of the Frisians, who occupied territory which today is partly Belgian, partly Dutch and partly German, is regarded as a private compilation made in the time of Charlemagne in which older material is used. Brunner conjectures that the first twenty-two articles represent a first draft of an official edition which for some reason was never issued. The remainder of the compilation deals in part with violations of law in Western and Eastern Frisia. As the East Frisians were still heathen, there is a curious difference between the rules laid down in the first and the second part of the compilation. In the first part labor on Sunday is forbidden; sanction is given to the peace of the church; sale of slaves to heathen purchasers is prohibited; and marriages forbidden by the law of the church are to be ended by separation. Ordeal by the drawing of lots in the church and oaths sworn upon relics are recognized.

In the second part, he who commits sacrilege in a temple may be slain by anyone and a mother may slay her newborn child without penalty. It is also declared to be the law of the East Frisians that he who robs a temple is to be taken to the sand washed by the sea and after various mutilations he is to be sacrificed to the gods whose shrine he has violated.

The *Lex Anglorum et Werinorum* is a compilation of Thuringian laws. In arrangement it was based on the Ripuarian law and it seems to have been influenced by Saxon law. It was probably compiled at about the same time as the law of the Saxons. It is of especial interest to students of Germanic law because it gives us the oldest evidence of a distinction in the law of movables between war-gear and domestic goods (*gerade*). It has some interest for students of English law because it is cited in the *Constitutio de foresta* traditionally ascribed to Canute but probably of later origin (Brunner, p. 350, note 2).

Passing from compilations of tribal law to royal ordinances, we note that in the Merovingian period the latter were designated sometimes as *auctoritates*, sometimes as *edicta* or *præceptiones* or *decreta*. In the Carolingian period they are all termed capitularies. The capitularies were distinguished as ecclesiastical or secular (*mundana*). They were distinguished from another point of view as those that were to be added to the tribal laws (*legibus addenda*), those that were to be written by themselves (*per se scribenda*) and those containing directions to the royal commissioners (*capitola missorum*).

The ordinances that were to be added to the laws were, as their name implies, measures modifying tribal law. Some were to be incorporated in the law of a particular tribe, some were made applicable to all the tribes of the empire. The rules laid down were to be used in judgments rendered in the popular courts. In principle these ordinances required the assent of the people of the tribe or tribes affected. Traces of the submission of these ordinances to the people are found as late as the time of Charlemagne. The capitularies to be written by themselves, on the other hand, are royal ordinances to be enforced by administrative authority. Many of them dealt with the royal domains and represented the proprietary authority of the king; in the main, however, they represented an exercise of the king's public powers. Some of them were what we might call special ordinances issued for temporary purposes, but others were to have permanent effect. The majority of these ordinances were administrative regulations dealing with the position and powers of the royal officials, with the temporal concerns of the church, with customs duties, money and trade. Many, however, dealt with the maintenance of the public peace and of public order, and practically created new general law affecting all the subjects of the Empire. In such cases they overrode tribal law.

Such ordinances the king could issue by virtue of his royal authority. There was, however, as previously noted, a growing custom by which the king submitted the more important ordinances to the magnates for discussion and secured their acceptance by the magnates at annual imperial assemblies.

Under Louis the Pious and his successors these assemblies were assuming more and more the character of parliaments and their assent was becoming more and more of a limitation upon the power of the crown. In some cases where the capitularies were to be incorporated in the tribal laws we find that the assent of the magnates seems to have been regarded as rendering acceptance by tribal assemblies unnecessary.

The *capitula missorum* were instructions issued to royal commissioners containing rules which they were to observe.

They contained, however, rules which they were to enforce; and when in the reign of Charlemagne royal commissioners rode circuit throughout the Empire, holding what amounted to royal circuit courts, these ordinances became important instruments for the development of substantive as well as procedural law.

The capitularies were issued in more or less numerous copies, and one copy at least should have been preserved in the royal archives. But no register or catalogue of capitularies was kept, the archives were not kept in good order, and copies seem frequently to have been lost. A compilation was made in 827 by Ansegisus, Abbot of Fontanella in the diocese of Rouen. He belonged to a distinguished Frank family and stood in intimate relations with the imperial court. "In order," as he says, "to rescue them from oblivion," he collected all the capitularies of Charlemagne, Louis, and Lothaire that he could bring together. He so arranged his collection that the ecclesiastical capitularies of each reign were brought together; and he added by way of supplement a number of the capitularies of the *missi*. He was able to collect very few, only twenty-nine altogether, which is the more surprising since in the latest and best modern editions it has been found possible to collect a hundred and twenty-four such capitularies for the period from the accession of Charlemagne to the year 827. This shows in what bad shape the archives were. Ansegisus endeavored to give correct texts without improvements or additions. His collection was much used, obtaining practically the authority of an official compilation.

Of a collection which appeared in the western part of the empire about a quarter of a century later, which purported to be a supplement to Ansegisus and which contained a number of deliberate forgeries, I shall speak later in discussing the sources of ecclesiastical law.

SECTION 22

The Frank Empire: Courts and Procedure

The organization of local popular courts differed in different parts of the empire. Among the Franks the court of the county was held successively in the different hundreds. It met at the time of the new moon or of the full moon alternately, so that there were some eight or nine regular sessions in the year in each county. This meant further that not more than two or three regular sessions were held in each hundred in the course of the year. Special sessions could be called in case of need.

In Germanic popular courts, as we have seen, the assembled freemen had nothing to do except to approve or disapprove a judgment rendered by the wise men or law speakers. Among the Franks these were known as *rachimburgi*. These were now selected by the counts from among the most esteemed, most experienced, and best informed men in the community.

During the period under review, as was indicated in Section 19, the duty of the common freeman to attend court was felt to be a serious burden upon the small landholders, to say nothing of the landless freemen. Moreover, since judgments were found by the counts and the *rachimburgi*, and the assembled freemen had practically nothing to do except give their assent, it seemed unnecessary to require their attendance. A capitulary of Charles the Great in the year 769 declared that every freeman must attend the regular session (*placita generalia*) of the court held in his hundred twice in the year, once in summer and once in winter. Later ordinances went even further in relieving the small landholders from the attendance of court. From attendance on special sessions, they were almost wholly relieved, since only those freemen were bound to come who were specially summoned by the count.

Given these conditions, it necessarily resulted that the *rachimburgi* who had to attend special as well as general sessions came to be chosen to an increasing extent from among the larger landholders or, as the contemporary phrase was, "from the better element" (*meliores*). There seemed to have been as a rule only about a dozen of these in each county and they regularly held office for life. They were coming to be called *schepen* or *schöffen*. Here we find the origin of the *schöffen* courts of the middle ages in which the right and duty of attending court and finding judgments was permanently associated with the possession of certain landed estates. In the rural districts of medieval Germany and France the local court thus came to consist (like the communal courts in Norman England) of nobles, knights, and yeomen.

In medieval cities, when these attained local autonomy and had their own city courts, the term *schöffen* or, in the French, *échevins* came to designate the officials of the city charged with administrative as well as judicial duties. Used in this sense, the term traveled from Holland to New Amsterdam and in the early records of this city you will find officials described as *schepen*.

In judicial procedure the increasing power of the state reveals itself in the limitation of self-help. The right of feud was narrowed, and extra-judicial distraint or pledge-taking for debt was forbidden.

Among the more important changes in procedure the following may be noted:

(1) The formalities of procedure were Christianized. Instead of invoking the heathen gods, the plaintiff, among the

Franks, had to swear a fore-oath or preliminary oath when the evidence of his right of or the defendant's wrong is not clear. In other tribes the complainant calls upon God and the saints to attest the truth of his complaint. The usual forms of oath are on "relics" or on the gospels. Of the heathen forms of oath only the weapon-oath remains. This became an oath sworn upon a consecrated weapon and was to be taken in special cases only. The Ripuarian Franks had an oath sworn on an oath ring and a hazel staff, which disappeared in the Carolingian period. The Frisians retained the oath described as the cattle oath, cursing all one's gear, but this was used only in cases of secondary importance. All ordeals were surrounded with Christian ceremonies. For a time a specifically Christian ordeal was introduced (the so-called cross proof). This ordeal was conducted by placing the complainant and the defendant face to face with laterally extended arms, and the person who could longest maintain this position was regarded as having triumphed in the ordeal. This, however, was forbidden in the year 819.

(2) Representation by attorney was not yet developed. As in all early legal systems, the head of the house represents wife, children, dependent members of the household and the stranger within his gates, but this was not regarded as representation. The head of the house represents his own interests as head rather than those of the person whose interests are primarily concerned. In this period, however, the party unfamiliar with the forms of complaint or of denial might avail himself of the services of a more expert friend. He himself must appear in court and must recite the necessary words, but he may be prompted by his friend. Later it was recognized as admissible that he designate the friend as his "mouth" or "forspeaker," or in the Latin *prolocutor*. In the Norman French this person is described as a *conteur*. In later medieval procedure a scheme was

developed by which if the forspeaker makes any mistake, he may be disavowed by his principal. In order that any such mistake might be promptly detected and corrected, it was not unusual in important cases for the principal to appear in court not only with a forspeaker but with a number of other experts known as "listeners" and "warners." It is their duty, if a forspeaker commits any error, to give prompt notice to the principal, who then withdraws the authorization given to the forspeaker. The latter, after paying a small fine for speaking without authority, may then be recommissioned and use the proper form of words. Here we have the earliest method of withdrawing and amending a complaint or answer. This method was in use in Norman England.

In the Frank Empire "forspeaking" was becoming a profession. In one of his capitularies Charlemagne warned his *missi* to be on their guard against the wiles of such professional pleaders because these by their superior skill were sometimes able to frustrate justice.

(3) The increasing authority and influence of the presiding official tended to lessen the extreme formality of the older procedure. In the oldest Teutonic procedure, the parties themselves had to formulate complaint and answer by the traditional spoken words, and the presiding official had no right of intervention unless one or the other of the parties failed to use the proper form: in which case he was regarded, as in other systems of early procedure, as having lost his case. In this period, however, the presiding official took a more active part; he and not the plaintiff called upon the parties to formulate their complaint or their answer, imposed the preliminary oath where this was required, and directed the judgment finders to propose a judgment. As in the earlier period, the decision of the case, whether by oaths or by ordeal, took place out of court, but the party who proved victor in the matter of proof could now obtain

through the mediation of the judge a declaratory judgment — that is, he could obtain judicial attestation of his triumph.

Summons of a defendant, which in the early law must be made by the complainant, might now be made by the judge at the complainant's request. The judge then summoned the defendant and could impose upon him a fine for failure to appear. This method of opening suit was described in opposition to the older *mannitio*, or personal summons by the complainant, as *bannitio*.

The local officer of the king, the count or viscount, developed wider powers in the punishment of criminals and in the matter of executing judgments. The wrongdoer taken in the act or pursued and captured after hue and cry was no longer to be slain upon the spot, except in case of resistance; he must be bound and brought before the royal officer. He was then granted no hearing nor any opportunity to prove his innocence. All that was necessary was that the party responsible for his arrest should swear regularly, with oath-help, that the prisoner was taken in the overt act; thereupon the royal judge could himself impose sentence.

In the execution of what may be called civil judgments — that is, judgments that impose the payment of compositions or fines — distraint upon the judgment debtor's goods could no longer be made except after judicial consent had been obtained. If the judgment creditor so requested, distraint could be made by the count or by one of his subordinate officials. This official execution of judgment naturally supplanted distraint by the judgment creditor. When judgment could not be thus satisfied, then unless the debtor were ransomed by his kinsmen or friends he was delivered into the hands of the judgment creditor who might deal with him as he pleased. Carolingian legislation permitted him to deliver himself voluntarily into servitude for debt and in such case limited the powers of the creditor.

In criminal procedure and in the punishment of criminals we find changes resulting from the fact that the peace of the people is coming to be supplanted and to some extent superseded by the king's peace. We have already noted that in numerous cases individuals were under the special protection of the king and that offenses against him are offenses against the king. Where this protection was granted, its withdrawal was viewed as a withdrawal of royal grace and favor. This was clearly the case as regarded members of the royal retinue and all royal officials. With the development of the higher feudal tenures these ideas were carried over into the relation between the king and his vassals. They were gradually extended to all people because an oath of allegiance to the king came to be imposed upon everyone in the empire when a new king came to the throne. Those graver offences which in the older Germanic period made the offender an outlaw, came now to be regarded as breaches of fealty which placed the offender in the power of the king or, as it was expressed in Anglo-Norman law, "in the king's mercy." From the power of the king to punish, there developed, accordingly, a series of new penalties: death, mutilation, banishment, loss of freedom — that is, degradation to the status of a slave — imprisonment or possibly, in accordance with the ancient and primitive *lex taliones*, delivery of the criminal to the wronged party or to his kinsmen.

Outlawry became banishment — that is, the offender was under the ban of the king or of the count.

In some cases the notion survived that penalty, even in the case of crimes, might be commuted by a payment of money — that the criminal might ransom himself; but where the fine imposed took the place of a new public penalty, it went into the royal treasury.

In the new as in the older law, when a man was put out of the peace there was no further legal protection of his property. In the Carolingian period procedure was developed for putting the property itself under the king's ban even where the offender was not put out of the peace. In these cases it was not the person but the property that was outlawed. This process became available for the execution of judgments rendered in what we should call civil cases. The estate put under the ban was held by the count for a year and if not then redeemed it was utilized to satisfy the judgment plaintiff and any residue went into the royal treasury.

Reforms were introduced in the matter of proof by oath and by compurgation. The compurgators or oath-helpers swore separately one by one. Where the party upon whom proof devolved had still the right to select his oath-helpers, he was no longer bound to select kinsmen, so that oath-help lost to some extent the character of a family or clan oath. In some cases the antagonist was allowed to outbid the party to whom the right of proof had been assigned, by offering to produce a larger number of oath-helpers.

Capacity to act as ceremonial witness to a transaction was made dependent upon the holding of a certain amount of property. And before such witnesses were admitted to swear, they could be examined to determine their competence — that is, their participation in and knowledge of the transaction. The production of opposing witnesses was permitted and, if a direct issue of veracity arose between the two bodies of witnesses, resort was had to the ordeal of battle between the two groups.

Like the older ceremonial oral transactions, documents and charters had to be supported by witnesses who confirmed them by their oaths. At Ripuarian law the scribe must also swear to the validity of the document and if this were challenged he also had to fight. The usual form of challenge was the piercing of the document with the adversary's sword. Royal as distinguished from private documents or charters were exempt from challenge.

Of even greater importance in the development of the law than the popular courts were the king's courts. In addition to the court held by the king or by his count palatine, special royal courts developed through the delegation of royal authority to commissioners, *missi*.

In the Merovingian period special commissioners were appointed, primarily in most cases to protect the rights of the king in his domains, frequently also to supervise local administration, sometimes to restore order in disturbed districts. Charlemagne divided the empire into missatic districts and appointed each year two *missi* to ride circuit in each district, partly to supervise the administration of the local officials, partly to protect the king's rights in his domains, but partly, and to an increasing extent, to supervise and supplement the administration of justice. The courts held by his *missi* became accordingly in the fullest sense regular circuit courts.

The *missi* of Charlemagne were instructed to make inquiry regarding crimes that had been committed and that remained unpunished. They were instructed in particular to see that justice was done to widows, to orphans and to helpless folk in general (*minus potentes*).

The royal courts were not bound to proceed according to any particular system of tribal law and, where it seemed desirable, they might disregard legal rules and decide according to their sense of justice, *secundum equitatem*.

In these royal courts was developed a new form of proof — namely, proof by inquest. This inquest procedure was employed in the Merovingian period. Where special *missi* sent out to protect the rights of the king in his domains found that these rights were disputed — found, for example, that controversy existed between the king and his neighbors in respect to the limits of the royal property or in respect to easements claimed by the royal steward or by the king's neighbors — or where they found doubt existing as to the status of persons residing within the king's domains, doubt whether a man were slave or serf or free, the matter was settled not by oath and oath-help but by the inquest. A number of neighbors or members of the community, usually more than six, frequently more than twelve, were summoned by the royal commissioner and to them he put the question in dispute. They were regarded as witnesses and were selected by the commissioner from among the most respected and trustworthy persons who could be expected to have knowledge regarding the point in controversy. They were not asked to testify what were the rights of the king or of his neighbors or what was the legal status of the person whose status was in dispute, but they were asked to state what had been according to their observation and recollection the existing state of things. Where was it generally supposed that the boundary between royal and neighboring estates had been situated? Had any right of easement been exercised in the name of the king or by his neighbors upon adjacent estates? What had been the actual position, as generally recognized, of the person whose status was in dispute? After the witnesses had been summoned and had taken oath to answer truly such questions as were put to them, the particular point in issue was submitted to them and they were asked what they knew about the matter. They then either gave a joint answer, after conference with each other, or they answered the question one by one. This latter method was more common in Italy and in southern Gaul. Usually they answered the question submitted without explaining the grounds of their answer — that is, without stating the facts known to them upon which their answer was based. But in some cases they merely stated the facts of which they had knowledge, thus giving to the commissioner a material basis for his own decision.

Because these witnesses were sworn to tell the truth, they were called *jurati* or collectively a *jurata* and their answer if unanimous was termed a *veredictum*. Neither party could impugn or challenge such a verdict. The royal commissioner, however, if cause were shown him to suspect perjury on the part of the witnesses, could require of them that they clear themselves by ordeal.

If the first inquest yielded no clear result, if the verdict were not unanimous, a new set of neighbors could be summoned and a second inquest held. If this also proved fruitless the plaintiff, the king's steward or the private claimant had to bring suit in the ordinary court according to the rules of the tribal law.

The underlying assumption in this whole procedure is that a state of things which has existed without interruption for a considerable period is presumably a legal state of things. This procedure was therefore originally limited to questions of land and of personal status.

Proof by inquest could be taken wherever it could be used in every royal court, not only in the king's court but in the courts held by special commissioners and, in the time of Charlemagne, in the circuit courts held by his *missi*.

Inquest procedure and proof by inquest were obviously developed, as indicated, for the protection of the king's rights in his domains or for the protection of the fiscal rights of the crown. In the latter case it was possibly a survival of Roman administrative practice. It seems, however, to have been recognized from the outset that the privilege of inquest proof attached to the royal domains traveled with the land when this was given by the king as a benefice or fief either to a secular magnate or to a monastery or abbey. Monasteries established on what had been royal domains appear to have enjoyed this privilege from the outset, and in the course of the period under review this privilege was extended to many other ecclesiastical establishments. In the reign of Louis the Pious the clergy tried to secure privilege of inquest for all church property. In this they were not wholly successful, but at the Diet of Worms they obtained the issuance of a law that if the church claimed thirty years of peaceable possession of land in controversy, the church could have this claim decided by inquest. The right of proof by inquest might be given by royal writ to an individual and went sometimes with the grant of royal protection to individuals, for example to alien merchants. Jews under royal protection had no general privilege of proof by inquest, but the counts were empowered and commissioned to resort to inquest in controversies between Jews and Christians in case witnesses to a transaction or to a document refused to give testimony against their coreligionists.

The king of the Franks, even in the Merovingian period, could on appeal draw any case from the jurisdiction of the ordinary courts for decision in the king's court or for decision by a royal official. In any such case, of course, inquest proof, if applicable, was employed.

The chief advantages of inquest procedure were that it substituted for oath and compurgation a more rational method of settling a controversy; that it enabled a party to prove his case although he had no ceremonial witnesses and was unable to obtain oath-helpers, and finally that the verdict could not be impugned by wager of battle.

We have seen that royal documents could not be so impugned either in the royal or in the ordinary courts. In order to secure this advantage in case of private transfers of land, resort was had to the machinery of a fictitious suit. The person to whom land was to be conveyed might, either by virtue of general privilege or by special writ, bring suit against the grantor in a royal court, and judgment would be rendered in his favor on the admission by the grantor that his claim to the land was valid. An authentic transcript of this decision took the place of any private deed or charter and enjoyed the advantage of immunity from challenge.

Where procedure by inquest was employed to bring suspected criminals to trial, the jury of inquest discharged the function of what came later to be known in Anglo-American law as the grand jury. The man who was indicated as a probable offender was tried in the popular court and his guilt or innocence was determined by ordeal.

There is ample evidence that royal inquests were very unpopular. Charlemagne had to caution his *missi* to see that such witnesses as had testified in favor of the royal treasury should be protected against their neighbors. We find also not infrequently that the privilege of inquest or that the privilege of decision through inquest granted to an ecclesiastical foundation was especially confirmed because the neighbors had refused to recognize it. When Louis II was crowned king of Italy his subjects complained that they had been harassed in his and his father's reign by needless inquests, and he had to promise that he would not extend this procedure further than it had been employed under Charlemagne and Louis the Pious.

This reaction against inquest procedure rested partly upon a very human antipathy to innovations, partly on the desire to maintain home rule against the encroachments of central government, but mainly perhaps upon the resentment aroused by the effective defense of the rights of the king and of the royal treasury against encroachments and evasions.

After the dissolution of the Frank Empire procedure by inquest, like many other progressive movements initiated in this period, was checked and disappeared in most of the new kingdoms and principalities. In Normandy, however, where the dukes succeeded in maintaining a strong government conducted largely on Carolingian lines, inquest procedure was maintained not only as a method of bringing criminals to justice but also as a method of deciding controversies regarding rights in land and personal status. The privilege of inquest trial was extended more and more widely to secular magnates and ecclesiastical foundations until, in the reign of Duke Geoffrey, the father of Henry II of England, it was made a general right of all Normans in those matters to which it could be applied. In England, Henry II introduced inquest procedure into all the royal courts; and under his successors the jury of witnesses was gradually transformed into a jury of decision and became the fully developed civil jury of Anglo-American law. That the English jury is historically traceable to the Frank inquest was first demonstrated by Brunner. His conclusions have been accepted by all modern English historians.

Whether the grand jury of Anglo-American law is of purely continental origin is, however, disputed. A somewhat similar procedure for bringing persons accused of crime to trial seems to have been employed in the Anglo-Saxon period.

The extension of trial by jury from civil to criminal cases was, of course, a purely English development; and the criminal jury was exported from England to the continent as a result of the French Revolution at the close of the eighteenth century and of the following revolutions in the nineteenth century.

BOOK III

DISINTEGRATION AND REINTEGRATION
(887–1500)

SECTION 23

Historical Data

After the final division of the great Frank Empire in 887 the rule of central and western Europe was divided, falling into the hands of a number of secular and ecclesiastical potentates. The German part of the old empire was placed under the nominal rule of an elected German king, and in the reign of Henry I (919–36) this new German monarchy was placed upon a firm basis.

Italy had at first a king of its own, Berengarius, the Marquis of Friuli. The Italian magnates, however, who, as the Italian historian Pertile says, preferred always to have two masters and to obey neither, set up Guido of Spoleto against Berengarius, and when both Guido and his son Lamberto were dead, they began to elect foreign kings. So it came to pass that in sixty-three years (888–951) Italy had ten kings, some of whom claimed the title of emperor.

In France there appeared also an elective kingship. The first of the separate French kings, like the first German and the first Italian kings, were of Carolingian blood, but in France the royal dignity passed to and ultimately became hereditary in the Capetian house.

Down to the middle of the thirteenth century the German monarchy was stronger than the French and played a predominant rôle in Europe. In the year 951 Otto I reunited the crown of Italy to that of Germany. The greater part of the territory between France and Germany, Lotharingia, fell under German control; Bohemia and Moravia were brought into the empire, and the lands of the Wends as far as the Oder became German through energetic colonization.

In all these kingdoms the royal power was more or less shadowy. The great vassals of the crown, ecclesiastical and secular, drew into their hands a considerable degree of political authority. Their powers, however, were limited in turn by those of their vassals. The lord of the manor owed specific and limited duties only to his immediate superior; each seigneur was practically a little king in his own manor. The cities also fought or bought themselves free from the counts or bishops who had ruled them in the early middle ages and obtained a high degree of autonomy.

In France after the middle of the thirteenth century the power of the kings steadily increased. In Germany, on the other hand, the attempt to maintain a European empire weakened the powers of the king. In the later middle ages the authority of the German king and Holy Roman Emperor became more and more nominal. Germany and Italy were each dissolved into a considerable number of independent principalities and city republics. In Italy there was not even a nominal central authority. Northern Italy was split up into a number of secular and ecclesiastical principalities and city republics. In central Italy the rule of the Roman pontiff was extended over the surrounding country, and these central states of the church remained independent until the nineteenth century. Sicily and southern Italy in the eleventh and twelfth centuries fell into the hands of the Normans. This south Italian kingdom was temporarily united to the Holy Roman Empire under the Hohenstaufen Frederick II; but after the overthrow of the Hohenstaufen dynasty it fell in 1267 under the rule of Charles of Anjou. This kingdom also maintained an independent existence until the nineteenth century.

The Moorish conquests stopped short of the mountainous northern provinces, and here there appeared a number of small kingdoms and principalities. The most important of these were Castile, Aragon, and Navarre, and the now independent Catalonia. These northern territories maintained practically continuous warfare with the Moors and gradually reconquered the entire peninsula. During these centuries of reconquest the separate kingdoms were gradually brought, chiefly by marriage, into larger personal unions, until in the fifteenth century through the marriage of Ferdinand and Isabella the entire peninsula was brought under a single monarchy, with the exception of Portugal, which had split off from Castile in the twelfth century.

During this whole period the administration of justice and the development of law were greatly decentralized. From the local courts of the manor, of the county or of the city there was as a rule no appeal to any superior tribunal. It was only about the close of the middle ages that the traditional right of the king to intervene where justice was denied or delayed could be effectively invoked. At the close of the middle ages a system of royal courts was established in each of the Spanish kingdoms, these being still connected with one another only by a personal union. In France also a system of royal courts was established, first in northern France and ultimately also in the south. In Germany the growing power of the great princes led to the establishment of a system of official courts with appeals running to the court of the prince, but the nominal supreme jurisdiction of the imperial courts was reduced to very scanty dimensions by the grant, to each of the more important secular and ecclesiastical territories, of the "privilege of not appealing."

As Europe emerged from feudal anarchy the modern state was gradually organized in the form of absolute monarchy. Spain remained a complex of distinct kingdoms under a single king, but France became a single state. Germany, however, became a loose confederation of ecclesiastical and secular princes and of free cities. In Italy the conditions were the same except for the absence of even a nominal union.

During the period under review, assemblies of magnates reinforced by deputies from the towns developed into something like parliaments. In some of the Spanish kingdoms, notably in Castile and in Aragon, these parliaments or *cortes* developed earlier and exercised greater powers than the English parliament. Delegates of the towns were brought into these assemblies in the twelfth century, while they did not appear in the English parliament or in the German imperial diet until the thirteenth century or in the French *états généraux* until the beginning of the fourteenth. From the thirteenth to the fifteenth century these Spanish assemblies played an important rôle. From 1217 to 1474, 149 such assemblies were held in Castile, and the longest interval between parliaments was eight years. The powers of these parliaments were better defined in some kingdoms than in others. Everywhere their consent was necessary to the levying of new imposts and was ordinarily obtained for the declaration of war and ratification of peace and for new laws. These three centuries may fairly be called centuries of constitutional government, and in Aragon and Catalonia the powers of the *cortes* were so great that we may fairly say that these kingdoms enjoyed parliamentary government.

In all these Spanish kingdoms, however, the powers of the *cortes* began to weaken in the fifteenth century.

In these Spanish parliaments the law of each of the separate kingdoms gradually assumed written form, but the laws of each remained distinct. Until the nineteenth century there was really no such thing as national Spanish law.

In France the Estates General seem never to have exercised such far-reaching powers as were exercised in the single Spanish kingdoms. With the development of royal absolutism their sessions became less and less frequent. In

Germany the imperial diets theoretically enjoyed general legislative power, but here, as elsewhere in Europe, the representatives of the nobles and of the cities were more solicitous to preserve their local autonomy than to establish uniform law.

At the close of the period, both in Spain and in France the royal power of ordinance was tending to become a power of national legislation. This was exercised, however, mainly for administrative purposes and not for the establishment of common law.

The ordinary private law, consequently, was almost wholly local in character.

During this period, however, certain great bodies of European law were developed. These were feudal law, ecclesiastical or canon law and later the law merchant. Royal courts administered feudal law, but as a rule they had jurisdiction only of controversies to which the immediate vassals of the crown were parties. Ecclesiastical law was administered and applied in special ecclesiastical courts, with appeals running to Rome. Commercial law was likewise administered by special commercial courts, in most cases without appeal from the ordinary court to any superior tribunal.

In the last four centuries of the period under review, through the revival of the study of the law books of Justinian and their increasing use in the administration of justice, a fourth great body of European law came to be recognized.

SECTION 24
Roots of Feudalism

When we speak of the middle ages, we think of them as characterized in part by the feudal organization of the time and partly by the position occupied by the medieval church, which in many respects resembled a world state.

The term "feudalism" covers many different things. When we say that the public law was feudalized, we mean that the power of the king or territorial prince was based chiefly upon his position as overlord of lesser feudal magnates and that each of these magnates held his lands and his powers in return for services to be rendered. Even the lands of the church were held in theory in return for services to the public.

From the point of view of social organization the feudal system represents a stratification of society into different classes, special rights attaching to the special duties discharged by each class. At the bottom of the whole system and forming its economic basis, we find the tilling of the land in the hands of laborers bound to the soil and placed under the practically uncontrolled authority of the lord of the manor. The degree of his authority is indicated by the statement that his manor is immune against interference by superior political authority.

Some of the roots of the feudal system, in particular serfdom and local immunity, ran back into the late Roman Empire. In that empire in the fifth century of the Christian Era small holdings of land in full ownership had practically disappeared; nearly all the land in the empire was owned either by the emperor or by municipal or ecclesiastical corporations or by secular magnates. The tillers of the soil, described as *coloni*, were practically serfs; they and their children were bound to the soil. In the Roman Republic and in the early empire the *coloni* were free tenants. Their degradation into the position of serfs was resisted by the imperial government; we can trace the struggle in the imperial constitutions; but social and economic forces prevailed over governmental policy; and at last the imperial constitutions merely assert that the rent paid by the *colonus* cannot be raised or changed from payment in kind into payment in money, and that he cannot be sold like a slave apart from the land. These were the conditions which the German conquerors found in the Roman province, and they made no attempt to change them. All that happened was that the king took over the fiscal lands while his chief followers and favorites took over the domains of the Roman secular magnates, or at least a part, varying from one-third to two-thirds of each domain. The ecclesiastical establishments held the lands which they had obtained before the conquest and received from the kings in many cases new and extensive grants of fiscal land. To his followers, either in reward for past services or to secure future fidelity, the kings made gifts of other fiscal lands.

The roots of the medieval immunity also run back to the Roman Empire. In the Roman Empire an immunity meant primarily exemption from the burdens of local government (*munera*), whether these consisted in personal service or in the payment of taxes. Immune in the later Roman Empire were all the lands of the *fiscus*, and immunity was granted by way of a privilege to many ecclesiastical establishments and to some of the secular magnates (*potentes*), especially in Gaul. What immunity meant was that the immune territory was taken out of the hands of the authorities who normally conducted local government. The normal authority in local government was the town or municipality; the open country was regularly governed from some central town. Immunity of fiscal or other lands meant that local government was placed in the hands of imperial stewards or of the ecclesiastical or secular owners of the immune district. In the Roman fiscal domains the imperial stewards (*procuratores*) always exercised over all tenants and serfs police jurisdiction. Civil cases in which both parties were resident in the domain were also tried in the court of the domain. Criminal cases were reserved for trial in the regular provincial courts held under the authority of provincial presidents. Even in criminal cases, however, it was customary for the provincial president to notify the procurator of the immune domain that the accused person was "wanted," and it was not unusual for the steward, when he brought the accused before the provincial court, to play the part of his protector and look after his interests. Much the same powers of jurisdiction seem to have been given to many ecclesiastical establishments in Gaul and to many of the secular magnates, by appointing a bishop or abbot or secular magnate "conservator of the peace."

This Roman immunity, as a delegation of local governmental power, carried with it no release from the authority and control of the central administration. Like the normal organs of local government, the municipalities, the authorities in the immunity exacted not only the personal services and taxes that were needed for local purposes; they also turned over to the central government the money and the men that were demanded for imperial purposes. The imperial steward, of course, turned over to the central government all the surplus of income collected within the domain. The secular and ecclesiastical authorities paid into the imperial treasury such sums as were required for imperial purposes. In each immunity men were recruited as required for service in the imperial armies. (Brunner, Vol. II, pp. 285-89.)

Under the rule of the Frank kings, as before noted, landholdings in the Germanic parts of the empire were becoming more and more unequal. Large tracts of land were granted to ecclesiastical establishments or to the king's followers and favorites, and at the same time an increasing number of small landholders were surrendering their lands to magnates, ecclesiastical or secular, and becoming tenants.

The extent to which the class of small landholders was disappearing is indicated by the fact that in later Frank legislation it seems to be assumed that the common man is under a *seigneur* (senior) who protects and is responsible for him.

In the Frank Empire, as in the Roman, the fiscal domains were not subject to the ordinary local government official — the count; not only their economic administration but also the local government was placed in the hands of the king's bailiff or steward. The immunity enjoyed by the ecclesiastical establishments in the Romanic parts of the empire was recognized, and similar immunity was bestowed to an increasing degree upon the ecclesiastical establishments in the Germanic territories. Immunity was also conferred to an increasing degree upon the leading secular magnates. It seems to have been held that all lands given by the king, either to ecclesiastical establishments or to secular magnates, carried with them the immunity from the authority of the count which they had enjoyed when they belonged to the king. Under the Frank rulers the exclusion of an immunity from the ordinary authorities and processes of local government was even more marked than in the Roman Empire. The king's count could not, as a rule, enter the immunity in his official capacity nor could he act directly upon persons or property therein. Civil jurisdiction over the people resident in the immunity was exercised even more fully than in the Roman Empire by or in the name of the lord of the domain — the *seigneur*. Criminal jurisdiction over the free persons in the immunity pertained, however, to the count, but it was apparently customary that he should ask the lord of the immunity to produce the accused person for trial. Only when the surrender of the accused person was refused was it regarded as proper for the count to enter the immunity in order to arrest him.

In the Germanic portions of the empire, immunity and private jurisdiction were not as fully developed as in the Roman territories; but the basis for such a development existed in the older Germanic law. By German law the head of the household was responsible for the misdeeds not only of the members of his family but of his slaves and of any stranger whom he harbored. He was therefore, of course, responsible for the conduct of all persons taken into his household as dependents. For the misdeeds of his free tenants the landlord was not at first responsible; but as the great German domains rounded themselves out and began to obtain immunity, it became usual for outsiders to appeal in first instance to the lord of the manor. This, however, was not legally required during the Frank period, nor in this period were controversies between free tenants taken out of the court of the hundred into the lord's private court.

As with the Romans, so in the Frank period, the inhabitants of the immune domain were not relieved of duties to the empire; they were freed neither from local service in the posse or in road and bridge building nor from the duty of military service. All these duties to the state were, however, enforced by or through the lord of the manor. He levied and led the military force of the immunity just as the count levied and led the armies of the county.

We have been considering the origin and nature of what

were known in the middle ages as the lower or base tenures. Of the higher feudal tenures the duty of rendering military service, and particularly knight service, was first fully developed in the Empire of the Franks.

In the fully developed feudalism of the middle ages, and especially in the higher military tenures, we find not only that land is held on tenure of service but that a personal tie exists between lord and vassal, between the immediate feudal superior and the inferior, which is characterized by reciprocal duties of protection and allegiance. This personal side of the feudal tenures runs back to the old relation between the lord and his retainers. Of this we have spoken in describing the early Germanic retinue or *comitatus*. The duty of service to the lord, which was based originally entirely upon this personal relation, was modified, and the connection of service with a grant of land began when the retainer was set out from the lord's house and placed upon land given him by the lord. Even then the duty of continued service was derived rather from the original personal relation than from the grant of land. The gifts of land made by the kings of the Franks to their followers did not at first carry any notion that the recipient was bound to render any definite services. He was, however, morally bound by his continued personal allegiance to render such aid as might be needed in any emergency. In case of failure to respond to a demand for service, the gift of land was indeed revocable, but only because according to early Germanic ideas all gifts were revocable if the donee displayed ingratitude. This underlying assumption that the gift or benefice could be revoked was not expressed, but its existence is shown by the fact that where gifts of land were not to be revocable this was distinctly stated in the deed of charter by which the gift was attested — a statement that is to be found in many of the grants of land to the church.

A more distinct understanding regarding the service to be rendered by retainers who received land from their lord first appeared among the Visigoths as early as the fifth century. The Visigoths had lived in more intimate association with the Romans than most of the other German tribes, and very many of them had served in the Roman armies. The retainers of the Visigothic kings were known as *bucellarii*. The name was derived from *bucella*, the military biscuit or hard-tack ("doughboys"). In the latter part of the fifth century in the laws of Eurich we find that some of these retainers are holding land on a distinctly military tenure, and the land is passing on the same tenure to their sons. The grant terminates if the grantee or his successor fails to render service. No arrangement as definite as this appeared in the Frank Empire until the eighth century.

In Saxon England we find developments similar to those noted on the continent in the earlier Frank period. The royal retainers of the earliest Saxon period were the *gesithas* mentioned in the laws of Kent and of Wessex. Even in these earliest laws these retainers were apparently settled on lands given them and had in their households both bond and free servants. If such a retainer failed to follow the king's summons to war he forfeited his land and paid a fine of 120 shillings. At a relatively early period these transplanted retainers had become a hereditary noble class; for men of *gesith* stock (*gesithcund*) had a higher *wergeld* than the ordinary freeman. King Alfred chose his shire-reeves from this stock. At the royal court there had developed meanwhile another set of household retainers, the *thegnas;* and these passed through the same development, some of them being transplanted to lands of their own and becoming a hereditary class of landed magnates. Even in the Saxon period it was to these magnates that the king looked for the levying and leading of the forces of the kingdom.

SECTION 25

Feudal Tenures in the Frank Empire

It was in the Empire of the Franks that the feudal tenure on condition of military service was first fully developed, and before the dissolution of the empire the conception of tenure based upon the duty of service was being extended to include not land alone but also offices, both secular and ecclesiastical.

The development of the military tenure, the knight fee, was associated with changes in the organization of the Frank army. At the outset the old Germanic idea obtained that every freeman was a member of the tribal army. The duty of service in war rested upon all freemen who were physically capable.

In consequence of the economic inequalities that were developing in the empire, it became increasingly difficult for the small freeholders to discharge their military duty, and there was a tendency to limit in such cases the call to military service. It was determined by royal ordinance to what extent this duty should be exacted at any given time. The controlling considerations were on the one hand the temporary needs of the empire, and on the other hand the capacity of the individual. As regards this second point, a certain amount of property fixed by royal ordinance and capable of modification by subsequent ordinance was treated as a unit on which personal service was to be demanded. Freeholders holding smaller parcels of land were grouped together so that, of three or four freemen, one only had to serve, the rest contributing to his support, *adjutorium*.

The raising of the levy in the county was entrusted to the

count; in immune domains, however, the duty of placing tenants and retainers in the field rested, in the Carolingian period, on the seigneur, the lord of the immunity, and not on the count. The military duty of all freemen was, however, maintained in principle; and in case of hostile invasion, every freeman capable of bearing arms was required to answer the call for the defense of the territory (*lantweri*).

While the crown was obliged to grant more and more relief to the smaller landholders, the value of the services which these men were able to render was steadily lessening because of changes in the art of war. The armies that had established the Frank Empire were of the old Germanic type — they were armies of foot soldiers; only the leaders and their retainers were mounted. Between the years 730 and 750, in the struggle with the Moors who had overrun Spain and made their way into Gaul, the need of larger and more efficient cavalry forces was keenly felt. The military problem was solved by the development of a heavy cavalry of armored and mounted knights to meet the light cavalry of the Moorish armies. At a time when land was practically the only important form of wealth, the economic basis of maintenance of this heavy cavalry had to be found in land. The land held by the crown and by the secular magnates was insufficient. Even after these had armed and mounted all their retainers, converting even their household slaves into knights, more cavalry was needed and therefore more land. To meet this emergency, Charles Martel, the Mayor of the Palace, and his successors who became kings, made extensive seizures of church lands. The church could not well protest when the issue was the defense of Christianity itself against Mohammedanism. The lands thus seized were distributed to secular magnates and trusty retainers who, by giving them in turn in small parcels to their followers, put these in an economic position which enabled them to equip more and more knights. The whole process has a singular resemblance to the award of a large public contract to a small number of responsible individuals who in turn distribute the undertaking among subcontractors. It is here perhaps that we have the origin of the medieval sub-enfeoffments which created a chain of intermediate authorities between the crown and the holders of knight fees. The employment of cavalry as the chief force in war and the development of definite feudal tenures go hand in hand. They appeared first in the southwestern part of the empire, in Aquitania. In Gaul or West Francia in the middle of the ninth century the armies were almost wholly composed of cavalry and consisted partly of free vassals and partly of *ministeriales* — that is, *knechte* equipped as knights. In the territories east of the Rhine, this development was not completed until after the dissolution of the empire.

At the time at which large tracts of ecclesiastical land were seized by the crown, even more high-handed measures were resorted to in order to utilize the resources of the church for the defense of the realm. In some cases laymen were appointed to such ecclesiastical positions as those of bishop and of abbot. When the Moorish onset had been repelled, the relations between the state and the church were readjusted. It was recognized that the ecclesiastical lands seized for military purposes were still lands of the church and were to pay tithes (*decima et nona*). At the same time it came to be recognized that, while church lands were held primarily for religious and charitable purposes, any surplus possessions not necessary for these purposes might justly be burdened with military duties. From the point of view of the state and its needs, the ecclesiastical superior was responsible for levying within the ecclesiastical immunity the fighting forces of his bishopric or monastery. Thus there appeared the fighting prelates of the later middle ages.

From the point of view of the state, the ecclesiastical offices themselves as well as the lands ruled by prelates were fitted into the scheme of lands held for service. Thus was developed the special feudal tenure which in the Norman French was called *frankalmoign*. Here the duty to be discharged was the maintenance of religious, charitable and educational services.

Not only ecclesiastical but secular offices came to be regarded from the same point of view. The position of a count holding a certain amount of royal land as the appanage of his office, the yield of the land representing his salary, was in fact so similar to the position of the lord of an immunity that it became more and more difficult to maintain any distinction. The count, like the secular or ecclesiastical lord of an immunity, conducted the local administration, exacted the payments and services required for such administration, held courts and collected fines. Each was responsible to the crown for such services as were due to the whole realm.

Toward the end of the Frank period, the benefice or fief held by tenure of military service was not yet distinctly heritable. The grant in theory was made for the joint lives of the feudal superior and his vassal. Almost from the outset, however, when the feudal superior died, his successor renewed the grant to the vassal who had faithfully discharged his duties, and it became increasingly customary in case of the death of the grantee to confer the fief upon his eldest son if there was a son capable of rendering the service due to the feudal superior.

As long as the Frank Empire held together, it was not in theory recognized that the count had even a life tenure of his office. Much less was it recognized that the son of a count had any right to inherit the office. It was usual, nevertheless, not only to permit the count to retain his office for life but it became increasingly customary to confer the office upon his son and preferably upon his eldest son if he seemed a suitable person.

Before the dissolution of the Frank Empire, accordingly, the feudal system, as we find it existing through the later middle ages, was substantially established. The whole system may be regarded as a system by which all the land of the realm was drawn into the service of the realm, or as a system by which those who render service to the community receive, in the form of the yield or produce of land, payment or salary for their services. The latter point of view, rather than the former, was dominant in the earliest phases of all these tenures. The tenure of military service, in particular, goes back to the personal relation of protection and allegiance between the lord and his retainers.

SECTION 26

Fully Developed Feudalism

After the dissolution of the Frank Empire, feudalism attained its full development. So long as land remained the most important source of wealth, the economic basis of the whole system was found in the land. It is on the yield of the land tilled by serfs bound to the soil that the whole structure of feudalism primarily rests. Not only is the fighting man, the knight, dependent upon this labor for his maintenance, but his feudal superior and that superior's superior and finally the king himself (where there is a king) has his own manors. The king and his court are maintained primarily by the yield of the royal domains.

Each feudal superior has against his inferior certain rights of economic value. Even when fiefs have become heritable, the feudal superior is entitled to a payment when the fief passes to the heir — the payment known as a relief and amounting usually to one year's income. If the heir is a minor, the feudal superior has the rights of a guardian, which again may involve payment for his services. If, as happened in many parts of Europe, the fief may pass to a daughter, if the deceased vassal had no son, the feudal superior has a voice in determining the marriage of the heiress; it is his right to see that she marries a man capable of discharging the duties that run with the fief; and the lord's consent to marriage may involve a payment and become an additional source of revenue. In certain emergencies the lord may call upon his vassals for aids or contributions — for example, to ransom him from captivity or to provide his daughter with a dowry when she marries. When such aids are demanded from vassals, they in their turn are entitled in this emergency to aids from their inferiors. Thus these taxes, as we may call them, are shifted down the line until they are paid in last instance in whole or in part by the serfs on the manors. There was a possible reversion of the fief to the feudal superior; it came back to him by escheat when there was no heir and by forfeiture in case of a breach of fidelity.

In the manor or demesne itself the servile tillers of the soil not only pay rent in money or in kind but owe to the lord of the manor certain services limited as to amount but not as to character. The serf or villein is bound to work for the lord only so many days in the week, but he must do whatever he is ordered to do. The villein may not give his daughter in marriage (at least, not to a villein on another manor), nor may have his son ordained a priest, nor may he sell a horse or an ox without the lord's permission. For leave to marry, the villein has to pay. His holding passes to his heir, but the heir pays heriot in cattle or other chattels or in money just as the vassal paid relief. The villein might also be called upon for an extraordinary contribution in a special emergency just as the vassal might be called upon for aids; and as already noted, the payment of an aid by the seigneur was an emergency to be met by contributions from his villeins. In the Norman terminology these contributions are described as *tallages*.

In so far as a fief included jurisdiction — and we have seen that the office of count, with the right and duty of holding the county courts, had come to be regarded as a benefice or fief — costs and fines collected in the administration of justice were a source of revenue.

Under the feudal system medieval society fell into marked classes. Above the serfs or villeins stood the knights and other nobles and in the nobility itself there were sharp gradations of rank. We find these most elaborately worked out in the thirteenth century in Germany. At the top of the social hierarchy stand the princes, secular and ecclesiastical. Then we have the free lords whose fiefs are held, not directly from the crown, but from ecclesiastical or secular princes. Then come the freemen who have seat and voice in the county court. These are for the most part knights, but where there were still peasant freeholders, these freeholders or, as the English called them, yeomen, are in the same class as the knights. In the next lower class stand the *ministeriales*, the knights of servile origin who were still in legal theory unfree but whose social position is higher than that of the landless freeman or of the burgess or townsman.

In other parts of Europe the social classification was less elaborate, but everywhere those feudal magnates who hold authority over considerable territories as the immediate vassals of the crown constitute the highest nobility, and everywhere the ecclesiastical magnates — bishops and abbots — belong to this class. Under them is the lower nobility, and then comes what the French call the Third Estate — the free burgesses or townsmen. In medieval Spain the feudal magnates were described simply as the rich men (*ricos hombres*); the lower nobility were described as sons of somebody or something (*filii alicuius, fijos d'algo*).

Regarded as a system of government, feudalism was capable of very different developments. Regarded as a system of tenures, the fact that all lands and offices were held in last instance from a supreme lord — from the king or, where there was no king, from the territorial prince — tended to consolidation of political power. Regarded, on the other hand, from the point of view of the personal bond between lord and vassal — that is, between the immediate feudal superior and his feudal inferior — it could be argued that the king or territorial prince could demand political services only from his immediate vassals and that these in turn could receive orders only from their immediate lord. This latter theory became dominant in western continental Europe. It was expressed in the saying, "The man's man is not the lord's man." This meant disintegration of political authority: it placed in the hands of the great territorial princes, dukes, marquises or counts, a degree of power which tended to make them largely independent of the crown. Until the middle of the thirteenth century, as already noted, the authority of the German kings, who had become also Roman emperors, was greater than the authority exercised by the kings of France. The disintegrating tendencies of feudalism had revealed themselves first in France. From the middle of the thirteenth century, however, German monarchy steadily grew weaker and the chief territorial princes, both in Germany and in northern Italy, became practically independent of the crown. In France, on the other hand, largely through the absorption in the crown of one or another of the great duchies, partly through escheat, partly through marriage, the power of the crown steadily increased. Of no little importance, of course, was the fact that the French crown had become hereditary while the German kingship concontinued to be elective. In Germany the right of electing the king passed into the hands of a limited number of great secular and ecclesiastical princes whose votes had to be purchased for each election by new concessions of territorial independence.

In Spain the practically continuous war between the Christian kingdoms of the north and the Moors, who in the eighth century had obtained control of the greater part of the peninsula, tended, as war always does, to strengthen the central power; and the Spanish royal authority in the separate kingdoms, all of which except Portugal were finally brought by intermarriage into the hands of a single family, became practically absolute at the close of the period under survey.

In England as a result of the Norman conquest the disintegrating tendencies of feudalism were successfully resisted. At the outset, William's victory over Harold placed in the hands of the conqueror all the English royal domains and the domains of Harold's supporters. A series of rebellions that were crushed and were followed by the seizure of the domains of the rebels brought practically all the land of England into the possession of the Norman crown. These lands William assigned for the most part to his principal followers; but, partly because these assignments were made not all at once but gradually, the holdings of the great vassals were scattered through various parts of the island. William and his successors, furthermore, rejected absolutely the continental theory that the man's man was not the lord's man. Not only did every Norman king of England follow the practice, which had been established in the Empire of the Franks and which had been perpetuated in the duchy of Normandie, of exacting from all the free inhabitants of the realm at the beginning of his reign an oath of fidelity to the crown, but the special oath of fidelity which each English vassal swore to his immediate feudal superior contained the clause "saving the faith that I owe to our lord the King." In the following centuries, although at times the barons in league against the king succeeded in imposing restraints on his authority, as especially in the time of John, on the whole the authority of the kings was maintained and increased until it reached its height under the Tudors.

When we consider the development of law on the continent we see that the disintegration of central authority made the development of national law an impossibility. The court of the king was a court for the immediate vassals of the crown and for them only. The courts of these crown vassals had jurisdiction only over their immediate vassals and only in matters of feudal law. The administration of justice, except in feudal matters, remained in the hands of local courts administering local customs. The tradition that the king had a supreme right and duty of drawing into his court all cases of delay or denial of justice never wholly disappeared; but the kings and even the great territorial princes had not the power to enforce this tradition.

When we consider the extent to which feudal law has influenced modern law, we note that little of the feudal system is left except in the law of real property. In so far as feudalism constituted a system of public law, its principles were superseded on the continent by the development of absolute monarchy in Spain and in France and by the development in Germany and in Italy of an equally absolute authority exercised by territorial princes, or by the development of independent or autonomous republics.

In considering feudalism as a system of land tenures, it is to be noted that, just as political authority was dissolved into fragments, so rights in land were separated in medieval jurisprudence into two great groups — *dominium eminens* and *dominium utile*. Eminent domain included at once the political authority of the feudal superior — not merely of the king but of each feudal superior in his relation with his immediate inferior — but it included also all the economic advantages, guardianship, marriage, reliefs, aids, etc., which accrued to the superior. *Dominium utile*, which we may perhaps translate as practical ownership, was held by the seigneur in that property which was under his immediate and direct control. It belonged equally to the king in the royal domains, to every mesne lord in his immediate domains and to the knight in his fee held on tenure of military service. Where, as was usually the case, the serf had a permanent and heritable right in land, we sometimes find that practical ownership was held to be his while the seigneur's right was that of eminent domain.

Practical ownership consists of a life interest, inalienable in most cases, and of a reversion or remainder which again, when vested, is simply another life interest. The heritable remainder does not go to all the children nor originally to all the sons. With the full development of the feudal system comes the succession of the eldest son, the rule of primogeniture. This rule originated in the impossibility or undesirability of recognizing the duty of knight service as a thing divisible. It was extended to fees held on other grounds than knight service because it was contrary to the interest of the feudal superior that the services due him by one person should be divided among many.

The system of primogeniture was carried over into the servile tenures. Here it was not so much the interest of the seigneur as that of the servile tenants that was decisive. The holdings of the serf should not be too small to support a family. Where peasant freeholds continued to exist — and in some parts of the continent such freeholds were numerous — these also go as a rule to the eldest son.

In the succession both to servile and to peasant lands, we find in some cases a different rule, that of ultimogeniture. The land goes to the youngest son. This is a thoroughly logical development of the notion that a holding barely sufficient for the maintenance of a single household should not be required to support at the same time too many generations. If the eldest son is to take the land, it has to support at the same time his parents, his wife and children, his younger brothers until these are old enough to leave the land and support themselves, and his younger sisters until they marry. Where, on the other hand, the land is to to go to the youngest son, his elder brothers will have left the land and become self-supporting and his sisters will probably have married before he marries and starts a family of his own. (Note the effect in France of the rule of the Code Napoleon compelling division of property among all children. Note also Prussian investigation of agricultural tenures in Westphalia.)

Under the feudal system it was impossible, of course, that the succession to real property should be determined by any last will or testament.

On the continent of Europe the modern law of real property shows few traces of feudal principles. Nowhere on the continent were landholdings even in the open country so thoroughly feudalized as in England. What was more important, in the European cities, when these became autonomous and developed each its own law in its own city court, all land was converted into freehold, and rights in land became alienable and capable of devise by will. With the reception of the law books of Justinian as subsidiary law, the Roman conception of ownership became applicable in all cases not governed by the existing local law or by feudal law. Feudal law, as such, had never been administered by any but feudal courts, and when feudal tenures were swept away by the great revolutions of the eighteenth and nineteenth centuries, real property previously governed by feudal law came to be governed by Roman rules. Almost the only important principle recognized today in the continental law of real property which was not recognized at Roman law is that permanent rent charges may be imposed on land.

Although in the medieval development of feudal law there existed for Europe no central judicial or legislative authority, this law was nevertheless substantially uniform. This was due in part to the similarity of conditions in most parts of Europe, in part to the fact that one of the earliest statements of feudal law came to enjoy general authority.

This was a private compilation made in Lombardy at the close of the eleventh or beginning of the twelfth century and known as the *Libri feudorum*. In the form in which this compilation has come down to us it consists of diverse elements belonging to different periods. It includes legislative measures adopted by north Italian diets held under the authority of the German rulers of the Holy Roman Empire and decisions rendered by the feudal courts of Milan, Pavia, Piacenza, and Cremona. This material is accompanied by interpretations or glosses. It is believed to have been compiled by a feudal judge of Milan. It was later subjected to further private revisions, so that the manuscripts of the thirteenth century show extensive variations. It was studied in the great law school at Bologna and it was inserted in all medieval editions of the Justinian law books. Many other compilations of feudal law were made in the twelfth and thirteenth centuries. Among the more important may be mentioned the following:

In Aragon a private compilation of noble law known as the Fuero of Tudela, which contains many rules drawn from and ascribed to an earlier Fuero of Sobrarbe (which has not come down to us), received in 1122 the sanction of an Aragonese *cortes*. In Castile a similar compilation of noble law commonly described as the *Fuero de los fijos-dalgo* but also known as the Book of Decisions and of Arbitrations and also, from the *cortes* which sanctioned it in 1138, as the Ordinance or Fuero of Nagera, is substantially a statement of public and of private feudal law. It was incorporated in later Castilian codes in the thirteenth and fourteenth centuries.

In the Norman kingdoms of the two Sicilies there appeared in the twelfth century valuable collections of decisions in feudal cases, and in the thirteenth century feudal law was very fully and systematically presented in a general code.

In Germany in the thirteenth century, provincial and local customs as administered in the ordinary courts (*landrecht*) and also feudal law (*lehnrecht*) began to be set forth in private compilations. In the famous *Sachsenspiegel* (1230) and in the *Schwabenspiegel* (about 1250) feudal law is separately treated.

In the eastern territories conquered by French crusaders and especially in the kingdoms of Jerusalem and Antioch not only was feudalism of the north French type introduced, but both in their political system and in their legal institutions feudal principles were developed to their extremest consequences. For this reason an especial interest attaches to the so-called assizes of Jerusalem and of Antioch compiled about the middle of the thirteenth century. Here we have a full and minute digest of feudal law based upon the decisions rendered in the feudal courts of these kingdoms. In the fourteenth century there appeared a similar treatise on feudal law as applied in Cyprus.

SECTION 27

The Christian Church in the Roman Empire

During the first three centuries of the Christian Era the Christian church and its members stood aloof from the heathen world. Christianity represented in the field of morals an energetic reaction against the growing corruption of the ancient world, particularly in sexual matters and also in antagonism to the religion of the empire. Christians could not accommodate themselves to the religious organization of the empire. Although the empire was tolerant of divergent religions and even gave the non-Roman deities a place in the pantheon, there developed first in the east and gradually throughout the empire a state religion based on the worship of the deceased emperors. The oaths imposed upon army recruits and in judicial procedure were oaths which a Christian could not take. The duty of Christians to keep themselves unspotted from the world thus not only kept them aloof from the ancient society but brought them at times into conflict with the institutions and laws of the empire. The result was occasional persecution of the Christians, which seems to have been especially severe under some of the ablest and most efficient of the Roman emperors.

The attitude of the Christians to ancient society suggested to Pliny that they were enemies of the human race.

Under these circumstances Christians were bound to each other by strong ties; each Christian church was a homogenous and very solidary group. The church gradually developed a hierarchic organization. It was first in the cities that Christianity gained a firm footing, and the surrounding open country was only gradually Christianized by missionary effort. The city churches exercised a considerable supervision and control over the country congregations, and the priest at the head of the city church became a bishop. A somewhat indefinite superior authority came to be attributed to patriarchs in different parts of the empire. The most important of these patriarchates was naturally that established in the city of Rome.

From the outset each Christian church exercised a certain moral control over the life of its members. Grave sin on the part of any Christian would involve his expulsion from the church unless he made public confession and did penance.

It became among the early Christians a point of honor, or perhaps rather of ethics, to secure the settlement of all controversies between fellow Christians without resort to the heathen courts. There was an increasing tendency to submit disputes to the arbitration of a bishop. For such procedure the Roman law afforded room and even encouragement. The decision of an arbiter chosen by the parties to a dispute was at Roman law conclusive as regarded the merits of the question. The decision of a Christian bishop was therefore recognized by the Roman law itself as final, not because he was a bishop but because he was an arbiter selected by the parties. As the number of Christians increased they were increasingly tolerated by the imperial government.

Under Constantine and his successors the Christian church was recognized and legalized. Its position at first was simply equivalent to that of other religious associations; it received this position through edicts establishing a principle of general religious freedom and of universal tolerance. By the end of the fourth century, however, Christianity became the state religion, and imperial legislation first penalized apostasy, then heresy, and later imposed penalties upon heathen practices. Ultimately all heathen temples were seized and either turned over to the Christians or devoted to non-religious public purposes. There were strong political reasons for the establishment of Christianity as a state religion. It had become, in the cities at least, the dominant religion, and the Christian church had developed a strong administrative organization closely corresponding to the political organization of the Roman world. By drawing this organization into the service of the empire, the authority of the empire itself was greatly increased.

In the Christian empire the emperor himself was the head of the church, confirming the elections of patriarchs and of bishops, presiding over general church councils and giving his sanction to their decrees. He had, of course, no such unlimited power of legislation in matters ecclesiastical as that which he enjoyed in secular matters; in matters of dogma and of morals the final authority was that of the general church council. The church exercised disciplinary power over the clergy and, what was much more important, it exercised a growing jurisdiction over the morals of the laity. The growing practice of periodical confession obliged the sinner to denounce his own transgressions and to perform the prescribed penances. The Christian who habitually refrained from confession or who, having confessed, refused to do penance, placed himself in a conflict with the church which might result in exclusion from the sacraments or finally in excommunication. These sanctions were psychical and moral rather than physical and legal. The penalty of excommunication, however, was one of great severity, for it meant not only that the salvation of the sinner was imperiled but that he was excluded from association with other Christians. Excommunication, as Maitland remarks, assumed the aspect of a boycott. The jurisdiction of the church over the morals of the laity was, however, not yet a legal jurisdiction in the proper sense, because the civil law attached no consequences to condemnation by an ecclesiastical court except in cases in which the sin condemned by the church had come to be recognized as a public crime, as for example, in cases of apostasy and heresy.

In the Christian empire it seems that the jurisdiction of the bishop over controversies between Christians was extended beyond its earlier limits. A law issued by the Emperor Constantine, A.D. 333, declared that if one party appealed to the decision of the bishop the other party had to appear and to submit the case to the bishop's decision (*Etiam si alia pars refragatur*). This means that the episcopal court had become a tribunal of first instance in ordinary civil cases with a jurisdiction concurrent with that of the civil courts. This law was included in the Theodosian code. It was not, however, included in the Code of Justinian.

An issue between the secular and the ecclesiastical authorities which was constantly raised during the middle ages appeared in the late empire. The Christian clergy were not exempt from criminal procedure in the ordinary courts, not even though the clergyman were a bishop. From the point of view of the church, however, it was scandalous that any clergyman should be brought into the criminal court as a clergyman; and the demand was made that the accused should first be tried by an ecclesiastical court to the end that if they found him guilty he might be unfrocked, and then delivered to the course of justice as a layman. To a large extent this privilege seems to have been conceded except in some cases where the accusation was of treason. Acquittal of the accused by the ecclesiastical court was, however, no bar to subsequent procedure in the ordinary courts.

SECTION 28

The Christian Church in the Frank Empire

In the different Teutonic kingdoms established after the overthrow of the West Roman Empire, wherever and so long as the Teutonic rulers clung to the Arian heresy, the relation of the Christian church to the Teutonic state was not intimate, was rather that of two independent powers. When, however, as ultimately happened everywhere, these rulers accepted the Nicene creed and became orthodox, the relation between state and church was substantially the same as in the late Roman Empire. It was, on the whole, one of coöperation in which the part played by the church was far more important than in the Roman Empire.

In order to understand the position of the church in the early middle ages, we must remember that it had new duties to discharge and that these carried with them new powers. The duties imposed upon the church were especially important in those territories in which Roman civilization had gained no footing — in Germany, in Scandinavia, and in Saxon England. Among these barbarous peoples the church represented all that survived of the civilization of the ancient world; it was the channel through which so much of that civilization as was to be immediately transferred to the modern world was passing. It fell to the clergy to teach the barbarian kings how they were to use their power; they became the counsellors and chancellors of those kings, advising them how to organize and helping them to conduct their governments. Many functions, moreover, which we regard today as functions of the state fell to the church, because the Teutonic state attempted so little. It confined itself in the main to protecting the frontier against foreign foes and maintaining peace at home. Even in the Roman Empire the relief of the poor had been left for the most part to the Christian church; and among the Teutonic peoples both charity and education became church functions. The jurisdiction over morals which the church exercised became of increasing importance because the rude Teutonic law left to moral sanction solely a far wider field of conduct than was left to morals in so highly developed and refined a system as the Roman law.

Each Teutonic king — Visigothic, Frank or Saxon — was the head of the church in his own kingdom, confirming the elections of bishops and presiding over councils. In the Visigothic Empire, as we have seen, the ecclesiastical magnates, in spite of the nominal superior authority of the king, obtained a controlling influence in political matters. In the Frank Empire they obtained no such authority. Under the Merovingian rulers the Frank church was not only subject to the supreme authority of the king, but it was in essentials independent of Rome. The Pope indeed was recognized as the first bishop in Christendom, and the Bishop of Arles claimed authority as his vicar until well into the seventh century. The kings, indeed, occasionally had relics sent to them from Rome, permitted or even requested the Pope to confer the pallium on their bishops, and listened to papal advice in ecclesiastical matters. The Pope, however, had no real supremacy in ecclesiastical matters, nor was great importance attached to the delegated authority of the Bishop of Arles. Without royal approval, it was inadmissible for the Pope to interfere with the Frank church. No right of legislation or of jurisdiction was accorded to him even in ecclesiastical matters. Ecclesiastical legislation proceeded from councils of the Frank church which met on the king's summons or at least with his authorization. Their resolves were not binding on the secular power unless sanctioned by the king. The king had a distinct veto power in matters of ecclesiastical polity, though not in matters of faith and dogma. In these the Frank church was autonomous. In mixed questions the kings exercised an independent legislative power through their ordinances without the concurrence of the church councils.

Bishops were appointed by the king; at least, his will was ordinarily decisive. The rule of the canon law that the bishop should be chosen by the clergy and congregation of the diocese is recognized in principle; but his election required royal confirmation and the bishop elect could not be consecrated until the election was confirmed. It frequently happened that the king indicated a candidate of his own and that the election was a mere form. In some cases the king appointed a bishop outright without even the form of election. Under the mayors of the palace, this practice was so frequent that Charles Martel was able to confer bishoprics upon laymen.

In the Carolingian period, as already noted, not only was there closer coöperation between church and state within the Frank realm, but there was an entente, which might almost be called an alliance, between the Pope and the Frank kings. In this alliance the kings not only protected the Pope against his Lombard neighbors, but supported the church more energetically than in the previous period in combating heresy and in forcing Christianity upon such German tribes as were still heathen. Within the Frank realm, however, the king exercised a supremacy over the church that was certainly not less and was perhaps in some points greater than in the Merovingian period. The king legislates even in ecclesiastical affairs; the clergy assembled in synod have only an advisory voice. If a parliament of magnates is in session, the ecclesiastical synod is simply a part of it. If the ecclesiastical magnates are summoned separately, the synod is simply a special ecclesiastical parliament. In the general parliament the ecclesiastical dignitaries usually deliberate separately, but even on ecclesiastical matters the secular magnates express their opinion. Like all resolves of these Frank parliaments, the resolves of the clergy require royal sanction. The king exercises through his ordinances power of legislating in matters of ecclesiastical polity without necessarily consulting either a general parliament or a synod. To what extent ecclesiastical rules are to bind the laity is determined by the king. If he issues no declaration on this matter, ecclesiastical resolves are supposed to bind the clergy only.

The appointment of bishops which the Carolingians had controlled as mayors of the palace they retained as kings. The royal power became even more sharply accentuated. Election by the clergy and congregation became exceptional; it occurred only where a special privilege of election had been granted to a diocese or where the king ordered an election to fill a vacancy. Even in such cases the king appointed commissioners who supervised the election, and the election required royal confirmation. If the bishop elect were unacceptable, the king simply appointed a new bishop.

Bishops and abbots were regarded as royal officials and, like the counts, they were placed under the supervision of Charlemagne's *missi*. On the other hand, they gained a steadily increasing influence upon the temporal affairs of the Empire by their appearance in parliament and their advisory voice in legislation; by their appointment as *missi* and consequent partial control of administration; by their appointment as assessors in the king's court and their consequent influence upon the administration of justice; by the development of ecclesiastical immunities with primary jurisdiction over their vassals and tenants; and by actual service in war when they led their vassals and tenants into the field.

Neither in the Frank Empire nor among the Visigoths or Saxons was developed as yet the separate and exclusive jurisdiction exercised by the ecclesiastical courts in the later middle ages. The church was able to secure such modifications of tribal law as seemed to it necessary, particularly in the matter of marriage and in the matter of deeds and testaments. It insisted that marriage must be monogamous and permanent, and it secured the recognition of charters and last wills. In Visigothic Spain the clergy seem to have exercised constant supervision over the administration of local justice. In Saxon England the bishop frequently sat with the sheriff in the communal court. In the Frank Empire the bishop seems rarely to have appeared in the county courts. Here the influence of the clergy upon the administration of the law was exercised, in and after the time of Charlemagne, through the supervisory powers of ecclesiastical *missi* and through the presence and voice of ecclesiastics in the central royal court.

As in the Roman Empire, the clergy were in principle subject to the jurisdiction of the ordinary courts. As in the Roman Empire, however, the church endeavored to secure the right of trying the accused clergyman in the proper ecclesiastical court, so that, if found guilty, he might be unfrocked. Over this matter there was more or less controversy. In the Merovingian period the church carried its point as regarded criminal proceedings against bishops. Where accusation was raised against a bishop, the king might cause investigation to be made in order to determine whether there was sufficient ground for prosecution. If this seemed to be the case, the bishop was tried in the ecclesiastical court and, if found guilty, was degraded and turned over to the court of the king for sentence. If he were acquitted by the synod, no further procedure could be taken against him.

As regarded the priests and lower clergy, the church was less successful in its effort to secure preliminary ecclesiastical procedure. The controversy was temporarily settled by an edict of Clothair II (614); but the wording of this edict is so ambiguous and its construction so tortuous that it is still a matter of dispute what the settlement really was. The edict was obviously amended and re-amended in the course of its discussion. A distinction was drawn between priests and deacons on the one hand and the lower orders of the clergy on the other, and a further distinction was drawn between major and minor cases. In the major cases priests and deacons were first to be tried in the ecclesiastical court, but an acquittal in such court was not a bar to further procedure in the secular court. In minor cases priests and deacons could be brought before the secular court, and in all cases clergymen below the rank of deacon could be brought before this court; and the only concession made to the church was that notice should be given to the bishop to enable him to aid the clergyman in the defense and to plead for mitigation of sentence.

To all these rules there was a thoroughly Teutonic exception where a clergyman was taken "in the act." In such cases even a bishop was treated as if he had pleaded guilty. He was debarred from all defense, and he was subject to condemnation in the secular court without previous ecclesiastical degradation. The church, however, always pronounced such procedure to be an unrighteous exercise of power.

In the Carolingian period, as in the Merovingian, an accused bishop was tried first by the synod. This, however, was no longer an independent body: it had become the ecclesiastical department of the king's court. The accused bishop appeared before the king and the synod, and the judgment rendered by the synod required royal confirmation. This, however, was probably seldom refused. The only case cited by Brunner to indicate that the king was not bound by the judgment of the synod is one in which the synod had condemned the bishop, and the king restored him to his diocese.

Criminal jurisdiction over all the rest of the clergy was, however, placed in the hands of the church. The accused person was tried before his bishop. If acquitted, he was not subject to prosecution in the secular court. If found guilty, he was sentenced and turned over to the secular authorities for punishment.

In matters purely ecclesiastical the church enjoyed full disciplinary powers over the clergy, and in matters of faith and morals full jurisdiction over the laity. In the Carolingian period the church received in these matters the support of the secular power. It was regarded as the duty of the government to see that the church had the assistance of the state in the discharge of its mission. A few examples will suffice. The count, and if necessary the king, lent aid to the bishops to compel the obedience of the abbots, the priests, and the lower clergy. When the bishop went through his diocese to investigate ecclesiastical offenses and to impose ecclesiastical penalties, the count or his deputy was to lend him all needed assistance. Every count was a "defender of the church" and was to stand by the bishop in suppressing heathen practices. In Saxony neglect of the sacrament of baptism, violation of church fasts, and the burning of corpses were made punishable with death.

What was most important for the maintenance and future development of ecclesiastical jurisdiction over the laity was that in the Frank Empire, as generally in medieval Europe, an excommunicated person who refused to make submission to the church and do penance was threatened with imprisonment and banishment. Behind excommunication the state thus placed the penalty of civil outlawry. This converted the authority of the church in matters of morals into a distinctly legal jurisdiction over sins. For the guidance of the clergy in the exercise of this jurisdiction, books were compiled, known as "penitentials," in which sins were catalogued and the proper penance for each sin minutely indicated. It is not easy to see why these penitentials should not be regarded as law books.

Under Charlemagne the coöperation between church and state which had existed in the late Roman Empire and in the Teutonic kingdoms established in the fifth and following centuries may be said to have reached its highest development. The reëstablishment of imperial dignity in the year 800 was the work of the church. It represented the idea of the unity of Christendom in state as well as in church. This unity was now visibly embodied in the two supreme heads of state and of church, the emperor and the Pope. As long as these two powers worked in harmony, their association was to the advantage of each and the church was satisfied.

After the death of Charlemagne the attitude of the church began to change. It was becoming clear that the unity of the empire could not be maintained. If the empire was to be dissolved and the church was to be the only representative of the unity of Christendom, it was obviously necessary that the position of the church should be strengthened. It must grasp and retain as much as possible of the imperial heritage; it would need greater independence against the multitude of petty feudal princes when there was no longer an emperor to protect it. We find, accordingly, in the ecclesiastical utterances of the period an increasing exaltation of ecclesiastical over secular authority and an increasing demand for the independence of the church and for its more effective organization under the authority of the Pope.

As early as 829 the Frank bishops at the synod of Paris, in an epistle to Louis I, expressed, in somewhat cautious terminology indeed, the idea that the spiritual authority has greater weight (*gravius pondus*) than the secular because the priests have to pass upon the conduct of kings in matters of religion (*in divino*). In the political crisis of 833, when Louis I had to bend to the will of his sons, the Pope appeared as umpire. The Frank prelates stripped Louis of his authority and in the following year formally restored him to the royal and imperial office. Pope Nicholas I (858–67) followed a deliberate policy of expanding the papal authority. Anointment and coronation by the Pope was recognized as the legal method of establishing the imperial dignity, and the anointment and coronation of the king was interpreted in the same sense. Charles II, in 859, recognized by implication the right of the bishops who had consecrated him as king to depose him by their judgment. He said that he ought not to be displaced or ousted "without hearing and judgment by the bishops by whose ministry I was consecrated as king and who are termed the thrones on which God sits and by which he makes known his judgments."

As a result of these tendencies, the royal power of legislation in ecclesiastical matters was greatly restricted. Pope Nicholas I asserted that ecclesiastical rules took precedence over imperial laws and ordinances. Charles II was constrained to recognize the supreme legislative power of the Pope in matters ecclesiastical, although he claimed the superiority of the imperial legislation in matters secular.

The Frankish synods became at once more independent of the emperor and more dependent upon the Pope. After the reign of Louis I, the Pope claimed the right of convoking Frank synods, and Nicholas I claimed that their resolves required confirmation by the Pope.

During this period the church succeeded to a large extent

in securing the election of bishops by the clergy of the diocese, although they did not dispute the necessity of a royal confirmation. In proceedings to depose bishops the church synod escaped from the control of the king and fell under that of the Pope.

These new tendencies found striking expression in two remarkable forgeries which appeared about the middle of the ninth century, the so-called Pseudo Isidoriana and the False Benedict. The first of these was perpetrated in the field of ecclesiastical law. An important collection of decrees of church councils and of papal decretals had been made in Spain in the sixth century. By modern historians this collection is termed the Hispana. In later manuscripts of this collection a preface was inserted which appeared also in the collected writings of Isidore of Seville, who died in the seventh century. Later it was assumed that this whole collection had been made by Isidore and it came to be known as the Isidoriana. Between the years 848 and 853 there appeared a new edition of this collection which contained some ninety new and forged decretals dated from the end of the first century to the end of the fourth. The earliest decretals contained in the Spanish collection dated from the end of the fourth century. These new and forged decretals were a curious mosaic of sentences taken from various ecclesiastical and secular sources, from genuine decretals and decrees of councils, from writings of the church fathers, from the Breviary of Alaric, and from Frankish capitularies. The objects which the forger had in view were in many cases gained by wresting single sentences from their context; but where it was necessary, words were altered. The general object of this forgery was to exalt the spiritual over the temporal power. A more special object was to exalt the authority of the Pope at the expense of the German and Gallican archbishops, giving to the bishops a right of appealing to the Pope against the acts and decisions of the archbishops.

At nearly the same time there appeared a collection of Frank royal capitularies the majority of which were forgeries. In this case also, the forged matter appeared in connection with older, genuine matter. The work was based on the compilation of capitularies made by Ansegisus in 827 and purported to be simply an enlargement. In the preface this new compilation was ascribed to a certain Benedictus Levita — that is, Benedict the Deacon. He was apparently an imaginary person. The forged capitularies in this compilation, like the forged decretals in the Pseudo Isidoriana, were made up of sentences dating from genuine sources: from the Theodosian Code, the Breviary of Alaric, the laws of the Visigoths and the Bavarians, genuine canons and decretals, also penitentials, the writings of church fathers, and the Bible. Here again sentences were separated from their context and words were altered. In these forgeries also, the object was to exalt the ecclesiastical over the secular authority and to lay a basis for greater independence of the church.

Both of these compilations were accepted as genuine. It cannot indeed be shown that the new and forged decretals were cited at Rome itself until the time of Leo IX, who died 1054, and who before being a Pope was Bishop of Toul. But in a council of the Frank church in 853 one of these forged decretals was cited. One of the forged capitularies was cited at a Frank synod in 858, and not long afterwards we find Charles the Bald referring to Benedict's collection of the laws of his predecessors, obviously without doubt of its authenticity.

SECTION 29

The Later Middle Ages
Ecclesiastical Jurisdiction and the Canon Law

The extension and consolidation of ecclesiastical power, delayed by internal conflicts at Rome, were fully realized in the eleventh and twelfth centuries. In the later middle ages the church was practically a world state. In the states of the church and in numerous other territories ruled by ecclesiastical princes it exercised a direct territorial sovereignty. In the rest of Europe it was organized as a state within the civil states, exercising legislative and judicial authority and lacking but one element of political authority, the power directly to enforce its mandates. These, however, were in the main enforced by the secular authorities: persons excommunicated by the church were civil outlaws.

The church possessed also great financial resources and with the support of the secular authorities exercised powers of taxation — for example, in the collection of tithes.

The government of the church was far better organized than that of any secular state on the continent. It was increasingly centralized; the Pope stood at the head of a well organized hierarchy. In addition to the secular clergy charged with the cure of souls, it possessed in the great monastic orders forces under the direct control of the papacy. Some of these orders, like the knights of the temple, amounted to a standing army.

The fact that many of the prelates of the church were great landholders with sovereign or almost sovereign powers of government was indeed a source of strength to the church, but it was also a peril. It was necessary to protect the church against the influences which were everywhere disintegrating the medieval state. It was the policy of the church to detach the ecclesiastical magnates from the secular control by depriving the secular kings and princes of anything amounting to a power of appointment. This gave rise to the great conflicts over investitures. In this matter the church was only partly successful. Another method through which the church endeavored to detach the entire body of the clergy from secular interests and ambitions was by enforcing clerical celibacy. Although the celibacy of the clergy had been increasingly favored, it was not unconditionally required before the time of Gregory VII (1073-80). The triumph of this policy outweighed in its results the partial failure of the church in the conflict over investitures; for though a prelate received his lands from the crown and might even be named by the crown, yet if he, like the rest of the clergy, were separated from society and free from secular ambitions he was likely in the long run to be faithful to the interests of the church. It is worth while to note that when after the Protestant Reformation the Grand Master of the Teutonic Knights in Prussia became a Protestant, he promptly married and converted the territory of the order into a hereditary principality.

In the later middle ages the ecclesiastical courts exercised a very extensive jurisdiction. The church not only secured a general exemption of the clergy from secular jurisdiction, but it extended its own jurisdiction over laymen. The aims of the church were greatly furthered by the disintegration of the medieval state. It was easy to secure from a king confirmation of the jurisdiction of the church in the territories of his great vassals whom he had so much cause to fear; and the great vassals were in turn inclined to support the claim of the church to exercise the same authority in the immediate demesnes of the crown which it exercised in their territories.

The claims of the church which were in the main realized were: that a clerk must not be tried in the secular courts for any crime or misdemeanor, although if tried and condemned in the ecclesiastical court he might after degradation be delivered to the secular authorities for punishment; that civil suits against clerks should be brought in the ecclesiastical court; that this court should entertain suits of clerks against laymen when the former could not obtain justice in the secular court; that under the same conditions the church should entertain suits of widows and of orphans and of helpless folk generally. It was also very generally conceded that the ecclesiastical courts should have jurisdiction over benefices and tithes and other property rights of the church, and in particular over simony or the sale of an ecclesiastical benefice, not only because the property rights of the church were involved, but also because simony was in itself a sin.

From the same point of view, that of jurisdiction over sin, the church took cognizance of such distinctly religious offenses as apostasy, heresy, schism, sorcery, witchcraft, and sacrilege. The latter term was broadly interpreted: violence offered to the person of a priest or to any person within consecrated buildings or grounds and the theft of articles used in religious service were acts of sacrilege.

From the same point of view, that of jurisdiction over sin, the church courts took cognizance of incest, adultery, bigamy, incontinence, and procuration. The church also dealt with falsification of measures, weights, and coin; forgeries of documents; libel and scandal; perjury, which included not only false witness under oath but failure to perform an oath or vow; and with usury, which in the middle ages meant the taking of any interest for the use of money.

Through its jurisdiction over vows, oaths, and usury, the church gained extensive jurisdiction over contracts. An obligation which the promisor had sworn to perform, although void or voidable at worldly law, must be performed for the sake of the promisor's soul; and even if no oath were sworn but faith was pledged, the position of the church was the same. In the middle ages the pledge of faith apparently had a spiritual significance: to pledge your faith was to give your creditor a lien on your hope of salvation; it was apparently a pledge of your soul, and if the creditor could not foreclose, doubtless the devil could. The handclasp to bind a bargain, which in primitive law probably meant that the creditor had a lien on the debtor's person, apparently came to symbolize a pledge of faith. Although in general an obligation supported by oath or pledge of faith must be performed, the case was complicated if the promise involved the doing of a wrongful act. In such cases it was possible to absolve the promisor from the obligation of his oath, and this might be done where the promise was not distinctly wrongful but merely rash and inconsiderate. In general, however, it was recognized that it was not expedient that absolution from oath should be lightly given. In a case in which a person had sworn to pay a debt with interest, Alexander III decided that the interest must be paid, but that when it had been paid the creditor would be compelled by ecclesiastical authority to surrender it. The decision does not state in whose hands the interest was left. If, however, it came back into the hands of the debtor he could hardly be regarded as having really performed his oath. It seems, accordingly, that the only safe place for this interest was in the hands of the church (Cap. 6, X, Book 2, Title 24).

In many of the above cases the church did not have exclusive jurisdiction but only jurisdiction concurrent with that of the ordinary courts. Many of the sins which it punished were also crimes or misdemeanors over which the secular courts had jurisdiction.

The most important and least disputed field of ecclesiastical jurisdiction was that which it exercised in matrimonial cases. This was based on the ground that marriage was a sacrament. It was not originally regarded as a sacrament that must be administered by a priest; it was a sacrament which the parties by their agreement to become husband and wife administered each to the other. Ecclesiastical celebration of marriage was not made requisite to its validity before the Council of Trent in the sixteenth century. Marriage was established, as in Roman civil law, by the consent of the parties; and, as in Roman law, the ages of consent were fourteen for males and twelve for females. At Roman civil law the consent of the *pater familias* was required without regard to the age of the party, and in case of wardship, the consent of the guardian was necessary for the marriage of the ward. At ecclesiastical law, however, consent of parent or guardian was not necessary. What was more important was that a private marriage without witnesses and without the coöperation of any priest was completely valid if consent of both parties was admitted. It was customary that notice of an intended marriage should be given in the proper church or churches, as it was customary that the troth plight or consent should be made *in facie ecclesiæ* and should be blest or consecrated at the altar; but before the Council of Trent, although non-observance of these forms might involve ecclesiastical censure and possibly penance, the marriage was nevertheless valid. The evils connected with clandestine marriage, especially in the case of minors, led to the requirement of ecclesiastical coöperation at the Council of Trent.

The law of the church included a formidable list of impediments to marriage. Some of these, described as impeding impediments, were of chief importance as grounds on which ecclesiastical coöperation might be refused; but so long as ecclesiastical marriage was not compulsory they did not affect the validity of the marriage. The most important of these impediments was the prior betrothal of one of the parties to a third party. Fatal impediments (*impedimenta dirimentia*) — impediments, that is, which made the marriage invalid and constituted grounds on which it might be declared null — were as follows: (1) Absence of valid consent. This might be due to nonage, to insanity, to fraud, or to mistake. Mistake in the person was, of course, fatal; and in the middle ages it seems to have been held that mistake as to social status of a person, as, for example, the supposition that a serf was free or a commoner a noble, particularly if the mistake was caused by misrepresentation, might furnish ground for annulment. (2) A marriage might also be annulled on the ground of impotence. (3) A bigamous marriage was of course null. (4) Further grounds of annulment were a previous vow of celibacy taken by either of the parties and (5) a difference of religion. Difference of religion, however, was fatal only when one of the parties had never been baptized.

The church also established far-reaching prohibitions of marriage based on consanguinity or affinity. Until the year 1215 consanguinity in the seventh degree was an impediment to marriage. In the pontificate of Innocent III the prohibition was restricted to the fourth degree — that is, to the marriage of third cousins. On the ground of affinity or connection established by marriage, marriage was prohibited before 1215 to the seventh degree and afterwards to the fourth degree. Before 1215 secondary affinity (*secundi ordinis*) was also a bar to marriage though not as regarded the more distant degrees. Ordinary or primary affinity, which alone was recognized in the Roman civil law and has alone been recognized since 1215, means that as a result of marriage each party is connected with the blood relations of the other party.

The church also recognized a spiritual affinity established by common participation in a sacrament. The sponsors who took part in baptism became thus spiritually connected.

Finally a so-called carnal affinity resulted from an illicit connection, each party being barred from marriage with a blood relation of the other party.

From most of the hindrances above noted based on consanguinity or affinity, dispensation could be obtained; but in the absence of such dispensation they constituted grounds for annulment. Annulment was possible only on grounds existing before marriage or at the time of marriage. Divorce on grounds that came into existence later was not permissible. Separation from bed and board could, however, be granted without dissolution of the marriage tie (*vinculum matrimonii*) — that is, without possibility of remarriage so long as both of the parties were living; and in granting separations the policy of the church was liberal.

For the extraordinary number of impediments to marriage and for the extraordinary extension of the forbidden degrees, particularly in the earlier middle ages, various explanations have been given. That given by the Protestants at the time of the Reformation was simple. They pointed out that, although the church refused divorce, the number and variety of grounds on which annulment could be decreed greatly facilitated the dissolution of the marriage tie with resultant right of remarriage. The whole system also was clearly a source of revenue to the church. Dispensation from impediments was regularly granted only for a price; and suits for annulment brought fees to the ecclesiastical lawyers and the payment of costs to the ecclesiastical courts.

While such fiscal considerations may particularly have buttressed the system once established, it seems unlikely that they explain its origin. Brunner, a Protestant, has pointed out that in the early middle ages after the extensive development of private property in land, there was among the Germans an increasing unwillingness to permit marriage outside of the kinship group. As village settlements were originally made largely by kinship groups, the result was an objectionable tendency to inbreeding or endogamy. Throughout the middle ages by reason of the difficulty of travel, the population of each village would but for the church have continued the system of marriage within the village or its neighborhood. The wide range of impediments based on consanguinity and the various forms of affinity counteracted this tendency and forced young men to seek wives and young women to seek husbands outside of the village. This system accordingly made for exogamy.

In the development of the ecclesiastical law of marriage there was apparently a degree of conflict and of compromise between Roman and German views. In the Roman law, betrothal (*sponsalia*) was a simple agreement which could hardly be called a contract, inasmuch as no damages could be recovered for nonperformance. In Teutonic law, on the other hand, the contract of betrothal established an inchoate marriage. Marriage was regarded as a process through three stages: betrothal, delivery of the bride, and cohabitation. There was a certain recognition of these ideas, first, in the rule that precontract was an impediment to marriage, though it was not finally regarded as an impediment which made annulment possible; and again, in the rule that a betrothal, if followed by cohabitation, established a valid marriage. In the twelfth century came a reaction chiefly in the Gallican church toward the Roman views. Under the influence of German ideas the word *sponsalia* had previously been applied indiscriminately to a betrothal and to the exchange of words of consent in the marriage itself. In the reversion to the

Roman view we find a sharp distinction drawn between *verba de future* (for example *accipiam*), and *verba de præsenti* (for example *accipio*). The use of words referring to the future is not even inchoate marriage. The established rule that betrothal followed by cohabitation amounted to marriage was not abandoned, but was explained by a presumption of present consent at the moment of cohabitation, a presumption which was absolute and irrebuttable. There is perhaps another trace of Teutonic ideas in the canonical rule that a marriage established by *verba de præsenti* may, if not consummated, be dissolved by dispensation or by a vow of celibacy taken by either party.

The jurisdiction of the church over marriage carried with it a jurisdiction over questions of the legitimacy of children. The church adopted the kindly Roman rule that illegitimate children were legitimized by the subsequent marriage of their parents. To this rule the church gave a greater extension. In the Roman civil law the rule applied only to "natural" children, which meant children born of a more or less durable union, such as concubinage. It did not apply to *spurii*. The church extended the rule to all illegitimate children except those born of adulterine or incestuous connections, provided always that at the time of marriage the husband recognized the wife's children as his. Another kindly rule established by the church was that where marriage was annulled the children were not thereby necessarily bastardized. If either of the parties to the annulled marriage had acted in good faith — that is, had been ignorant of the existence of any impediment to or defect in the marriage — the children were treated as legitimate.

The jurisdiction of the church over these matters of family law was based, as we have seen, on the theory that marriage was a sacrament. It received also not a little support from the fact that the church itself kept record of marriages and of baptisms.

The jurisdiction of the church over marriage carried with it some degree of control over matrimonial property relations, but in general these seemed to have been governed by local custom. In many parts of Europe and notably in England the church courts controlled the probate and execution of testaments and also the distribution of intestate property.

In the matters last noted — matrimonial property relations, testaments, and the distribution of property in case of intestacy — the jurisdiction of the church was largely confined to the field of personal property, because land was generally governed by feudal law. With the establishment of the feudal tenures, there could be no disposal of land by last will, and the inheritance of land was determined by the feudal law. Marriage settlements affecting land were also governed by this system.

As regards the legitimacy of children, there was conflict in many parts of Europe between ecclesiastical and feudal theories. Nobles and knights generally refused to accept the rule of legitimization by subsequent marriage. It was directly on this point that the English barons made their famous declaration at Merton: "We are unwilling to change the laws of England." It followed, as Maitland has remarked, that a child might be regarded as legitimate as far as regarded his right of succession to personal property, but not as regarded his right to inherit real estate. The same difference existed in many parts of the continent. In some cases we find town law in antagonism to the ecclesiastical rule, the guilds refusing to admit a bastard and refusing to recognize that such a one was legitimized by subsequent marriage.

For the exercise of its wide jurisdiction the church developed a system of courts far superior to any other that existed on the continent. The regular court of first instance was that of the bishop. He or the ecclesiastic whom he deputed to exercise his jurisdiction (such a delegation of authority being described as a *sub-rogatio*) was the "ordinary judge" or simply "the ordinary." There were also lower courts, such as those of the archdeacons, which exercised petty jurisdiction. This petty jurisdiction, however, reached further into the lives of the common people than the ordinary jurisdiction of the higher courts. Of course the same thing is true today of our police courts. In many cases, in accordance with feudal analogies, there were what may be called immunities within a diocese: the cathedral chapter, the abbey, the chapel royal, might have its independent court exercising ordinary jurisdiction to the exclusion of the episcopal court. From all these courts, however, as from the court of the bishop, appeals ran to Rome; and as against the papal court there was no local immunity.

Not only did the supreme ecclesiastical court at Rome hear and decide cases on appeal, but like the imperial supreme court in the Roman Empire, it had an original jurisdiction which was concurrent in all cases with that of the ordinary lower courts. The Pope was the "universal ordinary" of all Christendom, and to him any complaint could be brought in first instance. Like the Roman emperor, the Pope rarely tried such cases or had them tried in the supreme court at Rome; he regularly delegated the decision either to the local ordinary or to a special legate. Like the emperor again, the Pope was apt to send the case down with instructions as to the law to be applied if the facts were as stated. Both in the Roman Empire and in the medieval church, such direct applications to the central jurisdiction were usually made where there was doubt as to the law governing the facts, and in both cases the instructions sent to the lower court represented a decision by the central supreme court rendered on the facts stated. In the

Roman Empire the instruction set down in answer to the complaint was known as a rescript. In the church it was described as a decretal. Papal decretals, which were of the nature of ordinances, might be issued for the regulation of ecclesiastical administration or of ecclesiastical discipline, and in such cases they were a source of public canon law. Decretals of the sort above described based on direct application to the Pope in disputes of a private nature and containing instructions as to the law applicable to the case constituted one of the chief sources of the private canon law. In the ecclesiastical theory such decisions rendered in advance of the trial of a case were applicable only if it was found on trial that the facts were as stated; but for the development of the law such decisions had the same value as decisions rendered on appeal. In ecclesiastical theory, again, a decision established the law for the single case only, but if such a decision was approved and followed it was treated as authority of the highest order.

The procedure of ecclesiastical courts was modeled on that of the courts of the late Roman Empire. In criminal cases the judge could open proceedings either on accusation or on information. In all cases the judge heard the pleadings, examined the evidence and rendered decision. In the early middle ages Teutonic methods of proof — oath and compurgation and ordeals of various kinds — were often employed in the ecclesiastical courts in Germanic territories, but by the thirteenth century more rational methods were becoming general. In criminal cases the church procedure was inquisitorial — that is, it was based on the right of the tribunal to open an investigation either on the ground of special information or of common report. Today we associate with the word inquisition the notion of a procedure whose object was to secure by any and by all means the condemnation of the accused. It was only in its degeneracy, at the close of the middle ages, that procedure by inquisition became unjust and oppressive. The regulations established by Innocent III, about 1200, required the personal appearance of the accused and the communication to him of the names of those who had borne witness against him and of the substance of their testimony, to the end that he might controvert the accusation brought against him, which he was permitted to do by summoning witnesses or producing other evidence on his own behalf. It was when the inquisitorial procedure was employed principally to combat heresy that torture of the accused became admissible and that the names of the witnesses who had testified against him were no longer communicated to him. Then indeed procedure by inquisition became, as a contemporary Franciscan monk declared, of such a nature that the apostles Peter and Paul could not have escaped conviction of heresy.

Civil procedure in ecclesiastical courts became in the long run complicated and dilatory in consequence of the fact that testimony by deposition largely supplanted direct oral testimony before the courts, and that the pleadings were put in written form. In important cases the record of pleadings and testimony which was sent up on appeal became very great and procedure very dilatory.

The recognized sources of the canon law were as follows:

(1) The New Testament. The Old Testament was regarded as a source of law only in so far as it contained fundamental rules of morality.

(2) A work which can be traced back to the third century in Syria, known as the Teachings of the Apostles (*Didaskalia Apostolon*). This contained moral, liturgical, and some legal rules.

(3) A later work which is traced back to Syria in the fourth century, described as the Constitutions of the Apostles. This consists of extracts from the *Didaskalia* and from decrees of church councils.

(4) Decrees of councils. In the fourth and fifth centuries numerous synods and councils, local and general, were held and important decrees were issued by them. Like all the sources previously enumerated, these were set forth in the Greek language. Of the earliest Greek collections of decrees none has come down to us.

(5) In the fifth century numerous Latin translations and collections of decrees of councils made their appearance. The most important of these was a collection made toward the end of the fifth century by Dionysus, a Roman monk. It contained not only council decrees but a Latin version of the teachings of the apostles. About the year 500 Dionysus also made a collection of papal decretals, the earliest dating from the end of the fourth century. These collections of Dionysus had an extensive circulation throughout western Europe.

(6) As above noted, an important collection of decrees and decretals was made in Spain in the sixth century, which came to be known as the Isidoriana, although Isidore had nothing to do with its original compilation. It has also been noted that the forged decretals which were published in France in the middle of the ninth century were inserted in the so-called Isidorian collection. These forged decretals were accepted as genuine even by ecclesiastical authorities and were thus a source of canon law.

When in the eleventh century the study of the law books of Justinian was revived in the Italian universities and when in the twelfth century great law schools frequented by thousands of students from all parts of Europe were developed, canon law became a regular branch of university instruction. Those who devoted themselves especially to secular Roman law were known as "legists" or "civilians"; those who devoted themselves to the study of the ecclesiastical law were known as "decretalists" or "canonists"; and the law faculties gave degrees of Doctor of Civil Law, Doctor of Canon Law, and Doctor of Both Laws (J. U. D.).

The systematic study of the canon law in the universities produced numerous treatises and commentaries. Early in the twelfth century a great ecclesiastical law book was compiled which took the place of all earlier collections both in the study and in the application of the canon law. This was Gratian's "Concordance of Discordant Canons," generally described as Gratian's Decretum. It was compiled between 1139 and 1142. This was the first of modern digests. Gratian stated in his own words the leading rules or canons of ecclesiastical law and supported each canon with citations from Holy Writ, from the decrees of the church councils, and from the decretals of the Popes. These decretals, as already noted, were in many cases decisions rendered by the supreme ecclesiastical court at Rome, and it was from the decretals of this character that Gratian's digest was largely compiled. His work accordingly may be described as a digest of the statutory and case law of the church. All through Christendom Gratian's book was accepted as authoritative. Strictly speaking, his canons were only *dicta;* the law was to be found in the authoritative material which he cited. Practically, however, his presentation of the law was accepted as conclusive.

Later compilations of the law of the church were simply addenda or supplements to Gratian's Decree. The hundred years immediately following were, however, the period during which the canon law was most rapidly developed by decisions at Rome. Of the papal decretals issued after 1139, private digests were made, but these were superseded by an official digest made under the authority of Gregory IX and published in 1234. This digest was divided into five books, the first dealing with the ecclesiastical courts and their jurisdiction, the second with procedure, the third with the duties and privileges of the clergy, the fourth with the law of marriage, the fifth with the law of crimes. This arrangement was followed in subsequent collections of decretals. It was summarized in a hexameter: *"judex, judicium, clerus, Connubia, crimen."*

Of later decretals three official collections were made: one under the authority of Boniface VIII, in 1298, commonly described as the *Liber Sextus;* another in 1317 containing the decretals of Clement V (who died in 1314) which was described as the Clementinæ; and in 1582 a final digest of decretals subsequent to 1317 was published under the authority of Gregory XIII. Under his authority there was also prepared an amended and official edition of Gratian's Decree and of the earlier supplementary digests. It is this official publication of 1582 which is known as the *Corpus juris canonici.*

At this time Christendom had been divided for more than half a century by the Protestant Reformation, and the Pope's writs were no longer running in northern Germany, in the Low Countries, in Scandinavia, or in Great Britain. In all these countries, however, Protestant ecclesiastical courts long continued to exercise under the authority of Protestant kings and princes pretty much the same jurisdiction that the ecclesiastical courts had exercised before the Reformation. The law which they applied was the general canon law as it existed at the time of the Reformation, with such changes as seemed necessary. With the establishment of royal and princely courts in which the law was administered by trained jurists, jurisdiction over secular matters was gradually withdrawn from the special ecclesiastical courts and their jurisdiction limited to matters of ecclesiastical discipline. This process, however, was not everywhere completed before the nineteenth century.

At the present time the Roman Catholic church maintains throughout the world a system of courts in which the law of the church is administered and from which appeals still run to Rome. In matters — such, for example, as marriage — in which today even in Catholic countries secular legislation has taken the place of ecclesiastical law, it is still necessary for the Catholic who wishes to maintain his standing in the church to have recourse to those ecclesiastical courts. The parties to a marriage in France, for example, may obtain a legal divorce with rights of subsequent remarriage, but it is still necessary, in order that either of them may remarry and retain standing in the church, that the marriage should be annulled by an ecclesiastical court.

The law administered by the Catholic ecclesiastical courts is now contained in a new digest which was made at the initiative of Pope Leo XIII. This has of course superseded the *Corpus juris canonici* of the sixteenth century.

SECTION 30

Influence of Canon Law upon Modern Law

In consequence of the fact that for centuries the Roman Catholic church exercised legislative and judicial authority in many fields of the law which are today regarded as secular, its authority in these fields being unquestioned until the Reformation, and of the further fact that even after the Reformation Protestant ecclesiastical courts retained for longer or shorter periods the jurisdiction earlier exercised by the Catholic courts, secular law, both public and private, has derived many of its principles and institutions from the ecclesiastical law.

In international relations the Christian church rejected the notion that in the absence of a treaty the foreigner had no legal rights. It asserted that among Christian peoples peace and not war was the normal relation and that the Christian was entitled everywhere in Christendom to have his natural rights of person and property respected. It insisted that all Christian nations should be regarded as constituting a society of nations. All these ideas were introduced, indeed, not so much by the canon law as by Christianity itself.

In modern times this idea of a society of Christian nations has been widened by the recognition of a society of civilized nations.

The canon law affirmed that controversies between Christian princes and peoples are to be settled by negotiation in accordance with the principles of Christianity. The Pope was always ready to arbitrate international disputes, and his claim to be recognized as the proper arbiter was not infrequently acknowledged. Without recognizing any arbitral authority on the part of the Pope, international disputes were from time to time voluntarily submitted to his decision. The last case of this sort was the submission to the arbitration of Leo XIII of a dispute between Germany and Spain regarding their respective rights in the Caroline Islands.

The church made some efforts to humanize the laws of war or at least to diminish the cruelty of warfare. Innocent III anticipated certain rules of modern international law — such, for example, as that which prohibits the use of explosive bullets — by forbidding the use as between Christian peoples of certain peculiarly destructive catapults.

The organization and administration of the modern state owes something to the medieval church. The ideas of the church as to the relations between itself and the state have naturally not been generally accepted, and we can hardly speak of the direct influence of the canon law upon modern public law. The modern state, particularly on the continent of Europe, nevertheless borrowed its plan of organization to a large extent from that of the church; the ecclesiastical hierarchy furnished the model for the centralized system of administration adopted by the absolute monarchy.

In the field of criminal law and procedure the church represented ideas more liberal and progressive than those obtaining in the secular world of the time. In opposition to the German or primitive notion that penalty was to be regarded as a satisfaction due to the community or to the wronged party — a satisfaction of the desire for vengeance — the church represented the idea that punishment was an evil inflicted on the criminal for his violation of the divine order. From this view the step to the modern secular idea that penalty is inflicted because of the violation of the social order is a natural and easy one. In the Roman law of course this latter idea was fully developed, but it had to be reaffirmed in the medieval world.

The church developed further an important distinction between penalties. In addition to penalties inflicted as punishment required for the maintenance of the social order, it insisted on the recognition of healing penalties (*pœnæ medicinales*) which were imposed for the purpose of reforming the criminal. This notion is one to which our modern criminal law is only recently giving due weight.

In the canon law we find, moreover, in opposition to the later Roman law and to medieval German law, a distinct assertion of the great principle of equality before the law. In the administration of its law the church recognized no distinction between prince and peasant.

In the attempt to draw the line between criminal and moral offenses the church, on the whole, was not happy. The fact that its jurisdiction over sin was the root from which its entire criminal jurisdiction was derived naturally led the church to endeavor so far as possible to enforce every moral obligation and to punish as criminal every grave moral transgression.

The criminal procedure of the church, as already described, furnished the model on which the administration of criminal law was organized under the absolute monarchy. Until the revolutions of the eighteenth and nineteenth centuries, the administration of criminal justice on all parts of the continent was inquisitorial. One of the results of these revolutions was the introduction throughout continental Europe of jury trial in criminal cases. It may be noted that while in theory the transfer of the power of decision from judge to jury should modify the attitude of the judge in the conduct of criminal proceedings, should relieve him both of the duty and the right of inquiry and turn him into an umpire who is to see fair play as between prosecution and defense, this result has not been fully obtained today in the criminal courts of the continent. This transformation, indeed, was not at once achieved in England; consider, for example, the mode in which Chief Justice Jeffreys conducted criminal trials. A habit once developed is only slowly modified by changed conditions; and therefore it is not unnatural that in continental Europe, where the criminal jury is a comparatively new thing, judges still follow to a large extent the older inquisitorial tradition.

In private law the influence of ecclesiastical principles upon modern legislation has of course been greatest in the field of marriage and family law.

Other matters in which the church, to some extent under the influence of Teutonic ideas, introduced institutions unknown or imperfectly developed in the Roman civil law were agency and the execution of testaments. Modern civil law derives from the ecclesiastical law the notion that by the act of an agent he acquires no rights nor incurs any liability for himself, that rights and liabilities attach immediately to the principal. From the ecclesiastical law also, modern law has derived the institution of testamentary executors and the appointment of administrators in the absence of a last will. In Roman civil law the execution of testaments and the administration of intestate estates devolved upon the testamentary or statutory heirs.

The prohibition by the church of the taking of interest on loans, which was largely accepted by the secular courts, had some singular and interesting results. Business in its attempt to escape from this restriction resorted to various evasions of the law. Our very word "interest" is due to such an evasion. Contracts were so drawn that in case of default on the part of the debtor damages were fixed at a definite sum. The Roman phrase for damages was *quod actoris interest*. On the other hand, the Roman word *usuræ*, which meant interest on money owed, came to signify illegitimate or excessive interest.

Prohibition of interest had also a considerable influence in developing the institution of silent partnership under the name of the *commandita*. This is a partnership in which one or more of the partners has a definite sum invested in the business on which if profits are made he receives dividends, while if losses result he may lose his capital; but in no case is the *commanditist* liable for anything more than the sum invested, nor has he any voice in the management of the firm, nor may he sign for the firm.

When in the later middle ages royal and princely courts composed of learned judges replaced the popular courts, their procedure in civil as in criminal matters was based upon the procedure of the ecclesiastical courts, which in its turn was based upon the procedure of the Roman courts in the later empire. This procedure became cumbersome and tedious, and the administration of justice was seriously delayed by the development of technical rules of pleadings and of evidence and especially by the habit of putting the entire mass of pleadings and of evidence in every important case into writing. On the continent of Europe as in English-speaking countries, the modern tendency is to make pleadings in court oral, employing written pleadings only for preliminary indication of the points at issue before proceedings in court begin. The taking of testimony by deposition has also been greatly restricted; wherever possible, witnesses appear in court, give their testimony orally and are subjected to cross-examination.

SECTION 31

The Development of Self-governing Cities

In the Roman Empire the cities other than Rome itself, the *municipia*, enjoyed in the earlier centuries of the Christian Era a high degree of local self-government. As in republican Rome, the citizens elected their magistrates, and these at the end of their term of office became life members of a municipal council, which thus corresponded closely to the Roman republican senate. The members of the city councils were known as *decurions*. As the imperial government became increasingly despotic these municipal councils ceased to be recruited by popular elections. These councils themselves appointed the municipal magistrates, so that the final form of city government was that of a council perpetuated by coöptation.

In the late empire changes occurred in the status of the working classes. In the fourth and fifth centuries state control of industry became more and more complete, and the artisans in the imperial workshops became practically serfs bound to their benches as the agricultural laborers were bound to the soil. If they fled from the cities they were pursued and brought back as were the agricultural laborers who fled from their farms.

In the Teutonic kingdoms established upon Roman soil, the cities were placed under the jurisdiction of counts. With the development of the feudal tenures the rule of a city might be granted to a faithful follower of the king as a benefice or fief. In some cases it was entrusted to a bishop. If immunity was granted to the secular or ecclesiastical lord of the town, the town became practically a manor and its ruler a *seigneur*.

After the dissolution of the Frank Empire governmental authority of the secular or ecclesiastical lords was greatly increased. In many cases the bishop who ruled a city received the authority of a count.

The new cities that grew up in the Teutonic countries seem from the first to have been organized like manors. Here as elsewhere in Europe, we find in the cities at the close of the Frank period men of noble or knightly rank, free proprietors, tenants and serfs. As in the manors in the open country, the artisans were for the most part serfs.

As a result of the development of trade and industry in the eleventh and following centuries, cities grew in population and in wealth and strove, successfully in most cases, to obtain home rule, buying or fighting themselves free from their lords. As royal and princely power strengthened, cities received the support of the territorial rulers in this effort, as they in turn lent aid to the kings and princes against their common enemy, the feudal aristocracy.

In Spain there was a peculiar and interesting development of municipal autonomy. As the Christian states of northern Spain pushed their frontiers farther south in warfare with the Moors, the cities that were wrested from Islam became outposts marking and securing the Christian advance. In these towns the inhabitants were practically frontier garrisons until the next victories established a new frontier farther south. It was thought to be necessary to attract able-bodied Christians to these reconquered towns and to persuade them to stay there, and no attractions were found so useful as to grant the *populatores* freedom and equality, allodial tenures, exemption from feudal payments and services, and a large measure of self-government. These things were regularly conceded in the *chartæ populationis* or *cartas pueblas* granted by the kings. In some cases other or more questionable privileges were contained in these charters, such as the exemption of criminals, even murderers, from pursuit and prosecution and the release of debtors from the claims of their creditors — provisions which suggest that some of these frontier towns may have resembled Botany Bays. When, as the reconquest proceeded, the military necessities which had produced these concessions disappeared, the kings were disposed, as elsewhere in Europe, to protect the towns in their independence because the towns gave the kings aid and support against the feudal aristocracy.

As elsewhere in Europe home rule charters were granted to Spanish cities not only by the kings to towns of which they were direct lords but also by magnates spiritual and secular to towns within their domains.

All over Europe, as the cities became independent, the status of the inhabitants tended to become equal. There was a very general effort to crowd nobles and knights out of the towns, and a general tendency to make the half-free or servile artisans full-free. In spite of the disappearance of these legal distinctions, social distinctions tended to perpetuate themselves. The government of the medieval cities was at the outset aristocratic. It was largely in the hands of the merchants. Sooner or later the artisans strive for equal political rights, and in many cities the government becomes increasingly democratic.

In the old cities of France and of Italy we do not know how far the self-perpetuating councils of the late Roman Empire maintained their existence or how or when the form of government which prevailed in the medieval cities of Europe was first established. This new type of government was distinctly representative; the city council is made up in most cases of representatives of the city parishes. It is here perhaps that representative government, which the ancient world failed to develop, first appeared in Europe, and it is worth while to note that this is first developed in the Latin countries, just as the extension of the representative principle by the appearance of town representatives in the medieval parliaments first appeared in Spain. Spanish legal historians assert that the new form of city government by councils whose members represent the different parishes came with the reconquest.

In some parts of Europe and particularly in Italy, the free cities of the middle ages extended their authority over large tracts of neighboring territory. In some cases they establish transmarine settlements or colonies. Venice in particular established and held for centuries what may be described as an East Mediterranean empire.

Leagues of cities were frequently established for their mutual protection, and one of these, the famous north German Hansa, was for a time not merely a commercial but a political power in the Baltic and in the North Seas.

In the development of European law the medieval cities played an important part. It was in them that a general system of commercial law was reëstablished. In them also was developed a new and more progressive type of general local law.

SECTION 32

The Law Merchant

Trade and commerce develop transactions and relations which are different from those of ordinary life, especially from those of rural and agricultural life. The rules governing traders and merchants, their transactions and their relations, may be included in the general or common law, but these rules will still be different in many respects from the rules governing uncommercial persons, their transactions and relations; and the commercial law will constitute a distinct or at least a distinguishable part of the general law.

There is, however, a special reason why commercial law has tended to become a separate system. Commerce has always been impatient of territorial variations of law and of the resultant conflicts of law, for the reason that its operations are not local or territorial, but cross the frontiers of the different states. Commerce has always striven, and maritime commerce has striven with special energy, for rules that are universal; its ideal has always been world law, administered by special commercial courts in each state. And in fact there has existed for something like twenty-five hundred years, and perhaps for a longer period, a law merchant which has been substantially international, and which therefore has been distinct from the ordinary law obtaining in single states. For something like six hundred years, indeed, from the first century before Christ to the fifth century of our era, while the civilized world was living under the rule of a single state — that is, Rome — commerce was content to be governed by rules that were part of the universal Roman law; but when the Roman Empire went to pieces, commercial law gradually reappeared as *jus gentium* or law of all people, administered by special courts in each country. During the last two centuries, however, in consequence of the energetic development of national sovereignty and of national legislation, the universal law merchant has gradually been transformed into national law. Except in English-speaking countries it is still to be found in special codes, distinct from the general civil code, and its rules are administered by special tribunals. In England the special commercial courts, with the exception of the admiralty courts, disappeared almost three hundred years ago, and in the eighteenth century the commercial law became a part of the common law.

There has been little or no protest against this situation, because the commercial codes of the modern world have largely reproduced the previous international rules, and because the common law of England and of all English-speaking countries has in the main retained them. If, however, modern legislation should introduce important and disturbing changes in commercial law, there would be an energetic movement to reëstablish common rules by international treaties to which all civilized states should be parties. We find examples of treaties establishing common rules of commercial law among many of the Mediterranean states of the middle ages; and in those modern nations in which there have been, or are, a number of independent legislatures, we see the same tendency to create a common law by interstate agreements.

The history of commercial law, according to some modern writers, began at Babylon more than two thousand years before Christ. It is beyond question that at this period Babylonian law had attained a high commercial development. The contract bricks which have been unearthed in large numbers, and many of which have been deciphered, exhibit a highly refined law well adapted to commercial needs; and some of the institutions of the later Mediterranean law have their prototypes in Babylonian law. It has been assumed that this commercial law of Babylon was carried by the Babylonian traders into Phœnicia and into the Mediterranean world. The difficulty in sustaining this hypothesis is that it rests wholly upon the similarity of the Babylonian and the later Mediterranean institutions. A similarity of institutions, however, is by no means absolute proof of the derivation of the later institution from the earlier. By reason of the substantial identity of human nature, similar conditions produce similar results among different peoples. To prove specifically the derivation of later institutions of one country from the earlier institutions of another, it is necessary in every case to demonstrate the historic connection. In this case we are unable to show the necessary connecting links, because we know nothing of Phœnician law.

We first reach firm ground in the Greek law and especially in the Attic law, where we find institutions and rules adapted to the needs of commerce and some evidence of the existence of a general commercial law prevailing throughout the Mediterranean. At Athens we find that justice was administered directly to foreign merchants, and we find traces of special procedure in commercial cases. We find, also, that certain institutions of the later law merchant are already in existence — for example, the maritime loan. In the third century before Christ, Alexandria and Rhodes were the chief centers of eastern trade. At Alexandria we find drafts and other negotiable instruments in use; and at Rhodes maritime commercial law had reached a high development (*Lex Rhodia de jactu*).

In this same century Rome began that career of conquest which was to end in subjecting to her authority the entire

Mediterranean basin — that is, the entire civilized world — and in the fusion of the different systems of law prevailing throughout the Mediterranean into one great system. The latter process began at the court of the foreign prætor at Rome, about the middle of the third century before Christ. The international law merchant, which apparently already enjoyed general recognition throughout the Mediterranean, was systematized by Roman lawyers and incorporated into the prætorian edict. In the second and first centuries before Christ this law merchant was introduced into the law of the city itself. In the Roman law in its highest development — in the imperial law of the second and third centuries of our era — there was no separate body of commercial law. A separate commercial law was unnecessary, (1) because the Roman law had been thoroughly commercialized — that is, the law of personal property and of contracts had assumed such a form as thoroughly to satisfy the needs of commerce — and (2) because the Roman imperial law ruled the entire civilized world. While there was no separate body of law for merchants as a class, or for mercantile transactions in general, we find special rules governing bankers, carriers by land and water, and innkeepers; and we find special institutions of maritime law, like the implied authority of the shipmaster to contract loans, and the Rhodian law of jettison, worked out to their ultimate legal consequences. That the Romans had not themselves constructed this commercial side of Roman law they frankly admitted; the Roman jurists and judges ascribed the great commercial contracts — sale, hire, partnership, and agency — to the *jus gentium;* and that the rules of maritime law had to their minds a peculiar nonpolitical authority of their own is curiously emphasized in the saying of one of the Roman emperors: "I indeed am lord of the world but the law is lord of the sea."

A German historian of the law merchant, Goldschmidt,

gives a striking description of the development of commerce in the early empire:

"The world empire which extended from the Scotch highlands to the Euphrates and from the Sahara desert to the steppes of the Volga, including probably more than 90,000,000 inhabitants; which formed one immense economic domain of substantially free trade; in which, except for a few state monopolies, industrial liberty prevailed and general freedom of migration was recognized; which had established on land and on sea a hitherto unknown peace and legal security, suppressing war, crushing piracy, and restraining robbery by strict penal laws; whose wonderful military roads were also highways of commerce, such as have not since existed in the East and only in the nineteenth century again in the West — this empire included all the great commercial peoples and industrial areas of the ancient civilized world, and in it the commerce of the world attained a development that was not again equalled until the nineteenth century. Trade was carried on not only in the eastern Atlantic ocean and the North and Baltic seas, but on the eastern coast of Africa, in the Indian ocean, and even with China."

In the fourth and fifth centuries, even before the fall of the West Roman Empire, the prosperity of western Europe was declining and Mediterranean commerce was shrinking. The center of trade moved eastward again, locating itself in the old Byzantium, the new capital of Constantine. The barbarian conquests completed the economic ruin of the western Mediterranean world; but all through the early middle ages there was an active oriental trade at Constantinople; and here the Roman law lived on until the East Roman Empire fell into the hands of the Turks in the fifteenth century.

Modern commercial law took form in the self-governing cities of Italy, Spain, France, and Germany between the tenth and twelfth centuries. In the inland cities it was developed at the periodical markets or fairs (such as that held in our own day — at least until the World War — at Novgorod in Russia), fairs to which merchants came from great distances. In seaports visited by trading vessels at all seasons it was in continuous development. In the courts of the fairs and of the seaport towns the commercial customs of different nations met and waged a peaceful contest for mastery, in which the better custom tended to survive. The feeling grew strong that there should be a common law of merchants overriding the special rules of the towns in which the merchants came together; mixed courts were often instituted in which foreign and local merchants sat together and found judgments. The periodical judgments rendered in such courts tended to develop a customary law, distinct from the law of the town. Thus was developed the custom of the fairs and markets.

In the Mediterranean towns we can see that there was a long struggle between the immediate interests of the local merchants and the less direct but greater interests of commerce as a whole. There was much jealousy of the foreign merchants and disinclination to admit them to equal rights. Discrimination, however, of course provoked retaliation, and commercial interests ultimately led to the adoption of a more liberal policy; until, by comity or by special treaties, the foreign merchants gained substantially the same rights as the local merchants.

It was especially in the courts of the seaport towns that common commercial law was developed; and it was in the courts of the Italian cities that the Mediterranean custom was again formulated and became the maritime law of Europe. From Italy this law spread to Spain and to France and, following the line of sea trade, to the Low Countries, to Germany, to England, and to Scandinavia. From the seaports some of these rules which were applicable to trade in general struck inland, following the routes of land trade. Both by sea and by land other commercial customs spread which were not primarily maritime; and just as the maritime law of Pisa served as a model for that of Barcelona, that of Barcelona for that of Oléron, that of Oléron for that of Wisby, and that of Wisby for that of Bristol, so the custom of Lombard bankers spread throughout Europe and created a uniform law governing drafts and bills of exchange.

That Italy exercised a dominant influence in the development of the general law merchant was apparently due to the fact that the Italian cities first contested the supremacy of Constantinople in the oriental trade and first revived Mediterranean trade on a large scale; but it was due also to the fact that the Italian cities were not making wholly new law, such as was being made at the fairs and at the seaports of France and Germany; the Italian cities were in touch with the East, where the Mediterranean custom of merchants as embodied in the Roman law had never lost its force. Not only was there a revival of commerce in Italy during and after the crusades, but there was also a rebirth of the old *jus gentium* of the Mediterranean. Building on such foundations, the Italian cities built better law than was building in Germany or in France; and the books setting forth the Italian law merchant in Spanish, French, and German adaptations, became authoritative manuals of medieval law merchant.

From the tenth century to the close of the middle ages it was now one Italian city and now another that was more prosperous and more powerful, but Italy remained the central point of trade between western and central Europe on the one hand and eastern Europe, Africa, and Asia on the other hand. Only in the Hansa towns, in the later middle ages, was there any trade comparable in importance to that of the Italian cities.

The law merchant as developed in the Italian cities was largely based upon Roman law, but more upon the Roman law as it survived in the eastern Mediterranean custom than on the written texts. From the canon law, also, the Italian courts borrowed what suited them, notably the law of agency, which had not been fully developed in the ancient Roman law because slave agency met in a large measure the needs which are met today by free agency. From German law the Mediterranean courts borrowed the protection of the honest purchaser of movable property, and they developed new rules of their own to protect the purchaser in market overt.

It is commonly said that the law merchant of the middle ages was simply the custom of the merchants. But here, as in all cases in which custom is said to have made law, we notice that the only customs that were binding were those which were recognized and enforced by the courts. What enabled the merchants to transform their customs so largely into law was the fact that they had their own courts. At the same time many of the rules worked out in the courts of single cities attained wider importance from their incorporation in treaties of commerce and navigation between different cities.

In the Italian cities administrative and judicial functions were not sharply separated, and the old term "consul" was indiscriminately applied to magistrates and to judges, because the magistrates and the judges were frequently the same persons. The commercial court was sometimes the regular court of the city, presided over by consuls of the city; but the guilds also had their own courts over which their consuls presided, and in Italy, as elsewhere, the courts of the merchant guilds sometimes obtained jurisdiction over matters of foreign commerce. Such courts were known as *consulatus maris*.

In these courts, as in all the traders' and merchants' courts of Europe, there were peculiarities of procedure which differentiated them from other medieval courts. The whole procedure was summary; pleadings were informal; proof was mainly by document; defenses were limited; judgments were based on equity (*ex aequo et bono*) rather than on strict law. The interpretation of equity, however, was strictly commercial; and the limitation of defenses indicates that certainty was deemed as important as equity. Execution was summary and appeals were rarely allowed.

Foreign merchants were not always subjected to the local jurisdiction. A ship sometimes carried with it a traveling consul — that is, a judge. When many foreign merchants were resident in the same city, they often had a standing consul of their own. Such privileges were frequently guaranteed by treaties.

Certain compilations of maritime law obtained general recognition throughout Europe. In the thirteenth century there appeared at Barcelona a compilation which was described in the Catalan as *Costumes de la mar*. In later editions, in the fourteenth and fifteenth centuries, it was entitled *Libro del consolat del mar*. This work was translated from the Catalan into French, Italian, and Latin. In a widely circulated Latin version its title was *Consulatis maris* (Goldschmidt, pp. 208-9). This is essentially a book of maritime law. It includes public as well as private law — for example, rules regarding the treatment of private property in maritime war, especially regarding an enemy's goods on a neutral ship and neutral goods on an enemy's ship — and with its acceptance throughout Europe as a statement of commercial law, it became a source of public as well as of private international law.

Another early law book which exercised great influence was compiled in Oléron, near La Rochelle, France. The *Charte d'Oléron* belongs to the beginning of the thirteenth century, and contains judgments running back into the twelfth century. The compilation was also known as *Rolles des jugemens d'Oléron* and as *Jugemens de la mar*. This compilation deals almost exclusively with shipping law, and with the law of peace, not that of war. This enjoyed special authority in Flanders, Holland, and England. To account for its authority in England a curious legend was developed, which is gravely narrated in Reeves' History of English Law, that King Richard brought this law book from Oléron on his return from Palestine at the close of the twelfth century.

On the above French compilation was based a Low German law book known as the *Waterrecht* of Wisby, which obtained authority in northern Europe on the southern and eastern coasts of the North Sea and all about the Baltic.

These three compilations "form, as it were, a continuous chain of maritime law, extending from the easternmost parts of the Baltic Sea through the North Sea and along the coast of the Atlantic to the Strait of Gibraltar and thence to the furthest eastern shores of the Mediterranean."

SECTION 33

Local Law

The three great systems of European law — feudal, ecclesiastical, and commercial — by no means covered the entire field of law. Crimes came under the jurisdiction of the feudal courts only in so far as they were regarded as felonies — that is, as breaches of the allegiance due to the feudal superior. In the ecclesiastical courts crimes were dealt with from the point of view of sins, but from the secular point of view they came within the jurisdiction of the ordinary local courts. To a large extent the jurisdiction of the ecclesiastical courts in this field was concurrent not only with the feudal jurisdiction but also with the jurisdiction of the ordinary local courts. Commercial law dealt only with merchants and with mercantile transactions. The commercial courts had jurisdiction indeed over all controversies arising between merchants and their customers, but over controversies between two parties neither of whom was a merchant, the commercial courts had no jurisdiction. To some extent there remained, therefore, within the jurisdiction of the ordinary courts some part of the law of crimes, almost the whole of the law of torts, the law of real property as far as this was held on other than feudal tenures, and the law of personal property and of contracts in all cases where neither party was a merchant. In the field of matrimonial property law, jurisdiction pertained largely to the secular courts, feudal or local. Succession to allodial land was determined by the local law, and in the distribution of personal property in the absence of a testament the ecclesiastical courts on the continent obtained nothing approaching the jurisdiction assigned to these courts in England.

In consequence of the disintegration of political authority on the continent, this whole field of general or subsidiary law fell under the jurisdiction of local courts from whose decisions there was usually no appeal.

Of comparatively slight importance as regards its influence upon modern European law, but of great importance at the time as regarded the lives of the people of Europe, was the law administered and developed in the manors. After the dissolution of the Frank Empire, the immunity of the manors was greatly extended. Instead of dealing solely with minor acts the manorial court became exclusively competent in all cases. The jurisdiction of the ordinary county courts was maintained in cases where one of the parties to a controversy was not an inhabitant of the manor; at least, this party could proceed in the ordinary court if he failed to obtain redress in the court of the manor. Within the manor, however, the lives and fortunes of the inhabitants, all of whom became serfs, were wholly in the hands of the manorial court. In France in the later middle ages, as in other parts of Europe, a distinction was drawn between high, middle, and low justice; but until kings and territorial princes began to exercise a considerable degree of authority — until what has been termed the new monarchy began to develop — high and middle justice were not taken over by the governmental courts, nor could the traditional right of the sovereign to entertain appeals on the plea of delay or denial of justice be exercised.

In theory the court of the manor was composed of the persons who fell under its jurisdiction. They were in them the judgment finders; the lord or his bailiff was only chairman of the court. Wherever and so long as there were within the manor free tenants, there was one court for them and another for the serfs. With the disappearance of any outside control, however, the lord or his bailiff gained an increasing influence over the decisions of these courts. It was in consequence of this influence that the free tenants were gradually forced into serfdom; and in administering justice to serfs their voice in interpreting the custom of the manor weakened and largely disappeared.

So long as the cities were regarded and treated as manors the burghers were under the jurisdiction of a manorial court or courts. In the cities, however, there were ecclesiastics over whom only the ecclesiastical courts had jurisdiction; free knights, justiciable only in the county court, and free tenants, mostly merchants, who could not be forced down into the position of serfs and for whom a separate manorial court was maintained in which their voice continued to be decisive in interpreting the custom of the manor. When the cities began to buy or fight themselves free, their first demand was, as a rule, for the right of holding their own courts. Outside of the manors, throughout the later middle ages, the administration and development of the subsidiary law, which was neither feudal, ecclesiastical, nor commercial, lay in the hands, in the open country, of the old county courts; in the cities, in the hands of the city courts.

The county court consisted of the free landholders within the county. In many cases it was composed almost exclusively of the resident nobles and knights; but wherever there was allodial land tilled by free peasants, as was the case in many parts of Europe, these also had seat and voice in the county court. In England similarly the shire court, before it was supplanted by a royal court, consisted of the knights and the yeomen of the county. On the continent the development of the customary law was wholly controlled by these local courts. It was generally recognized that the custom which they administered was provincial rather than strictly local, but they were free to develop divergent local law, and such local law all over Europe prevailed over the more general provincial law.

After the dissolution of the Frank Empire, the system of the personal statute gradually disappeared and provincial and local law became territorial. Wherever the majority of the people had been living by Roman law, the territorial custom was naturally to a large extent Roman. But the Roman law was the simplified vulgar law which had begun to develop in Gaul and Spain before the overthrow of the Roman Empire. For a time such compilations as the Breviary of Alaric were used in the local courts; in southern France, for example, to such an extent that even before the reception of the law books of Justinian the provinces of this part of France were known as *pays du droit écrit*. In those parts of Europe that had been governed by Germanic tribal law, territorial custom remained largely Germanic. The written tribal laws, however, fell into desuetude, and the law became unwritten custom. In France, for example, the northern provinces were described as *pays coutumiers*. In Germany itself local and provincial custom continued throughout the middle ages to be described by ancient tribal names; the local courts were said to be administering Swabian law, Saxon law, etc. Similarly in north Italy the general local law was that of the Lombards. Nowhere, however, was the local custom or law purely Roman or purely Germanic. It was at the most either mainly Roman or mainly Germanic. In those parts of Europe, as for example in Burgundy, where neither the Roman nor the Germanic elements were preponderant in the population, the territorial custom exhibited curious blends and compromises.

In the European cities, when these obtained their own courts, the law applied was originally that of the province or of the county, but this was rapidly modified and developed to meet the new needs of city life. In the cities class distinctions were gradually obliterated. In many cities nobles and knights were either constrained to transfer themselves to the open country or found their environment so uncongenial that they did this of their own will. The half-free or unfree portions of the city population gradually became full-free. In Germany in the later middle ages, if a serf escaped from the manor and maintained for a year and a day unmolested residence in a self-governing city, he became full-free. This was expressed in the rule that in the cities "the air makes free." The converse rule also gained recognition; any person though of free birth who remained within a manor as an agricultural laborer for a year and a day became a serf; here it was said "the air makes unfree."

Since in the cities the dominant interests were those of trade and industry, the law was everywhere gradually commercialized. Feudal tenures disappeared; all land was held either in full ownership or by free lessees, and feudal charges and contributions were gradually bought off. The law of contracts was developed far more rapidly than in the open country.

Even in the cities the adaptation of the law to new social and economic conditions was retarded by the absence in these courts of experts trained in the law. The municipal magistrates by whose decisions the law was developed were not in any sense trained lawyers. In the open country where the courts were composed exclusively of landholders, the situation was the same. The absence of anything resembling a bar from which learned judges could be drawn seriously retarded the technical development of the law.

The decisions of lay courts are apt to develop equity at the expense of certainty of law; with them even more than with courts of learned judges, hard cases make bad law. It was the boast of the lay judges both in the country and the city courts that they found judgments "according to established custom and their own five sound senses."

If we may regard as normal the processes by which Roman

law and English law were developed, the development of European continental law from the dissolution of the Frank Empire to the close of the middle ages was distinctly abnormal. In early society, decisions are controlled and the development of the law is guided by experts — first by priests, later by lay experts who emerge by natural selection. At Rome for centuries these unofficial experts virtually controlled the rulings of the inexpert magistrates and the decisions of juries. In the early centuries of the Roman Empire, what we regard as a normal type of court was developed. This was done by appointing trained expert jurisconsults to all magistracies exercising jurisdictional powers. In England in the reign of Henry II the same step was taken; from the body of unofficial, naturally selected, "law speakers" or "wise men" the king selected five *sapientes* to hear all the clamors of the realm. This was the origin of the court of common pleas and the first step in the development of the learned judiciary in England. In continental Europe, in the later middle ages, on the other hand, the decision of cases by lay judges was without expert guidance. The naturally selected experts had disappeared, but the artificially selected expert, the learned judge, did not appear. Among the lay judges who sat in the court by virtue of their holdings of land, there appeared of course sporadically legally-minded individuals, whom we may call natural lawyers, who exercised a strong influence in the finding of judgments, and who in some cases wrote books setting forth the law with which they had become familiar. Some of the most important and authoritative expositions of local or provincial custom were written by such men. On the whole, however, the satisfactory development of law in the local courts was retarded by the absence of trained experts; the judges were unlearned and nothing like a barrister class was developed except in one direction. There were naturally selected expert pleaders. These were at least familiar with formal pleadings but not necessarily or usually versed in other branches of the law.

In another and important respect the development of continental law was abnormal. At Rome in the early empire there was established a supreme court with appellate jurisdiction. It is obvious that better law is developed where numerous cases come up from a wide area to a single central court than where the cases submitted to a court are those originating in a single locality. In the development of law, as in that of the natural and social sciences, generalizations are valuable in almost direct proportion to the number of data on which they are based. In continental Europe such appellate courts were not developed anywhere in the twelfth century, and in many parts of Europe they were not established even at the close of the middle ages. The local custom developed in these lay courts was for the most part unwritten until the thirteenth century. Legal historians describe the tenth, eleventh, and twelfth centuries as the "diplomatic" period, because our knowledge of the law depends so largely upon deeds and charters. Written statements of the local law first appeared in the tenth century in a few of the self-governing cities of Spain and of Italy. The earliest date from the tenth century; there are very few of these, nor do many more appear in the eleventh and twelfth centuries. Books setting forth provincial and local customs outside of the cities are produced only in the thirteenth and following centuries.

Most of these earlier compilations were made by private individuals. Official statements of the law appeared when legislative power was developed and exercised. This happened first in the self-governing cities of Spain and of Italy. When a wider legislative power was developed, as was the case in some of the separate Spanish kingdoms, statements of the laws were formally enacted. In many cases these enactments represented a legislative confirmation of a private compilation which had come to be recognized as authoritative; in nearly all cases these earliest legislative compilations were avowedly nothing but statements of established usage.

One reason why written statements of provincial and local customs became more numerous in the thirteenth century was that the law books of Justinian had been minutely studied in European universities for more than a century — first in the Italian universities, later in universities established in other parts of Europe. In not a few cases, individuals concerned in the administration of local law who had become more or less familiar with Roman law were moved by a desire not only to see their local law put into written form but also by a desire to utilize their training in Roman law by giving to the local law something like a scientific arrangement and statement. In some cases, as we shall see, they used Roman law to fill up gaps in the local customary law.

When, in the later middle ages, the Roman law was "received" in most of the continental countries and the law books of Justinian became authoritative subsidiary law, compilations of provincial and local law were made for another reason. In proportion as the popular courts were replaced by official courts composed of learned jurists — that is, of men trained in the Roman law — there appeared in these official courts a tendency to apply the subsidiary Roman law wherever contrary local law or custom was not pleaded and proved. Because of the difficulty of proving rules of unwritten custom, a natural desire to preserve local customs from being submerged by the rising tide of Romanism furnished a new and cogent reason for the reduction of unwritten custom to written form. This motive, however, became more strongly operative in the sixteenth and following centuries than even in the later middle ages.

Since from the local courts in the open country and in the cities no appeal could ordinarily be taken, the local law applied in each jurisdiction tended to vary increasingly from that applied even in neighboring jurisdictions. There were, however, certain forces at work that checked, in some degree at least, this tendency to indefinite variation. Aside from the fact that like conditions and needs tended to produce similar law, certain unifying forces were at work. First of all, there was imitation, and secondly, downright borrowing. This was particularly the case with city laws. From the cities which first gained independence and developed important trade, neighboring and sometimes distant cities borrowed their laws. In some cases the first compilations of city laws, which were largely digests of the judgments of the city courts, seemed to have been made in order that the request of a younger or less important city for the good laws of the older and more important city might be gratified. Thus among the medieval city laws there were, as legal historians express it, "mother laws" and "daughter laws." Controversies arising in the application of the borrowed law were not infrequently referred to the judges in the mother city, and in this way appellate instances were developed to which cases were carried from whole groups of cities. The development of such courts of appeal was promoted by the establishment of city leagues or federations, which were formed primarily for reciprocal protection against the feudal magnates. Of these city leagues the most conspicuous was the Hansa, but there were smaller leagues in western and southern Germany and in other European countries.

In the following sections I shall speak briefly of the development of local and provincial law in the principal west European countries.

SECTION 34

France in the Later Middle Ages

Down to the middle of the thirteenth century, in consequence of the weakness of the French monarchy, each locality developed its own customary law. The system of the personal statute disappears and custom becomes territorial. A sharp distinction is to be noted in the legal development respectively of northern and of southern France. Between these sections there was a real difference in national type and even in language. In northern France, with its stronger Germanic element, we have the *langue d'oïl;* in southern France, the *langue d'oc.* The customary law of north France was substantially Germanic except as modified by rules of ecclesiastical law, and later, after the revival of the study of the law books of Justinian, by the acceptance of some specific Roman rules. In south France, where the great majority of the population had continued to live by simplified or vulgar Roman law and where such compilations as the Breviary of Alaric were still used, the customary law was fundamentally Roman. For this reason the southern provinces were known as the *pays du droit écrit*, while the northern provinces were known as the *pays coutumiers*. Even in south France, however, the written Roman law had only subsidiary application. Each province and locality had its own *coutume*.

In those parts of France in which there had been a very considerable mixture of Germanic and Latin elements, the local custom often represented more or less of a fusion of the two systems. In some cases, as in Auvergne, the line of division between north French and south French law ran through and divided the province.

Until the thirteenth century, comparatively few local or provincial customs were put in writing. The earliest written laws are those of the cities. To written charters granted by the king or the immediate feudal superior, there was gradually added a certain amount of civil and criminal law, developed mainly by the decisions of the city courts.

In the thirteenth century a considerable number of local laws were put into written form. These compilations of the customary law were, in France as elsewhere, mainly the work of private and in many cases unknown writers. One of the most important and most famous of these private compilations was the *Grand coutumier* of Normandy, which was put into shape in the later part of the thirteenth century (between 1270 and 1275). This compilation is remarkable for its lucidity and its methodical arrangement. It was the work of a man of unusual ability and of wide knowledge. Internal evidence indicates that the author was a churchman but was well versed in the decisions of the secular courts of the province.

In a royal English inquest held in the Channel Islands early in the fourteenth century, the inhabitants of these islands declared that they had adopted as a statement of their customs a collection composed by a Norman named Maucael, after Normandy had ceased to belong to the king of England. This compilation was known as the *Somme de Maucael*. This, says the French legal historian Tardif, was obviously the *Grand coutumier* of Normandy which in many manuscripts is entitled *Summa de legibus Normandiæ*.

This compilation was in fact first written in Latin, but was translated before the end of the thirteenth century into French. It obtained such general recognition and authority in Normandy that when, at the close of the middle ages, official compilations of provincial and of local customs were made under the authority of the crown, one of the very last of the customs to be revised was that of Normandy (1577-83); and the only reason why the Normans asked Henry III to have their customs revised was that the old French in which it was written was difficult to understand.

Besides compilations of local custom, there began to appear also in the thirteenth century systematic treatises. The most famous of these was a book dealing with the custom of Clermont in Beauvoisis, by Philippe de Remi, Sire de Beaumanoir. This nobleman was bailiff or seneschal successively of various counties and was a member of the parliament of Paris. His book, written in 1283, attained in north France general recognition and a high degree of authority. The author did not confine himself to an exposition of the custom of Clermont but added a comparison of this custom with other north French customs. He was obviously acquainted with Roman law but was not dominated by it. He was, however, progressive in his tendencies and in sympathy with reformatory ideas.

Among the various statements of city law there were some that exercised a strong influence upon the development and formulation of other and later city laws. One of the most important of these, naturally, was the custom of Paris. A special importance attaches to this custom because it was introduced in all the French colonies and formed the starting point of their legal development. French Canada, for example, was governed by the custom of Paris, supplemented by later legislation, until the nineteenth century.

The thirteenth century marks a turning point in French legal development by reason of the increasing power and influence of the crown. Uniform national law begins to be created by royal ordinance. The reforms which began in the reign of Louis IX dealt primarily with the administration of justice. Seigneurial and municipal jurisdiction were not abolished, but their extent was defined and gradually limited. High and middle justice were increasingly withdrawn in the local courts and exercised by royal officers. Procedure in the royal courts was regulated. The first step in this direction was the abolition of the ordeal of battle in the royal courts by Louis IX (1257-58). The royal ordinances dealt, however, mainly with administrative law and with judicial organization and procedure, less frequently with criminal law, and hardly at all with private law.

Of greater importance in the field of private law was the organization of royal courts with appellate jurisdiction. From the council of state there emerged a supreme court known as the Parliament of Paris, to which, at the end of the thirteenth century, appeal could be taken from all the northern French provinces. By the decisions of this court there was gradually developed a body of north French law which indeed did not derogate from established local custom but supplemented it. This body of subsidiary judge-made law was in the main as Teutonic in character as the common law of England, but gaps were increasingly filled by the acceptance of Roman rules. In the fourteenth and fifteenth centuries other parliaments — that is, royal courts with appellate jurisdiction — were established in south France, in Burgundy, and in Bordeaux. In these courts the subsidiary law, applied where local and provincial customs were silent, was the Roman law as set forth by Justinian.

Before the close of the middle ages, as already noted, official compilations of provincial and local customs, which were in many cases revisions of older written sources, were made by royal commissioners.

SECTION 35

Spain in the Later Middle Ages

In Spain the Visigothic code remained in force during the later middle ages in Leon, Castile and Catalonia. It is assumed, but upon very scanty evidence, to have been in force also in Navarre and in Aragon. It everywhere became, however, subsidiary law, for everywhere there developed customary law of the most varied character, and recourse was had to the Visigothic code only when customary law was silent. The names by which the various systems of local law were designated — "usages," "observances" and "customs" — sufficiently indicate their character.

When these customs were first reduced to writing, originally in Latin, later in Spanish, and when they were confirmed as *fueros* by kings or parliaments (*cortes*) — a movement which began apparently in the eleventh century — we find two clearly marked groups: the *fueros* of the nobility and those of the towns. There were also, but in much smaller number, *fueros* for the tenants of noble seigneuries and of church domains. How these bodies of law originally worked out is not in any way doubtful. Nobles were justiciable only in the king's court, and the customs of the nobles were the rules established by decisions in that court supplemented by rules laid down in arbitrations. Similarly the *fueros* in the towns were worked out in the proceedings of their courts. Doubtless also the customs of the manors were worked out, as we know was the case in France and Germany, by decisions in manorial courts.

In consequence, however, of the disinclination which most continental jurists have until recently shown to recognize that decisions make law, nearly all the Spanish legal historians lay chief stress upon the fact that these compilations of noble law and of the *fueros* of royal towns were confirmed by kings or *cortes*, and they sometimes deny that the rules under which nobles and towns had lived for generations were really law until they were so confirmed. The facts and the documents which they themselves cite prove the opposite. In the prologue to the old *fuero* (*Fuero viejo*) of Castile as revised by the king and the *cortes* in 1356, we have the following history of the compilation: "In 1212 Alphonso VIII confirmed the charters granted by Alphonso VI and VII and charged the magnates and nobles to search out their records (*istorias*) and write down the good laws and customs and decisions which they had and to suggest amendments. This done, the king, in spite of many appeals, withheld his sanction. But judgments were rendered according to this *fuero* as written in this book and according to these decisions [that is, according to this unauthorized compilation] until in 1255 Alphonso issued the *Fuero real*." Where *fueros* of other than royal towns were confirmed by the lord of the town, Spanish legal historians similarly insist that royal confirmation was necessary. In many cases, however, there is no evidence of such confirmation. One of the best and fullest of the codes of Spanish town law that have come down to us is that of Tortosa in Catalonia. This *fuero* was put in writing in 1279 after long disputes between the town and the lords of the town (in this case the knights of the temple) as to the existing law of the town. The disputes were settled by protracted negotiation between a legal representative of the templars and the syndics of the town, and a written formulation of the town laws was agreed upon.

Not only in this case but in other cases where customary law was confirmed by kings or by lords, the transaction resembles contract much more than legislation. The distinction is not easy to draw when the written law is confirmed or adopted by the *cortes;* but all legislation by medieval parliaments was substantially agreement or contract between the king and the Estates.

Of the nobiliary codes, so classed because they contain substantially the law observed by the nobles, although in some cases legal rules referring to other classes are included, the most interesting is the *Fuero de los fijos-dalgo.* This is also known as the Book of Decisions and Arbitrations and also as the Ordinance or *Fuero* of Nagera. This latter title indicates that it was sanctioned by a *cortes* held in 1138 at Nagera.

Municipal *fueros* are said to have been issued or sanctioned by kings or town lords as early as the ninth century, but none has come down to us that dates back of the eleventh century. In the eleventh and following centuries they became increasingly numerous until there was hardly a town of any consequence that had not its own special law. The later town laws not only contained the charters that set forth the privileges of the town but embraced more or less complete statements of the private law observed in the town.

The earliest attempts to set forth the general law prevailing in any of the separate kingdoms were the *Fuero* of Leon and the Usatici of Catalonia (1068).

In the thirteenth century the publication of *fueros* setting forth more completely the custom of each realm and bringing both noble and municipal law into a single code became general. In Castile appeared in 1212 the so-called Old *Fuero* (*Fuero viejo*) and in 1255 the *Fuero real.* Successive revisions of the Castilian law were made in the following centuries: the ordinance of Alcala in 1348, the ordinance of Montalvo in 1485, the laws of Toro in 1505, and the *Nueva recopilación* in 1567.

For the history of world law a special interest attaches to

the law of Castile because it was introduced into all the Spanish colonies as was the custom of Paris in the French colonies.

In Aragon a general collection of laws commonly known as the *Fuero* of Huesca was made in the thirteenth century (1247). This was supplemented by later collections. In Navarre a general *fuero* was enacted in 1234 or 1237, and this was revised in 1330. In Valencia general *fueros* were published in 1239 and revised in 1270. This old code was practically supplanted in 1548 by a private compilation of Valencian law which came to be regarded as authoritative. In Catalonia the old Latin code of 1068, the Usatici, was supplanted by a *recopilación* of 1413, and this again by a further revision in 1588.

At the close of the middle ages, accordingly, there existed no general law for Spain. Although the several kingdoms had gradually been brought into personal union, each kingdom retained its special parliament as long as parliaments continued to exist, its own separate judicial organization, and its own special bodies of law. In the codes of these separate kingdoms the general law set forth in no wise swept away the distinctions between noble law and town law, nor did it prevail over established local law.

SECTION 36

Italy in the Later Middle Ages

In Italy there was no such semblance of national organization as existed in France and in Germany. The elected king of Germany as Holy Roman Emperor held a nominal sovereignty in north Italy; but real governmental power was in the hands of spiritual and secular princes and of city republics. In central Italy the lands of the church were under the supreme authority of the Pope. Southern Italy and Sicily, conquered by Norman adventurers, were brought under the rule of a single Norman king. As a result of the failure of the male line and the marriage of the heiress to a Hohenstauffen prince, this southern kingdom was for a time brought into personal union with Germany under the Emperor Frederick II.

In northern Italy, on account of the mixture of races, the personal statute survived longer than in other parts of Europe. As late as the beginning of the fifteenth century it was recognized that there were here men living by the law of the Franks and others by the law of the Lombards. In southern Italy, where the irruption of Saracens and of Normans had produced other racial mixtures, the system of the personal statute obtained even longer. For a considerable time the *scabini*, or lay judges, in northern Italy were frequently so chosen as to represent the principal groups living under the system of the personal statute. Everywhere, however, as in France, there was gradually developed territorial law. In the mixed districts there was some blending of the different racial laws; in districts where there was little mixture of races the dominant personal statute became territorial law at an early period.

In Lombardy even before the disruption of the Frank Empire an interesting attempt was made about 830 to set forth the general rules of Lombard law in systematic form. This Latin compilation was entitled *Concordia de singulis causis* or *Capitula legis regum Langobardorum*.

Written statements of city law began to appear at an early period: that of Genoa in the tenth century, that of Pistoia in the eleventh, and that of Pisa in the twelfth century. In the thirteenth century there appeared many more compilations of city law. In many cases legislation was active. Dante derided the Florentines for changing continually their laws, their coins, and their costumes.

In Italy also there was imitation and borrowing. Parent or mother cities for Sicily were Palermo, Catania and Messina. The laws of Bologna seem to have been imitated in Florence and in later revisions of the laws of Pistoia. The laws of Milan formed a model for those of other Lombard cities.

In some cases, as in Spain, the general law of a province was put into written form. In the fourteenth century the collected statutes of Milan in eight volumes covered the whole county and diocese. In this and in the following century, Venetian legislation covered all the territories of the republic. In the fifteenth century the statutes of Rome similarly covered all the states of the church.

In the kingdom of the Two Sicilies we have a legal development closely resembling that which took place in the larger Spanish kingdoms. There was considerable legislation by the states of the kingdom in the twelfth century. In 1231 a systematic collection of Norman-Sicilian laws was made under the auspices of Frederick II. This so-called Constitution of the Realm of Sicily was one of the best codes of the time. Book I dealt with public law; Book II with judicial procedure; Book III with feudal law and to some extent with general law. It contained, however, very little private law: in this field local custom remained dominant. This code remained nominally in force until 1819.

In north Italy down to the thirteenth century, periodical diets were held under the auspices of the emperor as king of Italy. The legislation sanctioned by these diets was published in the form of imperial constitutions. This legislation dealt mainly with public law and with feudal law. After the revival of the study of the law books of Justinian, not a few of these imperial laws were included first in manuscripts and then in printed editions of the law books of Justinian in the form of an appendix to the codex.

In Italy, accordingly, as in France and Spain, the development of private law was essentially particularistic, and here as elsewhere in continental Europe the more local law regularly prevailed over the more general.

SECTION 37

Germany in the Later Middle Ages

In Germany the written laws of the Frank Empire, both the statements of tribal law and royal capitularies, went out of use. In many cases they had become inapplicable in consequence of changes in the social and political organization. Their disappearance, however, was probably due in part to the fact that they were all written in Latin, with which the lay judges, *schöffen*, were seldom acquainted. From the tenth to the thirteenth century, accordingly, the law applied in the local courts reverted to the form of unwritten traditional custom.

Here, as elsewhere, the manorial jurisdiction removed large numbers of people from the jurisdiction of the county courts. For a time the unfree knights were under the jurisdiction of the lord whom they served as vassals. For them a separate manorial court was held, distinct from that to which the tenants of the manor were subjected. With the disappearance of the distinction between free and unfree knights they escaped from the jurisdiction of the manorial court. As regarded their fiefs, they were subject to the ordinary feudal court; as regarded other relations, they were subject to the general law administered in the county courts, in which, by virtue of their holdings of land, they themselves became *schöffen*.

The customary law applied in the county courts was based on the older tribal law prevalent in the territory. To a considerable extent it was still described by the older tribal names: it is Saxon law or Swabian law, etc. Written statements of local law appeared in the thirteenth century. The most noted and most important of these was the *Sachsenspiegel*. Its author, Eike von Repkow, was a Saxon knight and *schöffe*. It was composed probably about 1230. It was originally written in Latin; but at the suggestion of Count Hoyer von Falkenstein, Repkow translated it into German. It consists of two parts: the first deals with ordinary law administered in the county courts (*landrecht*), the second with feudal law (*lehnrecht*). The law set forth in the first part is that actually applied at the time in the bishoprics of Magdeburg and Halberstadt. Repkow was a very conservative person, holding fast to tradition.

When we compare this statement of Saxon law with Beaumanoir's contemporary treatise on north French custom or when we compare each of these with Bracton's contemporary treatise on the laws of England, we notice interesting differences. The Saxon law seems to belong to an earlier stage of development, is more popular and is inferior in technical analysis. This is especially apparent when we compare it with Bracton's treatise, in which the law set forth is the custom of England as developed by central royal courts.

The *Sachsenspiegel* was largely used throughout the entire domain of Saxon law — that is, over a considerable part of north, central and northeastern Germany.

About the middle of the thirteenth century there appeared in south Germany a treatise purporting to deal with German law in general and called *Spiegel der deutschen Leute*. This was based on Repkow's work. The first book of his treatise and part of the second were modified to accord with south German customs; but the remainder of the work was simply translated from the Low German into the High German with little change.

On the basis of this work and with some use of the older written laws of the Frank period, an unknown ecclesiastic worked out what he called a *Kaiserliches Land- und Lehnrecht,* which, on account of the attention paid to south German and especially to Swabian customs, came to be generally known as the *Schwaben Spiegel.* It seems to have been published somewhere between 1259 and 1275.

Like the *Sachsenspiegel,* this south German compilation gained wide circulation and a high degree of authority. In the fourteenth century both compilations were regarded as products of imperial legislation and were cited as such in the courts. The Mirror of the Saxons was not only circulated in Latin and Low German but was also translated into Dutch and into Polish; the Mirror of the Swabians was translated into Latin, French and Bohemian. Both compilations were repeatedly "glossed" — that is edited with extensive marginal comments — and in the later glosses a certain amount of Roman law was introduced. Their popularity furnished an incentive to many less important compilations of territorial and local law.

These works on the substantive law, territorial and feudal, were supplemented by treatises on procedure in the territorial and in the feudal courts (*richtsteige*). There appeared also a smaller number of treatises on manorial law (*hofrecht*).

In the thirteenth century there appeared also numerous compilations of city laws. As elsewhere in Europe, the starting point is the city charter granted by the king or territorial lord. To this is added a statement of the customs developed by the decisions of the city court. In and after the thirteenth century, ordinances of the city council were incorporated as well as special decisions of the *schöffen.* The latter often ran over into declaratory legislation.

In most of the more important German and in Bohemian cities records of decisions, "books of judgments," were kept. By reason of the obvious advantage of putting transactions between individuals into the judicial records, it became usual to insert in these records notes regarding conveyances and mortgages of property and the establishment of ground rents. The insertion of such transactions was obtained at first through the machinery of the fictitious suit (compare the English fine and recovery). Later such transactions are inserted in the records as a matter of course; and in some of the towns separate records were kept of transactions affecting real property. Some of these so-called land books (*grundbücher*) were kept on what we call the lot and block system.

Literary presentation of city law as of territorial law begins in Saxony. Here the law of Magdeburg was the model usually employed. One of the earliest of these compilations, known as the Saxon *Weichbild*, consists of a digest of decisions followed by a treatise on the jurisdiction and procedure of the city court. In the form in which it has come down to us it seems to be a collection of separate treatises written by different authors. The oldest manuscripts date from the end of the thirteenth century. This work was translated into Latin, Polish and Bohemian, and it was to a large extent cited as authority in Polish and Bohemian city courts. This compilation was frequently glossed, and here also some Roman law was worked into the later glosses.

In the fourteenth and fifteenth centuries numerous other works appeared treating of the law of special German cities.

Until the thirteenth century there was little imperial legislation. Under the Hohenstaufen a number of constitutions were issued with the assent of the magnates assembled in imperial diets. Most of these constitutions (from the Concordat of Worms, 1122, to the Golden Bull of 1356) were organic or constitutional laws.

There was also some imperial legislation in the field of criminal law. The central authority was too weak to check feuds and breaches of the peace by direct administrative action. Resort was accordingly had to compact between a king and the more important territorial princes. From time to time the kings issue "land peace laws" (*landfriedensgesetze*), each for a definite term of years, swear to observe them, and obtain similar oaths of observance from the magnates. These compacts contain not only dispositions relating to breaches of the peace but also rules regarding other criminal offenses and provisions concerning procedure and preventive police measures. The first of these compact laws dates from 1103; the last was the perpetual land peace (*ewiger landfriede*) adopted in 1495 at the Diet of Worms. This was reënacted, with amendments, by several other later diets.

In the later middle ages, from the thirteenth century on, the authority of the German emperor-kings steadily diminished and the ecclesiastical and secular princes obtained increasing power and independence within their several territories. They gradually obtained general legislative power, laws being passed with the assent of the magnates of each territory. In this way a considerable body of territorial legislation came to be established in the thirteenth and fourteenth centuries. This legislation was mainly administrative or penal. There was little interference with ordinary private law.

There was through the whole period a royal court. It was attached to the person of the king and was held at first wherever the king happened to be. Judgments were rendered not by any permanent judgment-finders, but by the magnates, royal officials, and royal retainers who happened to be on hand. Before the end of the middle ages permanent imperial courts distinct from the royal council were organized. Neither the itinerant royal court nor the standing courts later established were able to develop general German law. Before the thirteenth century the royal court, as in other parts of Europe, dealt mainly with controversies between the magnates; at the close of the middle ages, when the standing imperial courts were in theory courts of general jurisdiction, no appeals ran to them from the more important territorial courts. In all the more important territories the princes had obtained the "privilege of non-appeal" (*de non appellando*).

SECTION 38

Reactions against Lawlessness

The disintegration of political authority on the continent of Europe not only impeded the development of national law but crippled the administration of local law. There were no efficient political organs for the preservation of the peace. Not only was there in many parts of Europe a recrudescence of feud as a method of settling disputes, but there was much open disregard of law and of private rights. It was the age of the robber barons.

We have seen that in Germany particularly attempts were made to preserve the peace by compacts between the crown and the territorial princes. The enforcement of these so-called territorial peace laws rested mainly in the hands of the territorial princes. They, however, were in many cases unable to control the action of their vassals.

The church did what it could to lessen the evils of feud or private war. It forbade fighting in sacred places. It endeavored to lessen the duration of violence: by the so-called Truce of God, there was to be no fighting in any week from Friday to Sunday inclusive, nor in Christmas week, nor in Holy Week.

Leagues of cities were formed in many parts of Europe, partly to protect their own independence, partly to protect trade. The greatest and most efficient of these leagues was the north German Hansa; but smaller city leagues were established in south Germany, in France, and in Spain. In Spain the city leagues were sometimes termed *comunidades*. In some cases in Spain the cities and the nobles formed territorial leagues for the defense of their rights against the crown or simply for the maintenance of public order. Both the city leagues and the wider leagues of cities and of nobles were commonly called brotherhoods (*hermandades*). Brotherhoods of the latter type for the maintenance of public order were not only tolerated but encouraged by the kings. One of the greatest and most efficient of these law and order leagues was the so-called Holy Brotherhood (*Santa Hermandad*) 1476–98.

There was a similar development in other parts of Europe. The most famous of all these leagues was the Holy *Vehm* (*Fehm*). Its organization and activities have attracted the attention of writers of novels and romances (Anne of' Geierstein). This league started in Westphalia. Here popular courts of the older Frank type maintained their organization longer than elsewhere in Europe. They consisted in yeomen and knights of the respective counties; but since the number of yeomen or free peasants was here much larger than in other parts of Germany the noble element was less dominant. Here also the authority of the territorial prince was developed more slowly than in other parts of Germany.

In the later middle ages the Westphalian counties were subdivided; at the head of each was a free count (*freigraf*) who in many cases held his little county in fourth or fifth hand — that is, through a chain of intermediate feudal lords — but who still received his *bann* directly from the German king. In each of these smaller counties a county court held regular and special sessions throughout the middle ages under the chairmanship of a free count. The members of each court were the knights and free peasants. Membership in the court, attached as elsewhere to the land, was described as a *freistuhl*, and the members of the court were called *freischöffen*. The jurisdiction of these courts extended over crimes, and their procedure was of the older Germanic type with certain modifications introduced in the Carolingian period. Of these the most important was the right of inquest: the court could take jurisdiction of a case on information in the absence of a private accuser.

In the latter half of the thirteenth century there appears in the body of free *schöffen* an inner and secret organization of so-called *wissende* or "initiates." These might and did hold secret courts. Before long this body of initiates outgrows the larger body in which it originated. Any honest born freeman of good repute and in possession of civil rights could be made simultaneously a *freischöffe* and a *wissender* although he had no seat in the county court. This wider secret organization which came to be known as the *vehm* was thus a great Westphalian vigilance society. It attained its greatest extension and power in the fourteenth and fifteenth centuries. In the fifteenth century all the higher and lower nobles and most of the city councellors in Westphalia were members of this league. At the same time its membership and its activity were gradually extended all over Germany, including the territories of the German Order in Prussia, and also into Switzerland and Bohemia. The Emperor Sigismund, Elector Frederick I of Brandenburg, many other princes and many bishops became members not only of the league but of the inner circle of initiates.

Sessions of this league might be either public or secret. To its public or open courts in Westphalia all the free *schöffen* of the county were of course summoned. To a secret court initiates only were summoned. It seems probable that in the earlier and narrower Westphalian organizations secret courts were held only when accusation was brought against an initiate. As the *vehm* assumed more and more the character of a vigilance committee, secret courts were held to pass upon charges raised against all offenders, whether initiates or not. In the fourteenth century the *vehm* had definitely cut loose from its original basis, the Westphalian county courts, and all its courts are secret.

The procedure of the courts of the *vehm* was conducted substantially on old Germanic lines. Whenever a criminal was caught in the act by at least three members of the *vehm*, no judicial procedure was required. The criminal might at once be hanged on the nearest tree. In other cases procedure is by inquest (*rüge*). All the members of the *vehm*, all free *schöffen*, were permanent and official *jurati* in the Carolingian sense of the word. In other words, all members of the *vehm* were permitted and bound to raise accusation on their own knowledge or on information which they had received. If the alleged crime was one of which the *vehm* took cognizance, then on accusation raised the accused was summoned. If his whereabouts was unknown, summons was posted at crossroads, on church doors or on other places of public resort. If his whereabouts was known, he was served with secret personal summons. In case of his failure to appear at the secret session to which he had been summoned, the accuser with six oath-helpers might swear that he was guilty and he was then put out of the law (*verfemt*). In such cases one or more of the free *schöffen* was designated to execute the sentence of the court. All initiates were bound to lend their aid if demanded. The sentence was always executed by hanging.

If the accused put in his appearance the case was decided on old Germanic lines. Wager of battle, however, was inadmissible. Ordeals of every sort were abandoned after the year 1215. The decision was then obtained by oath and oath-help. The accused was nearer to the proof and could swear himself free "self seventh." He must, however, find his oath-helpers among the members of the *vehm*. Over-bidding was admissible; if the accused offered to swear himself free "self seventh," the accuser might offer to substantiate his charge "self fourteenth." Then the accused could free himself only by swearing "self twenty-first."

Probably his original six oath-helpers might be included in the twenty.

With the great power which the *vehm* obtained came almost inevitable corruption. Membership in the order was employed for selfish and even for mercenary ends. The destruction of the *vehm* was ultimately brought about by its arrogance. The Emperor Frederick III was summoned to appear before it under threat of outlawry. It disappeared before the end of the fifteenth century. The need for such an organization had also disappeared; for by this time the growing power of the territorial princes had enabled them to develop a fairly efficient administration of justice.

There were sporadic survivals of the *vehm* in Westphalia and elsewhere down to the beginning of the nineteenth century. These may be described as local private courts with a vague jurisdiction over the morals of the peasants.

SECTION 39

Revival and Reception of the Roman Law

The revival of the study of the law books of Justinian, the intensive prosecution of this study first in the Italian universities and then in the leading universities of western Europe and even of England, not only the acceptance of the general principles of that law as authoritative, but also its practical application in most of the courts of western continental Europe — all this is on its face a very singular chapter of legal history. It is on its face strange that law books framed in the sixth century, written in a language known only to scholars, should be applied centuries later, not only in countries that had formed part of the Roman Empire, but also in countries which the Romans had never ruled. It is strange also that the old Roman law should have been accepted as living law in spite of the extensive changes which had developed in the social and political organization of the medieval world.

It is to be noted, however, that even where the Roman law was received as authoritative law it did not in theory derogate from any existing later legislation nor from established local or territorial custom. It was received as subsidiary law. Its relation to laws and customs of later date was precisely that attributed in our country to the English common law. It was generally described and, until it was superseded by modern national codifications, it continued to be described as the "common law" of continental Europe.

The fundamental reason why Roman law was received as the subsidiary law of Europe was that in the later middle ages there was increasing need of new law adapted to new economic conditions. From an economic system in which land constituted the chief form of wealth, Europe was rapidly passing to a system in which personal property was increasing in importance and in the variety of its forms. The basis as well as the measure of wealth was no longer land but money. These economic changes of course required a more refined and highly developed body of private law than was in existence anywhere in continental Europe. Since the ancient Roman law had been adapted to an economic system that was even more advanced than that of medieval Europe, its principles and rules met all the needs of the time —and to a great extent meet the needs of the modern European world.

A further reason for the reception of the old Roman law was the absence in most parts of continental Europe of organs, legislative or judicial, which could develop the new rules that were needed. The feudal courts were not concerned with personal property or with contracts. The ecclesiastical courts dealt with personal property to a limited extent only and only in so far as there was question of matrimonial relations or of succession in case of death; and they dealt with contracts only when performance was sworn or faith pledged or where a contract was usurious. The commercial courts took no jurisdiction of personal property or contract cases except where at least one of the parties was a merchant. For the settlement of controversies touching personal property or contracts in which neither of the parties was a merchant, the ordinary local courts were alone competent. Why these were unfit to adapt local custom to the new economic conditions has been explained in preceding lectures.

The acceptance of the law books of Justinian as living law was not caused but was generally facilitated by the theory, or if you choose the fiction, of continuous empire. It was assumed that all political authority in the medieval world was derived from the old Roman Empire, that the kings and princes were in some sense successors of the Roman emperors, and that for this reason the Roman law was still applicable in so far as it had not been superseded. The roots of this theory have already been indicated. We have seen that in the Teutonic kingdoms established in the fifth and following centuries in Roman territory there was a persistent effort to legitimize the new authority by connecting it with the Roman Empire. This theory gained a new basis when the Frank kings became Roman emperors and further strength later when the title of Roman emperor came to be connected with the German crown. In the tenth and eleventh centuries we find kings of Germany who were also Roman emperors—for example, Otto III and Henry II and III—introducing in their edicts rules borrowed from the Roman law and referring to these as the laws of their most sacred predecessors. In the twelfth and thirteenth centuries we find the Hohenstaufen emperors, Frederick I and Frederick II, in their conflicts with the papacy, citing Roman law texts and using these to prove the invalidation of papal decretals. In 1165 Frederick I declared that he followed in the footsteps of his predecessors, the sacred emperors, especially Constantine the Great, Valentinian and Justinian, and that he revered their sacred laws as divine oracles.

These were something more than claims advanced by the Holy Roman emperors: the theory of continuous empire was generally accepted both in Germany and in Italy. The Italian jurists indeed went further than the German emperors: they declared that all Christian peoples properly belonged to the Roman Empire and were to be governed by Roman law. An Italian canonist, Huguccio, wrote about 1200: "The Roman law binds the Romans and all who are subject to the Roman emperor. What of the French and English and other ultramontanes, are these bound by the Roman law and held to live by it? I answer, certainly; for these either are subject or ought to be subject to the Roman emperor, for in the Christian world there is but one emperor although in the different provinces there are different kings under him."

This theory was of course not accepted by the kings of England, of France or of Spain, but it was sufficiently prevalent to cause them apparently some discomfort. It is recorded that on one occasion when a German king who was Roman emperor wished to visit England he was not permitted to land until he had expressly disclaimed any political authority in that island. It seems also to have been due to the prevalence of the theory of continuous empire that the rulers of England and of Spain were sometimes described as emperors. Queen Elizabeth, for example, was not infrequently described as an empress. This may perhaps be regarded as an attempt to indicate that even if all political authority was derived from the old Roman Empire, it had been so divided that the Holy Roman emperor of the German nation was in no sense the superior of these western kings.

For the practical reception of the law books of Justinian — that is, for their application in the courts — two things were necessary. In the first place it was necessary that a sufficient number of persons should study the Roman law and study it thoroughly enough to plead it in litigated cases. In the second place it was necessary that men trained in Roman law should be able to attain judicial positions in order that Roman law might be employed in rendering decisions. The first of these problems, the training of students in Roman law, was solved in the universities. The second problem was solved only when the kings and princes of continental Europe were able to do what the kings of England had done centuries earlier — establish governmental or official courts composed of judges learned in the law. These were in fact established almost everywhere in western Europe in the later middle ages, earlier in some countries, later in others. As in England, these courts superseded the older popular or communal courts composed of lay judges. German legal historians speak of this last movement by which the reception of the Roman law was practically completed as the development of a learned judiciary; but it is obvious that the development of the learned judiciary became possible only in so far as the communal courts were replaced by courts of the official type. The periods at which Roman law was practically received and the degrees of authority attributed to the law books of Justinian varied in different parts of western Europe. The whole process began with the development of systematic study of the law books of Justinian, and this was first organized in Italy.

SECTION 40

Roman Law in Italy

There appeared in the middle ages a legend which still figures in some English and American histories that the Roman law as set forth by Justinian had no recognition either as law or as juristic science except in Sicily and in Sardinia; that it first became the object of serious study in northern Italy at Bologna in the twelfth century; and that this study was made possible by the discovery at Amalfi in 1135-36 of a manuscript of the Pandects of Justinian which was taken to Pisa and brought to the attention of north Italian jurists. This legend was questioned as early as 1720 by the Italian writer Donato d'Asti and was absolutely discredited by Savigny nearly a century ago in the *History of Roman Law in the Middle Ages*. Savigny showed that there were texts of the Justinian law books in monastic libraries throughout western Europe from which ecclesiastical writers drew citations throughout the earlier middle ages.

More recent investigations have shown that the study of the law books of Justinian did not begin at Bologna in the twelfth century. From the seventh to the eleventh centuries, inclusive, there were in many Italian cities ecclesiastical and secular schools of grammar and rhetoric, and in these schools there was some elementary study of Roman law, civil as well as ecclesiastical. In these schools were trained notaries who here acquired some notion of the significance of the traditional forms of contract and of testament to be employed in cases where their clients were living under Roman law. There were also schools that dealt independently with the elements, at least, of Roman law, with more or less use of the law books of Justinian. These were free schools — that is, private schools — and their importance and the character of the instruction given in them at any particular period depended on the learning and ability of the teachers. Schupfer and Salvioli think it certain that such a school existed at Rome down to the middle of the eleventh century and that this school was or claimed to be the successor of the Roman law school to which Justinian granted important privileges. It is certain, Salvioli asserts, that the Ostrogoths maintained this school at the cost of the treasury, although under Lombard and Frank rule it existed only as a private institute. The continuous existence of such a school at Rome is, however, questioned by later Italian historians. It seems to be established, however, that there were law schools at Pavia and at Ravenna earlier than that of Bologna. The school at Pavia exercised an important influence upon the development of the Lombard law, and this influence is attributed to the fact that there were teachers in this school who supplied the advocates and judges of Pavia with information regarding Roman law. In the eleventh century this school enjoyed a great reputation and was frequented by students from southern France, who carried home not only some knowledge of the Roman law but the manuals or handbooks of Roman law which were at the time in use in Lombardy. Some of these were afterwards recast on the other side of the Alps. Thus originated one of the most famous of medieval Italian manuals dealing with Roman law — *Petri exceptiones*. The existence of a law school at Ravenna from the beginning of the eleventh century can be proved, and it may have existed even earlier. It drew students from Tuscany and from the Romagna.

In these schools was developed a juristic literature consisting of texts with glosses or comments and of manuals. In consequence of the scarcity and great cost of the Justinian law books, compendia were prepared, sometimes in the form of alphabetical glosses. Among the later of these works were some in which the rules laid down were substantiated and explained by illustrations and by theoretic comments. The most important of the products of this early Italian study of Roman law were the Exceptions of Peter already mentioned, in which there are direct citations from the Digest of Justinian, and the *Brachylogus juris*, sometimes also called *Corpus legum*. This latter work was divided into four books, following the system of the Institutes of Justinian with reference to his Digest and Codex and also to Roman ecclesiastical literature.

After 1100 we hear nothing of the school of Ravenna. Bologna takes its place, and, by the more scientific direction given to legal studies, it obtains an extraordinary reputation. Without accepting the tradition that the school at Bologna was established by Theodosius or by Charlemagne, it is probable that it had existed for a considerable time before it became famous, and it is certain that, in addition to the customary instruction in liberal arts, Roman law was taught by masters and doctors of law before Irnerius. This teacher (1085-1125) inaugurated the period of the glossators, or commentators. In his glosses he went beyond grammatical interpretation of the sources and endeavored to formulate the rules and doctrines of the law. He was called "the lamp of the law" (*lucerna juris*). Among his most famous successors in the twelfth century were Bulgarus and Martinus. The former was more inclined to interpret the sources strictly, the latter attempted to find equitable interpretations. They were regarded as the founders in this period of these two schools of interpretation.

This body of teachers established the reputation of Bologna as *la dotta*, and about the year 1200 the university is said to have had ten thousand students.

Bologna professors played an important rôle in the political controversies of the twelfth century. In the struggle between the emperors and Popes over the investiture of bishops, Irnerius and the other legists defended the imperial claims, while the canonists supported those of the church. The Bologna legists drew up in 1158 the Constitution of Roncaglia, defining the rights of the crown (*regalia*), with copius references to the Novels of Justinian. They also drafted a constitution in which Emperor Frederick I gave special rights to the students and professors of Bologna.

The popularity of Bologna and the extent to which it drew students from foreign countries led in the course of the twelfth and thirteenth centuries to the establishment of law schools in twelve other Italian cities. The number of foreign students was so great that the student body in Bologna and in some of the other Italian universities was organized in "nations." Many of these students came from countries such as Germany, the Netherlands, northern France, and England, where at the time Roman law was not recognized as having even subsidiary authority nor cited in any courts except those of the church. Many of these foreign students were doubtless preparing themselves for practice at the ecclesiastical bar and for this purpose were studying not only the canon but the civil law of Rome. More numerous, however, were the foreign students who had no such intention and who confined their studies to the Roman civil law.

For what career were these young laymen preparing themselves? The only answer seems to be that they were preparing themselves for a career, that is, for administrative office. In the earlier middle ages the kings and princes of Europe were forced to depend upon churchmen for all services which could be rendered only by educated men, because the only educated class was the ecclesiastical. While these men usually rendered faithful service in political offices, there was always the possibility, because they were churchmen, of a divided allegiance. A systematic study of the Roman civil law was now producing a large body of learned laymen to whom public offices could be entrusted without any such misgivings as might be felt in the case of ecclesiastics. It seems probable, accordingly, that in the twelfth and to some extent in the following centuries the north Europeans who were studying Roman law, first in the Italian universities and later in such universities as Leyden and Paris and Oxford, were preparing themselves for public service, possibly in the councils of the kings and princes. If such greater prizes did not fall to them, they were at least eligible for minor administrative positions particularly in the cities. In the educational terminology of our time we should say that they were students primarily of political science. As a matter of fact we find that this new learned class of legists gradually supersedes the old learned class of ecclesiastics in many branches of public service.

Coming back to the development of legal science in Italy, special mention should be made, among the later glossators, of Azo, a Bologna professor who died in 1230. His *Summa* which may be described as a rather expanded volume of institutes of Roman law and his readings (*Lecturæ*) in the code were said to have been studied in the thirteenth century more faithfully than the law books of Justinian. Of him it is said, "Chi non ha Azo, non vada a palazzo." The method of instruction pursued by the glossators in their lectures was that of reading titles from the Digest or from the Codex with explanation and comment. This method also determined the form of much of their published literature. In addition to these they published in some cases collections of contemporary decisions, general systematic treatises like that of Azo, and monographs on special subjects. The exegetic labor of these glossators for a century and a half was summarized in the thirteenth century in the so-called standard gloss of Accursius. This came to be recognized as the authoritative interpretation of the law books of Justinian: "*quod non agnoscit glossa, non agnoscit forum.*"

The school of the glossators was subjected in later times to much criticism and even ridicule. They had little knowledge of Latin literature and made in some cases absurd mistakes in Roman history. They were, however, acute lawyers who by their comments and cross references brought the law books of Justinian into such shape that they could be used conveniently in the medieval courts. In many cases it can be shown, as it was shown by Savigny, that they misinterpreted the Roman rules. A later German jurist, Bruns, has, however, shown that in many cases what Savigny regarded as an ignorant misinterpretation was really an attempt to adapt Roman rules to medieval conditions. At the close of the middle ages, however, when jurists like Cujacius were enriching the study of Roman law through their knowledge of Roman history and Latin literature, they applied to the glossators such adjectives as ridiculous, absurd and foolish. Rabelais, who was not only a humanist but had studied the Roman law very thoroughly, compared the law books of Justinian to a garment of the most precious material adorned with jewels and surrounded by a border of muck. To appreciate this description it is necessary only to open any of the earlier printed editions of the *Corpus juris civilis* and to note that on every page a central square of the text of Justinian is completely surrounded in smaller type by the standard gloss of Accursius.

Throughout the middle ages, however, Italian jurisprudence dominated Europe. From 1250 to 1500 the Italian school of jurisprudence was described as that of the postglossators. They devoted much attention to definitions and to distinctions. Their chief object was a thoroughly logical formulation of the rules of law. Their method was essentially scholastic. They were criticized later as paying too little attention to original texts and too much to the standard gloss. Of them Cujacius said: "They use the empty language of ignorance; in matters of no consequence they are verbose and prolix; on hard questions they are silent." Among them, however, there were some famous names: in the fourteenth century particularly, Bartolus, a pupil of Cinus who was a friend of Dante; and Baldus, a pupil of Bartolus. Bartolus was one of the earlier writers on conflicts of law. A distinction which he drew regarding law governing inheritance is still frequently cited as an extreme illustration of purely verbal interpretation. If the law says, "Let the immovable go to the first born," that is a real statute; but if the law says, "Let the first born take the immovables," that is a personal statute. This of course meant that in the first case the law of the site was to govern, in the latter case the law of the descendant's domicile.

The practical reception of the Roman law — that is, its application in the courts as subsidiary law — came very rapidly in Italy after the revival of the study of the law books of Justinian. Here as elsewhere in Europe, the reception was complete only when doctors of law were associated with or took the place of the lay judges in princely and city courts. In the cities especially, need was felt for a more general, more certain and more equitable law.

Political considerations also promoted the reception. We have seen that in their controversies with the Popes the emperors were provided by the legists with texts that could be used against those contained in the canon law. It followed that all the Ghibellines in Italy — that is, those who took sides with the emperor and in general with secular authority as against ecclesiastical claims — favored the application of Roman law. Roman law was favorably regarded by the emperor and by the princes, as by kings and princes in other parts of Europe, by reason of certain texts in the Codex of Justinian which set forth the absolutist principles of the later Roman Empire, such as the assertion "*princeps legibus solutus*" and "*quod principi placuit legis habet vigorem.*"

As a result of the use made of the Roman law to support princely rights against papal claims, Pope Honorius III in 1219 forbade the ordinary clergy — that is, not the secular clergy — to study Roman civil law. Inasmuch, however, as acquaintance with the Roman civil law was of great value in the development of the ecclesiastical law, this prohibition did not seriously interfere either with the study of the Roman civil law by ecclesiastical lawyers or with the practical reception of the law books of Justinian in the Italian courts.

SECTION 41

Roman Law in France

In the twelfth century, as we have seen, the revival of the study of the law books of Justinian in Lombardy drew numerous students from southern France, and in southeastern France itself there was some literary activity in the field of Roman law. In the twelfth century French students thronged to Bologna, and for nearly two centuries French jurisprudence was dominated by Italian influences. At the close of the thirteenth and the beginning of the fourteenth centuries France developed an independent school of Romanists. They tried to vivify and fructify the customary institutions of their time through principles borrowed from the Roman law, and they endeavored to formulate in the light of the Roman law the theories underlying the French customs.

This original development was short-lived. By the middle of the fourteenth century Italian influence was again dominant, and down to the sixteenth century the writings of the Italian doctors furnished the schools of law and the courts of justice with their interpretation of Roman law. The gloss of Accursius enjoyed the same authority in theory and in practice as in Italy.

In the sixteenth century France wrested from Italy and assumed in Europe the leading position in the study and presentation of the Roman law. The leaders of the new school of jurisprudence were not only jurists but also humanists. An effort was made to give to Roman legal institutions their true force and original significance by examining their development. In other words, we have here the beginning of modern historical jurisprudence. There was also an endeavor to construct a new and independent system of Roman law. Characteristic of the new French literature, which was still written in Latin, was the superior quality of its Latinity. The barbarous and medieval Latin used by the glossators and post-glossators was replaced by the polished and elegant Latin of the humanists. The most distinguished representatives of these new movements were Cujacius and Donellus. Both were professors at the little university at Bourges. Cujacius was especially interested in the reconstruction of Roman legal history, and his work in this field is still of value. Donellus attempted to bring the rules of Roman law into more systematic arrangement. His great work, *Commentaries on the Civil Law* was published in twenty-eight volumes.

Donellus was a Protestant and after the revocation of the Edict of Nantes lived in Holland.

In those parts of France in which the territorial custom was in the main Roman and in which, in theory at least, the people were living by Roman law, the practical application of the law books of Justinian came very rapidly after the revival of their study. As elsewhere in Europe, the reception became complete in proportion as royal courts of learned justices supplanted the popular courts. Here, as elsewhere in Europe, the Roman law was not held to derogate from established custom; it had subsidiary force only.

In northern France, where royal courts of appeal had been active since the thirteenth century and by their decisions had constructed a subsidiary common law for north France, the law books of Justinian were not received. Roman law was cited as argument only, not as authority. In the judicial development of north French law many rules and principles had indeed been borrowed from the Roman law;

there had been what is sometimes called a particular reception of rules and principles but no general reception. It was neatly said that in so far as Roman law was applied in north France, it prevailed "*non ratione imperii sed imperio rationis.*"

SECTION 42

Roman Law in Spain

In Spain, where legislative organs had been developed, at least in the separate kingdoms, earlier than in most European continental countries, the law books of Justinian were fully received as subsidiary authority only in three provinces: Barcelona (the modern Catalonia), Valencia and Navarre. The completeness of the reception in these three provinces seems to have been due to the close connection of Navarre with southern France — the kingdom of Navarre having originally included territories north as well as south of the Pyrenees — and the almost equally close connection of Barcelona with Valencia on one hand and southern France and Italy on the other. The vernacular speech of Barcelona was substantially identical with that of the Provence, and the trade relations between eastern Spain and Italy were frequent and intimate.

In Navarre Roman law was received in the medieval form and with the Italian glosses; and in 1576 the *cortes* of Pamplona expressly recognized its subsidiary authority.

In Barcelona the subsidiary authority of the law books of Justinian was recognized by juristic writers as early as the eleventh century. They called their own local law "municipal" and the Roman law "common" (*dret comu*). The code of territorial law adopted in that century, the Usatici, contains a citation from the Digest of Justinian and other passages which are taken to show knowledge of eleventh-century Roman law literature. In the middle of the thirteenth century James I of Aragon, who was at the same time king of Barcelona and of Valencia, endeavored to drive the

Roman law out of Barcelona. This king had become involved in disputes with the papacy and seems to have distrusted anything that came from Rome. In 1251, with the advice of his council, he decreed "that in secular cases no Roman or Gothic laws, decrees or decretals be received, admitted, used in judgment or pleaded, and that no legist shall presume to appear as advocate in any secular tribunal, unless in his own case; provided always that in such case the aforesaid laws and bodies of law be not pleaded, but that pleas be made in every secular case according to the usages of Barcelona and the approved customs of that place where the case shall be tried, and that in default of such customs the suit shall be conducted according to natural law." This prohibition was apparently little respected and fell into oblivion. In 1409 the *cortes* of Barcelona declared that the court of chancery should administer justice according to the usages of Barcelona, the laws passed by the *cortes*, local and personal customs, privileges, immunities and liberties, common law, equity and sound reason.

In Valencia during the reign of this same James I a compilation was made of the laws of this province, but no attempt seems to have been made to exclude the subsidiary use of the Roman law. In the reign of James II Roman law was expressly recognized as having subsidiary authority.

In Aragon itself the policy of James I was more successful. The compilation of Huesta, published in 1247, declared: "Where, however, the said [Aragonese] *fueros* are not sufficient, let recourse be had to natural sense or equity." Of course the legists were convinced that Roman law represented natural sense and equity in the highest degree, and the prestige of the Roman law and the influence of the universities brought much of the medieval doctrine of Roman law into Aragonese practice; but something in the temper of this province kept its law more purely Spanish than that of any other part of Spain. As in north France, the Roman law might be cited by way of argument but was never recognized as having even subsidiary authority.

In Castile Ferdinand III (1217-52) and his son Alphonso X (1252-84) favored and encouraged the study of the Roman civil as well as that of the Roman canon law. In the university of Salamanca, founded early in the thirteenth century, Alphonso X maintained two Roman lawyers and three canon lawyers. It will be noted that no provision was made for instruction in the law of Castile. In 1401 this university had twenty-five instructors, of whom six were canonists and four legists, but there was still no teacher of Spanish law. A similar situation obtained in all the Spanish universities through the eighteenth century. Spanish law was systematically taught only in independent law schools described as *academias*.

These two kings also brought legists into their councils and into the royal court. The law books of Justinian were not received as such, but Roman law as taught in the medieval universities was introduced in the form of a special Castilian code, the famous Law of the Seven Parts.

It was in the reign of Ferdinand III that a plan was formed to set forth in the Castilian vernacular a systematic statement of Christian theology, canon law and Roman civil law. A fragment of such a treatise was completed; it is commonly described as the *Setenario* because it begins with a disquisition on the mystic properties of the number seven. In the reign of Alphonso X the plan was fully carried out in a work consisting of seven books, of which five only have come down to us and only in a single manuscript. This is commonly described by Spanish legal historians as the *Especulo*, although in his testament Alphonso X described it as the *Setenario*. This compilation (1256-65) is not yet the Code of the Seven Parts but only a first draft of that code. It is doubtful whether it was ever meant to be enacted as a code of positive law. It was probably intended either as a manual for the education of Castilian princes or as a treatise for the instruction of the lettered class in general and the judges in particular.

Almost a century later this compilation was subjected to a certain amount of revision and it was published as a law book to which subsidiary authority was expressly given by the Ordinance of Alcala, in 1348.

Since this code had important influence on the later development of Castilian law and since Castilian law obtained in all the Spanish colonies, something should be said of its form and character. Part I treats first of law, usage and custom and then sets forth the principal doctrines of the orthodox Catholic faith and the Catholic system of church discipline. Part II treats of the king and his relation to his people; of the estate and duties of the nobles; of the law of war at sea and on land; and of the organization and government of universities. The law set forth in this part is substantially the Spanish law of the time. Part III treats of the organization of the courts and of legal procedure. The law here set forth is mainly Roman but partly Spanish. It deals then with property, its acquisition, its protection and its loss. This is pure Roman law. Part IV treats of marriage and of the family. The law of marriage is pure canon law; the law of matrimonial property sets forth the Roman dotal system, which at the time had no existence in Spain; the community system which actually obtained is not noticed. Then this fourth part treats of masters and slaves (slavery was practically extinct in Spain) and finally of *seigneurs* and vassals. This last of course is general feudal law. Part V sets forth the Roman law of contract and the law merchant of the time. Part VI treats of succession *ab intestato* and of testaments. This is pure Roman law. Part

VII deals with criminal law. This part is thoroughly medieval. It includes rigorous provisions against apostasy, heresy and blasphemy.

In this résumé I have omitted to mention the philosophical, philological and historical excursions with which this code is decorated from beginning to end. This Law of the Seven Parts is quite as much a *summa* of the university wisdom of the time — medicine only being omitted — as a code of law.

Since this code was to have subsidiary force only and since the Ordinance of Alcala through which it obtained legal authority contained a fairly full statement of existing Spanish law, it is clear that a great part of its provisions were wholly inapplicable. Nevertheless where the local *fueros* and the general Spanish law were silent this code brought in Roman law; and with judges on the bench who were trained in Roman law; at the universities and who regarded the older Castilian law as a somewhat barbarous product, there was a tendency to construe Spanish law, local or general, very strictly and to find as many open places as possible which might be filled from the *partidas*.

The net result of this whole development may be summed up as follows: The Roman law as set forth by Justinian and as interpreted by the Italian glossators was received as subsidiary law in Navarre, Catalonia and Valencia. Roman law was also received in Castile but not so that the law books of Justinian received direct legal authority. In Aragon the law books of Justinian were not received directly or indirectly; although as in other parts of Europe gaps in the law were filled by a particular reception of special Roman doctrines and rules.

SECTION 43

Roman Law in Germany and the Netherlands

While France began to consolidate herself, Germany went more and more to pieces. As I have said before, the German monarchy was more powerful in the tenth, eleventh, and twelfth centuries than the French. While the French monarchy, however, devoted itself in the main to the establishment of its domestic authority, the German monarchy wasted its energies in the dream of universal empire, especially in the attempt to rule Italy. The revival of the imperial dignity in 962 was fatal to the German kingship. In order to obtain the support of their German vassals in their Italian politics, the emperors made constant concessions to these vassals, so that the territories became more and more independent of the central authority.

While the French monarchy became hereditary, the German monarchy remained always elective. The result was, of course, that at any election the new king was obliged to confirm all previous concessions and to grant new ones.

The year 1250, the date from which a firmer legal organization in France may be considered to have begun, marks in Germany the downfall of the last powerful imperial house — that of the Hohenstaufen. The dynasty was entirely annihilated, as you know, in the conflict with the papacy.

During the two following centuries, the period during which France laid the foundation of her later political and legal organization, we have in Germany, first, a long interregnum, then a series of emperors chosen purposely from different houses, in order to avoid anything like the semblance of hereditary succession. Finally in the fifteenth century the independence of the territories is so far established that they no longer fear the establishment of a powerful imperial dynasty, and the imperial dignity is authorized to remain constant in the house of Hapsburg. And the Hapsburgs in fact make no effort to reëstablish German unity, or to reinvigorate the empire; they confine themselves to the policy of increasing the territorial power of their own house. Under these circumstances it was naturally absurd to look to the king for any effective measures of legal reform. He was, indeed, the source of all judicial authority; but he had given the exercise of that authority away. He had still the right of interfering if justice was not done in the territorial courts; but he had not the power to make such interference effective.

The phenomenon which the Germans call the reception of the foreign law is the reception of the canon and the civil law. Since the existing emperors could give no relief, recourse was had to the older emperors and to the Popes — the legislative authority of the latter being, as I have already said, generally recognized. The fact that the Roman Empire of the German Nation — that is, the Holy Roman Empire — was regarded as a continuation of the Roman Empire was of material importance. The idea of the imperial continuance was no mere fiction under which the reception of the Roman law was cloaked and legalized: it was a general and deep-seated belief.

In the fourteenth century the first German university was established — that of Prague in 1348, followed in the same century by the establishment of universities at Vienna, Heidelberg, Cologne, and Erfurt. In the fifteenth century ten more universities were founded. We observe that the canon law was taught first in these universities, while the Roman law was not taken up until the end of the fifteenth century. It came to be considered necessary for the German who intended to embrace a public career to study law and make his doctorate. The emperors, as we have seen already, and the territorial princes also, began to choose doctors of the two laws (*doctores utriusque juris*) as chancellors, councillors, envoys, etc. The degree conferred upon its holder both social position and political influence; and in the middle of the fourteenth century Charles IV decreed that all *doctores juris*, no matter what their origin, should be deemed nobles and should become members of the lower nobility — *propter scientiam*.

The reception of the foreign laws had begun before the doctors had got hold of the actual administration of justice. A popular literature of Roman law had developed in Germany; brief collections of leading rules were made, and these collections had begun to be used in the courts. Moreover, the doctors had begun to draw up contracts, testaments, and other documents, in accordance with the principles of Roman law. Then, if the transactions were doubted by the *schöffen*, a doctor would appear in court as advocate for the parties and cite Latin by the hour until the bewildered *schöffen* either gave his client the case or refrained from giving any decision whatever. Experiences of this sort had naturally hastened the disappearance of the *schöffen* and the establishment of a learned judiciary.

The attitude of the German doctors to the German law was very different from that of Beaumanoir and his successors to the north French *coutumes*. The doctors in Germany were convinced of the perfect completeness of the Roman law and the absolute worthlessness of the ordinary German law. They term the German law *jus barbarum, lex sine ratione, jus per homines barbaros et ratione carentes conditum*. Hence, although in theory the *Corpus juris* of Justinian is accepted only as subsidiary and its rules are only to be applied if the German law is silent, in practice the

German law was to a great extent superseded. German law was recognized only as "local usage," and the party who alleged this usage had to prove it. The practical activity of these doctors in the administration of justice and the general application of the Roman law in the courts began in the fifteenth century. In the fifteenth and sixteenth centuries the *schöffen* disappear and a learned judiciary takes their place. The method in which the change took place is simple enough. At the court of the emperor and at the courts of the territorial princes the nobles and knights were gradually superseded by the doctors. In some cases the old court of noble *schöffen* is retained for a while — the chancellor, however, developing a concurrent jurisdiction. The same development took place in the cities; and the old lay *schöffen* were finally crowded out. The whole movement seems to have occurred spontaneously. It is not as if the *schöffen* were suppressed; they were simply superseded by force of circumstance. No one has any confidence in their law, nor any respect for their irrational form of procedure — no one will have anything to do with them. So they go and the doctors come in their place.

One of the methods of obtaining judicial decision much resorted to in the period of transit from the old popular court to the new learned court was the submission of cases to the legal faculty of some German university. This began in the fourteenth century and was greatly extended in the fifteenth and sixteenth centuries.

Commercial development, which Germany in common with most of Europe experienced at the end of the middle ages, made German law inadequate. A highly developed commerce demanded a highly developed law, and the German law was exceedingly crude. An extensive commerce demands a *common* law; diversity of legal rules in adjoining territories constitutes a serious check upon commercial activities. Commerce finally, like all business, demands above all a *certain* law; the merchant must know by what law his acts and contracts are to be governed. Now there was no common German law, and the local usages which supplied the place of a common law were for the most part uncertain, as is the nature of local usages. The German law therefore was inadequate, and the particularism into which Germany had fallen rendered the reform of the German law impossible. The Roman law, on the contrary, met these demands. The Roman law, according to the idea of the time, was the common law, if not of all Christendom — and many went so far as to assert this — at least of all who lived under the Roman Empire of the German Nation. It was at least a common law for Germany, Holland, and Italy. The Roman law was a certain law, having been reduced not merely to writing but also to the form of a code. And the Roman law was an exceedingly highly developed and refined law, a law whose provisions were certainly sufficient for the economical conditions of the time. The reception of the Roman law was accordingly on the whole an advantage. It was not the best thing that could have befallen Germany; it would have been better to have developed a common German law, using the Roman law to correct and supplement the German institutions. This was, however, impossible because of the lack of any central authority; and the reception of the Roman law was undoubtedly a better thing than the retention of the German law as it was.

The complete reception of the Roman law and its application in practice had unquestionably evil results. In spite of the universal character of the Roman law, it contains much that is specifically national in character and which, because it was chiefly Roman, was not suitable to Germany. The institutions of one nation cannot be imposed simply and *in toto* upon another nation without resultant inconveniences, at least, if nothing worse. And the way in which the Roman doctors attempted to suppress or ignore everything German made the matter worse. In some cases the results were disastrous in the extreme. For example, all the German peasants who did not own their land, but who on the other hand had not become serfs, sat on leased land. The lease gave the lessee a *real right* and was usually perpetual and hereditary (*erbpacht*). Now came the doctors with their Roman law and refused to recognize this relation, because at Roman law lease (*conductio*) was a relation of contract simply. So far from establishing a real right the lease, at Roman law, did not even give the lessee legal possession; the legal possession remained with the landlord. Not having legal possession the tenant was not protected against arbitrary ejectment, and his only remedy lay in the action for damages for breach of contract! A hereditary lease was unthinkable, of course, under these circumstances, for the parties could not contract for their heirs. Think for a moment now of the effect of this construction of lease upon the position of the peasant in general and the hereditary tenants in particular. They were delivered over completely into the power of the landlord, and all their rights against him were swept away!

Fortunately circumstances proved to be too strong for the doctors; and in most parts of Germany the *erbpacht* maintained itself as local usage. No better illustration can be found, however, of the danger of applying the law of one nation to the relations established by another; nor can any better illustration be found of the fanatic intolerance with which the doctors attempted to enforce their gospel of pure Romanism.

Although the Roman law had at first been popular in Germany, and although the substitution of a learned judiciary for the old *schöffen* courts had been brought about to a great extent by the demand of the people, it was natural that as soon as the doctors got possession of the courts and began to apply the Roman law in disregard and defiance of local German usage, a reaction set in.

With the completion of the reception of Roman law in Germany begin to appear protests against the *fait accompli*. These came mainly from the knights and peasants, more rarely from the cities. So in 1497 the Bavarian knighthood complained "that many things are done in contravention of established usage, whence arise deceptions, errors and confusions; for those professors of the law do not know our customs, nor if they knew them would they be willing to make any concession to them." Similar complaints came from the estates in Württemberg in 1514. The duke is requested to appoint as councillors and chancery officials persons born in the territory; furthermore he is asked to appoint as judges in his court "honest and sensible men from the nobility and the cities; and *such as are not doctors*, that verdicts may be rendered in accordance with established usage and that his Highness' subjects may not be unsettled and confounded." Protests of this kind were voiced also in the diet of Tyrol in 1567, 1619, and 1632. In 1513 there was a riot in Worms, and the rioters demanded the expulsion of the doctors from the courts and councils. The municipal council of Lübeck protested against the application of the "imperial laws" — that is, the Roman law — in 1555. Finally in the demand advanced by the insurgent peasants, in the general peasant insurrection of 1525, we find that nothing less was demanded than the complete suppression of the doctors. Article IV of the so-called "reformation" declared that "no doctors of the laws, be they clerks or laymen, shall be suffered in any court, in any trial, or in any princely or other council; but they shall be completely abolished. " For," the complaint goes on to state, "the law is harder for them to unlock than for the laymen, nor are they able to find the key until the parties are both impoverished and ruined." It is further suggested that they be "employed to read and preach the Holy Gospel instead of ruining folk by their delays and coercions."

When a national law reaches that height of development at which it becomes necessary for its application to be entrusted to a special class, the jurists, and when such a law outgrows the popular stage and ceases to be intelligible to the layman, one always finds a certain tension between laymen and lawyers, expressing itself in more or less abuse of the legal profession. This abuse gives a pretty accurate measure of the extent to which the layman is dependent on the lawyer, and also of the amount he has to pay for legal advice and service. When the jurists are so happy as to be able to give advice for nothing, as in the Roman republic, they are naturally well treated. In Germany, however, where the law was a foreign one, concealed in a foreign tongue, one might indeed expect to find a still greater jealousy and dislike of the lawyer manifested, especially if we consider the way in which the lawyers treated the local usages. No language, accordingly, is so rich in abusive taunts directed at the greed, the unscrupulousness, and the pedantry of the advocates as the German. The advocates were made directly responsible for all faults in the working of the law. They are the men who thwart justice by their chicanery and pettifoggery. These ideas gained so much influence and these views of the legal profession were so generally accepted that Frederick William I of Prussia attempted to suppress the advocates and to substitute for them paid officials, attached to each court, who should be bound to plead gratuitously all cases brought to them. It is evident today that the unusually wide breach between the lawyers and the laity in Germany and the unusually bitter hatred of the legal profession was in the main a result of the reception of a foreign law clothed in a dead language.

In the Netherlands the development was on the whole parallel to the German, although the union with Germany at the time of the actual reception of the Roman law was merely nominal. In many districts, as in Germany, we have a gradual, theoretic reception of the Roman law during the thirteenth and fourteenth centuries — that is, the gradual development of the belief that the Roman law is subsidiarily applicable. At this time we also observe its first application in contracts, testaments, etc. In the Netherlands, as in Germany, a practical reception of the Roman law took place in the fifteenth and the first half of the sixteenth centuries through the agency of a learned judiciary. The study of the Roman law in the universities facilitated this reception. At the university of Louvain, founded in 1425, Roman law was taught at the outset.

The practical application of the Roman law in the courts, however, is not demonstrable before the latter half of the fifteenth century. As late as the year 1424 the judges are directed by the Duke of Burgundy to judge according to established usage and their own five senses. In 1462, however, Charles the Bold instructed his representative (*statthalter*) in Leyden to proceed according to the content and form of the written laws — that is, the canon and civil laws.

As to the method in which the *Corpus juris civilis* was received and the extent of its legal authority, we notice the same development as in Germany. In other words, although in theory Roman law is only subsidiary, in fact it supersedes local law by demanding local usage to be proven in each case.

SECTION 44

Roman Law in Other European Countries

In the period most decisive for the reception of Roman law in Germany, Switzerland had severed her connection with Germany. No princes encouraged in this country the study of the Roman law or called learned doctors into the courts in place of the *schöffen*. And finally in the comparatively simple condition of Swiss life the old Germanic law was not found inadequate as in Germany. Switzerland had developed no extensive commercial connections, and the economic conditions were equally simple.

On the whole, accordingly, the Swiss law remained during the fifteenth, sixteenth, and seventeenth centuries a Germanic law, differing as suited the Germanic particularism in each canton. Roman law found little acceptance. A characteristic anecdote has been handed down of an unsuccessful attempt of a learned doctor to smuggle Roman law into Thurgau. He was a doctor from Constance and had the audacity to cite Roman law to the *schöffen* in Frauenfeld, Thurgau, before whom he was arguing passages from the writings of Bartolus and Baldus. Whereupon the *schöffen* interrupted him: "Hark ye, doctor, an *eidgenoss* [Swiss citizen] will none of your Bartolus or your Baldus or any other doctors; we have customs and laws of our own." After which explanation they put him out; and no Roman law was cited to them.

In the eighteenth and nineteenth centuries, however, Switzerland has undergone what may be called the theoretic reception of the Roman law — that is, through the universities the Roman law came to exercise a great influence upon the scientific construction and upon the development of the Swiss law. Today Roman law is taught in the Swiss universities just as in the German universities, and Roman law is cited, or argued at least, in the courts.

In Spain, as we have seen before, the Gothic king issued in the seventh century a code intended to bind both the Romans and the Germans. This code naturally contained not a little Germanic law, and hence the Spanish law through the middle ages remained considerably tinged with Germanic ideas. The influence of the renaissance of the Roman law in Italy showed itself in Spain in the thirteenth century. Alfonso the Wise summoned distinguished jurists to his court and encouraged the study of the Roman law. In 1265 the *Ley de las siete partidas*, which was based on established usage, introduced, nevertheless, much that was new. It borrowed, of course, also, as has been pointed out above, from the Roman law. The innovations contained in this code aroused great hostility, so that it was not put in force during his reign, nor indeed till 1348. Then the Law of the Seven Parts was published with subsidiary force; in other words, local usage was to take precedence, and when that failed, the provisions of Alfonso's code were to be applied.

The Spanish jurisprudence held itself in the main to the Law of the Seven Parts; that is, this compilation was studied rather than Justinian's code. A reception of the latter consequently did not take place in Spain, except in so far as the incorporation of many principles of Roman law in the code of Alfonso may be called a reception.

In Norway and Sweden the Germanic law developed itself through the middle ages in probably greater purity from any foreign admixture than elsewhere in Europe; so that the Scandinavian sources are of the greatest importance in the comparative study of old Germanic law. From the end of the middle ages the Roman law seems to have exercised a certain influence upon Danish jurisprudence, and so, indirectly, upon the Danish law.

In England, as you know, the administration of justice was thoroughly organized by the monarchy much earlier than on the continent. The basis of this organization is firmly laid in the reign of Henry II. He it was who revived the Carolingian institution of the *missi*, under the name of *justiciarii itinerantes*, or justices of eyre. He also made the jury a regular part of civil procedure. During the twelfth century, under Richard I, the court of Common Pleas came into existence. The development of the English common law was thus made possible, and that development began at once — partly by means of royal statutes under the Edwards, partly by acts of Parliament, but in still higher degree by judicial decisions. Simultaneously with these reforms begins the study of the Roman law at Oxford. A Lombard jurist named Vacarius lectured on the Roman law at Oxford from 1149 to 1170. We see the effects of this study of the Roman law clearly in the oldest English juristic writings — not in that they attempt to incorporate legal rules borrowed from the Roman law, but that they use Roman categories, Roman definitions, and Roman terminology in their treatment of the English law. The keenness of their analysis and the clearness and precision of their statements show also, I think, unmistakable proof of the thoroughness with which they had studied the Pandects. Especially typical in this respect is Bracton, the first of the great English jurists, the greatest name before Littleton. Bracton in his five books *De legibus et consuetudinibus Angliæ* took a considerable part of his work almost verbatim from Roman sources. He used the *Corpus juris civilis* directly, to some extent; but still more, a popular Italian work of the period: Azo's *Summa*. What he takes from the Roman law is, however, for the most part, only definitions and explanations of German legal principles.

All that we can positively affirm concerning the influence of the Roman law upon the common law is that the older jurists used the categories and conceptions of the Roman law for the scientific construction of the common law. Phillimore asserts that the judges of Westminister Hall had frequent recourse to the *Corpus juris civilis*, especially when new questions arose for which no earlier decisions had established precedents. Such a statement may be accepted as more or less probable; it is impossible, of course, to prove it. In theory, the judges found the law in their own brains. Practically, however, it would have seemed much trouble then to go to Justinian. But when we consider that the Roman law was diligently studied in England in the twelfth century, it seems not improbable that they did what Phillimore says they did.

The study of the canon and civil laws continued to be prosecuted during the middle ages. The study of the Roman law had, however, less effect upon the English bench and bar than was the case upon the continent, because in England acquaintance with the Roman law was not regarded as a sufficient preparation for a legal career nor even as a necessary part of a legal education. From the middle of the fourteenth century it may be considered as an established rule that admission to the bar or to the bench could be gained only by study of the English law in the Inns of Court. But in the Inns of Court, as far as I know, the Roman law was not studied.

That English equity jurisprudence was considerably influenced by the Roman law is, I think, unquestionable. The chancellors from Becket to Wolsey were regularly ecclesiastics. That they knew and used the canon law is certain. That they also studied and used the civil law may be accepted as probable in most cases.

Finally, English commercial law, especially as developed

by the decisions of Mansfield, is largely based upon Roman law. Mansfield himself was a diligent student of the Pandects, and himself, according to Phillimore, avowed that this was the basis upon which he had built.

LITERATURE AND REFERENCES FOR COLLATERAL READING [1]

BOOK I

BACHOFEN, J. J., Das Mutterrecht, 1861. (French trans. by the Groupe français d'études féministes, Paris, 1903.)
BRUNNER, HEINRICH, Deutsche Rechtsgeschichte, Leipzig, Duncker & Humblot, 1887-92, 2 vols., vol. 1, secs. 6-23.
FUSTEL DE COULANGES, N. D., La cité antique, 22d ed., Paris, Hachette & Cie., 1912.
GIRAUD-TEULON, ALEXIS, Les origines du mariage, Genève, A. Cherbuliez, 1884.
JHERING, RUDOLF VON, Geist des römischen Rechts, 4th ed., 1883 (French trans. by Meulenaere, 4th ed., 1888), Buch I, Abschnitt 1.
LIPPERT, Geschichte der Familie, 1884.
McLENNAN, JOHN F., Studies in Ancient History, London and New York, Macmillan & Co., 1896.
MAINE, SIR HENRY J. S., Ancient Law, London, J. Murray, 1907.
—— Village Communities in the East and West, London, J. Murray, 1871.
—— Lectures on the Early History of Institutions, New York, H. Holt & Co., 1888.
—— Dissertations on Early Law and Custom, New York, H. Holt & Co., 1886.
MORGAN, Lewis, Ancient Society, New York, H. Holt & Co., 1877.
POLLOCK, SIR F., and MAITLAND, F. W., The History of English Law before the time of Edward I, Cambridge, Univ.

---

[1] Students are especially advised to read in connection with these lectures all cited passages in Brunner, Pollock and Maitland, and the General Survey of the Continental Legal History Series. [Ed.]

Press, 1895, 2 vols.: vol. 1., chapter 2, Anglo-Saxon Law.

POST, ALBERT H., Ursprung des Rechts, 1876.
—— Die Anfänge des Staats- und Rechtslebens, Oldenburg, Schulze, 1878.
—— Bausteine für eine allgemeine Rechtswissenschaft, Oldenburg, Schulze, 1880-81, 2 vols.
—— Die Grundlagen des Rechts und die Grundzüge seiner Entwickelungsgeschichte, Oldenburg, Schulze, 1884.
—— Einleitung in das Studium der ethnologischen Jurisprudenz, Oldenburg, Schulze, 1886.
—— Studien zur Entwicklungsgeschichte des Familienrechts, Oldenburg and Leipzig, Schulzesche Hof-Buchhandlung, 1889.
STARCKE, CARL NICOLAI, Die primitive Familie. Eng. translation in The International Scientific Series, Amer. ed., vol. 66, New York, D. Appleton & Co., 1889.

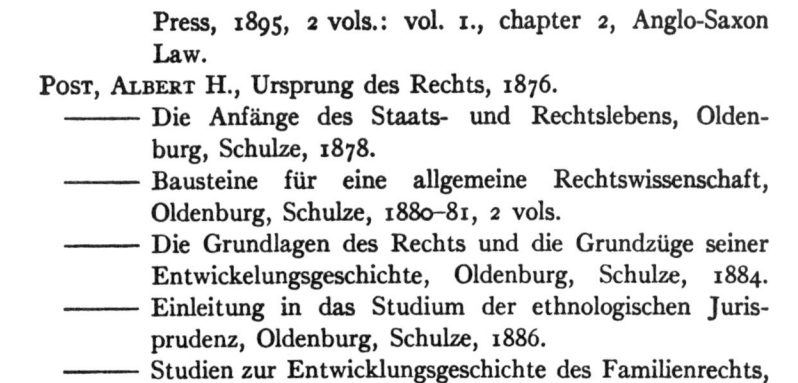

BOOK II

BETHMANN-HOLLWEG, MORITZ AUGUST VON, Der Civilprozess des gemeinen Rechts in geschichtlicher Entwicklung, Bonn, A. Marcus, 1864-73, 5 vols.
—— Der germanisch-romanische Civilprozess in Mittelalter, Bonn, A. Marcus, 1874.
BRUNNER, HEINRICH, Deutsche Rechtsgeschichte, Leipzig, Duncker & Humblot, 1887-92, 2 vols.
CONRAT, MAX, Geschichte der Quellen und Literatur des römischen Rechts im früheren Mittelalter, Leipzig, J. C. Hinrichs, 1891.
Continental Legal History Series, vol. 1, General Survey, pp. 9-19, 23-70, 95-99, 109-12, 594-601. (Boston, Little, Brown & Co. 1912-).
FICKER, JULIUS, Forschungen zur Reichs- und Rechtsgeschichte Italiens, Innsbruck, Wagner, 1868-74. 4 vols.
PERTILE, ANTONIO, Storia del diritto italiano, 2d ed., Torino, Unione tipografico-editrice, 1892-1902; 6 vols. in 8.

SAVIGNY, FRIEDRICH KARL VON, Geschichte des römischen Rechts im Mittelalter, 2d ed., Heidelberg, J. C. B. Mohr, 1834-51, 7 vols. (French trans. by Charles Guenoux, Paris, C. Hingray, 1839.)
SCHÄFFNER, WILHELM, Geschichte der Rechtsverfassung Frankreichs, Frankfurt am Main, J. D. Sauerländer, 1845-50; 4 vols. (2d ed. in 1859).
SCHRÖDER, R. K. H., Deutsche Rechtsgeschichte, Berlin and Leipzig, G. J. Goschen, 1912-13. 2 vols.
SIEGEL, HEINRICH, Deutsche Rechtsgeschichte, 3d ed., Berlin, F. Vahlen, 1895.
STINTZING, RODERICH VON, Geschichte der deutschen Rechtswissenschaft, München and Leipzig, R. Oldenbourg, 1880-1910, 3 vols. in 5.
STOBBE, OTTO, Geschichte der deutschen Rechtsquellen, Leipzig, Duncker & Humblot, 1860-64; 2 vols.
VIOLLET, PAUL, Droit privé et sources. Histoire du droit civil français, accompagnée de notion de droit canonique et d'indications bibliographiques . . . 3 ed. du Précis de l'histoire du droit français, Paris, L. Larose et L. Tanin, 1905.
WARNKÖNIG, L. A., and STEIN, L. VON, Französische Staats- und Rechtsgeschichte, 2d ed., Basel, Schweighauser (H. Richter), 1875., 3 vols.

BOOK III

BAXMANN, RUDOLF, Die Politik der Päpste von Gregor I bis auf Gregor VII, Elberfeld, R. L. Friderichs, 1868-69, 2 vols.
BRACTON, HENRY DE, De legibus et consuetudinibus Angliæ, ed. by Geo. E. Woodbine, 2 vols., New Haven, Yale Univ. Press, 1915-22.
Continental Legal History Series, vol. 1, General Survey:
    For secs. 23-26 [of the Development of European Law]
        "   "   see pp. 71-80, 112-13, 325-27;
                27-30 see pp. 92-95, 113-17, 335-36, 344-46, 466-67, 634-36, 705-24.

For secs. 31–32 see pp. 159–68, 222–24, 242–44, 313–14, 327–30.
" " 33–37 " " 80–83, 104–7, 203–5, 213–22, 224–30.
" " 38–44 " " 19–22, 87–92, 95–104, 108–9, 117–58, 206–13, 252–58, 334–72, 620–23, 627–34, 645–53.

DOVE, De jurisdictionis ecclesiasticæ progressu, 1855.
FRANKLIN, Beiträge zur Geschichte der Reception, 1863.
FRIEDBERG, EMIL ALBERT, Corpus juris canonici, Leipzig, Tauchnitz, 1879–81, 2 vols.
——— Lehrbuch des katholischen und evangelischen Kirchenrechts, Leipzig, B. Tauchnitz, 1879.
GAUTIER, Histoire du droit français, 2d ed., 1884.
GÜTERBOCK, KARL E., Bracton and His Relation to the Roman Law, trans. by Brinton Coxe, Philadelphia, Lippincott & Co., 1866.
HINSCHIUS, PAUL, Geschichte und Quellen des kanonischen Rechts, in Holtzendorff's Encyclopädie, 5th ed., 1889.
LAURENT, L'église et l'état, 1866.
MAASEN, F. B. C., Geschichte der Quellen und der Literatur des canonischen Rechts im Abendlande bis zum Ausgange des Mittelalters. Gratz, Leuschner & Lubensky, 1870.
MODDERMAN, W., Die Reception des römischen Rechts . . . Autorisirte Übersetzung, mit Zusätzen, hrsg. von Dr. Karl Schulz, Jena, H. Dufft, 1875.
MUTHER, THEODOR, Römisches und kanonisches Recht im deutschen Mittelalter, Rostock, E. Kuhn, 1871.
NIEHUES, Kaiserthum und Papstthum im Mittelalter, 1863.
RICHTER, Beiträge zur Kenntniss der Quellen des kanonischen Rechts, 1834.
RIFFEL, Geschichtliche Darstellung der Verhältnisse zwischen Kirche und Staat, 1836.
SCHAEFFNER, WILHELM, Das römische Recht in Deutschland während des zwölften und dreizehnten Jahrhunderts, Erlangen, T. Blaesing, 1859.
SCHMIDT, Reception des römischen Rechts in Deutschland, 1868.

SCHULTE, J. F. VON, Die Geschichte der Quellen und Literatur des canonischen Rechts von Gratian bis auf die Gegenwart, Stuttgart, F. Enke, 1875-80, 3 vols. in 4.

SCRUTTON, SIR THOMAS EDWARD, The Influence of the Roman Law on the Law of England, Cambridge, Univ. Press, 1885.

STINTZING, RODERICH, Das Sprichwort "Juristen böse Christen" in seinen geschichtlichen Bedeutungen, Bonn, A. Marcus, 1875.

STOLZER, Entwickelung des gelehrten Ritterthums, 1872.

TARDIFF, A. F. L., Histoire des sources du droit canonique, Paris, A. Picard, 1887.

INDEX

INDEX

A, meaning of, 66
Abduction, a case of "blood and honor," 31; payment of composition for, 32
Accursius, standard gloss of, 268, 271
Action of theft. *See* Theft, action of
Adrianople, defeat of Romans at, 78
Africa, North, division of, by Genserich and Valentinian, 78
Agency, law of, influence of church on, 211
Agobard, Bishop of Lyons, quoted, 117
Agriculture, little importance of, to early Germans, 9; growth in importance of, 72
Alaric, king of Visigoths, invasion of Italy by, 78; Breviary of Alaric, 88, 95, 189, 190, 230, 236
Alcala, ordinance of, 242, 277, 278
Aliens, conscription of. *See* Conscription
Aliens, status of, in Frank Empire, 116, 117; in Lombardy, 117; protection of, by treaty, 117; protection of, by king, 117
Allemanni, adoption of name by united Swabian tribes, 72; conflicts with Romans and Burgundians, 72; influence of, on British legions, 76; legislation, 126
Alliteration, use of, in early German rules of law, 67
Alphonso X, study of Roman law in Spain encouraged by, 276
Amalfings. *See* Carolingians
Ampurias, early Greek colony in Spain, 89

Anefang action, not limited to search for missing cattle, 54; ancestor of English action of trover, 55
Anjou, Charles of, 150
Annianus, breviary of, 94, 95
Ansegisus, Abbot of Fontanella, compilation of Frank capitularies by, 133
Antrustiones, 22
Apostasy and heresy, public crimes, 179
Apellate courts, development of, 233
Arbitration, international, influence of Pope on, 209
Arian kingdoms, overthrow of, by orthodox Christian armies, 84
Arminius, campaign of, against Romans, 15
Army, Germanic, division of, 14
Army, Roman. *See* Roman army
Arson, 28
Asega, functions of, 37
Assembly. *See* tribal assembly
Azo's *Summa*, 267, 290

Babylon, commercial law of, 218, 219
Bailments, 63
Banish, origin of term, 35
Bann, defined, 35; etymology of term, 35; imposed upon property of judgment debtor, 44
Bannitio, method of opening suit, 138
Barbarus, technical name for soldier, 77
Barragania, legal recognition of, in Visigothic law, 100
Basques. *See* Iberians

Batavi, location of, during third century, 74
Bavarians, origin of union of tribes of, 73; rule of Franks over, 102, 103; compilation of laws of, 130
Beaumanoir, treatise on north French custom, 248
Berengarius, king of Italy, 149
Betrothal (*sponsalia*), under Roman and Teutonic law, 198, 199
Biesterfrei or *vogelfrei*, 26. *See also* Outlawry
Bishops, appointment of, in Frank Empire, 183; increase in importance of, reasons for, 183, 184; election of, by clergy, 189
"Blood and honor," cases of, 31, 32
Bologna, law school at, 264, 265, 266
Books of judgments, German and Bohemian city records, 249
Bot dinge, 35
Brachy ogus juris, the, 265
Bracton. treatise on laws of England, 248, 290
Breviary of Alaric, 88, 95, 189, 190, 230, 236
Britain, invasion of, by Angles, Saxons and Jutes, 80
Brunner, cited, 23, 35, 68, 95, 110, 130, 131, 157, 186, 198
Bucellarii, retainers of Visigothic kings, holding land on military tenures, 160
Bulgarus, glossator of twelfth century, 265
Burgundian law, compilation of, by Gundobad, 87; application of, 87, 88
Burgundians, establishment of settlements west of the Rhine by, 79; defeated by Aëtius, 79; defeated by Huns, 79; migration into Gaul and establishment of kingdom of, 79; legislation of, 87
Burgundy, conquest by Franks of, 88

Cæsar, quoted, 57
Canon law, xxi, xxii, 153, 182, 191–207; sources of, 203, 204; Gratian's *Decretum*, 205; digest of papal decretals by authority of Gregory IX, 205; collection of decretals under Boniface VIII, Clement V (*Clementinæ*), and Gregory XIII (*Corpus juris canonici*), 206; digest of ecclesiastical law, made at initiative of Leo XIII, 207; influence upon modern law, 208–12; influence upon commercial law, 224. *See also* Church
Capitularies, royal ordinances of Frank Empire, 131 f., 189, 190, 247; compilation by Ansegisus, 133, 190; compilation of forged capitularies, 190
Carnal affinity, bar to marriage, 197
Carolingians, unification of Frank Empire under, 102, 103; royal ordinances or capitularies, 131; *legibus addenda, per se scribenda*, and *capitola missorum*, 131, 132
Carthaginians, rule of, in Spain, 89
Castellani. *See Milites limitanei*
Castile, law of, 243
Catalonia, annexation of, by Franks, 103
Cattle, importance of, among primitive Germans, 8
Cattle oath, 63, 136
Celibacy, enforcement of clerical, 192
Celtic law, early, 4
Charlemagne, Frank Empire under, 103; coronation of, at Rome as emperor, 103, 104; compilation of laws by, 127, 128, 129; supervisory powers of ecclesiastical *missi* during time of, 184; coöperation between church and state in reign of, 187
Charles of Anjou, reign of, 150

Charte d'Oléron, 226
Chindasvind, compilation of laws by, 96
Christianity, conversion of Germans to, 72; abolition of heathenism in Roman Empire, 177, 178
Church, acquisition of land by, 107; status of slaves on church lands, 111; seizures of church lands by Charles Martel and his successors, 162, 163; readjustment of relations with state, 163; Christian church in Roman Empire, 176–79; jurisdiction of, over morals of laity, 178; jurisdiction over civil cases in Roman Empire, 179; church in Frank Empire, 180–90; ecclesiastical legislation, 181; jurisdiction, 184–87; jurisdiction and canon law during later middle ages, 191–207; power of, during eleventh and twelfth centuries, 191; civil and criminal jurisdiction, 192 ff.; jurisdiction over marriage, 198 ff.; influence upon modern law, 208–12
City government, development of, 213–16; election of magistrates, 213; perpetuation of city councils by coöptation, 213; struggle for municipal autonomy, 214, 215; commercial and political power of Hanseatic League, 216
City republics, in Italy and Germany, 150, 151
Civil jurisdiction. *See* Jurisdiction, civil
Civil procedure. *See* Courts and procedure
Civitas, division of, 14
Clementinæ, collection of papal decretals, 206
Clergy, unfrocking of, 179, 184, 185
Clovis, conversion to Christianity of, 101

Code Napoleon, xxv, 55, 173
Coloni, German captives settled on Roman soil as, 74; reduced to serfdom in Gaul and other parts of Roman Empire in fourth and fifth centuries, 106, 155; free tenants in Roman republic, 155
Comitatus, 16, 20 f.; responsibility of lord for acts of retainers, 21; rights and duties of lord, 21, 22; relationship between lord and retainer, 21–22; effect upon feudal system, 23, 159
Commandita, institution of silent partnership, 212
Commercial law, development of, xxii, xxiii, 153, 217–26; difference between English and continental systems of, xxiii; *jus gentium*, 218, 220; national codes of, in continental countries, 218; Babylonian law, 218, 219; Greek law, 219; *Lex Rhodia de jactu*, 219; development of, in Roman Empire, 220; in self-governing cities of Italy, Spain, France and Germany, 221, 222; importance of seaport towns, 222–23; maritime law of Barcelona, Oléron, Wisby, Bristol, 223, 225, 226
Common law of England, development of, 290
Common Pleas, court of, establishment during twelfth century of, 290
Complaint, formulation of, 39; "staff saying" or "bestaving," 39
Composition, 29, 31; choice between feud and, 31–32; insistence upon reciprocity (equality oath), 31–32; suit for, in popular court, 32; payment of, in cattle or horses, 32; payment of "peace money," "wite," or "lawbreach," 32–33. *See also Wergeld*

Comunidades, establishment of, in Spain, 253

Concordia de singulis causis, 245

Conflict of laws, in Frank Empire, 117-23

Conscription, aliens on Roman soil subject to, 76

Consortes, relationship between Roman owner and German invader, 82

Constitutio de foresta, origin of, 131

Constitution of the Realm of Sicily, 245-46

Consulatis maris, 225

Consuls, judicial functions of, 224, 225

Conteur, functions of, 135

Continuous empire, theory of, 259, 260

Contract, 61-65; importance of form in early law, 61; origin of *wed* contract or *wadiatio*, 62; bailments, 63, 64; executory and executed agreements, 65; sale, 65

Corpus juris canonici, prepared under Gregory XIII, 206, 207

Corpus juris civilis, gloss by Accursius to the, 268

Corpus legum, the, 265

Cortes, development of, in Spanish kingdoms, 152

Counts, attempts of, to establish independent personal holdings at expense of tenants, 109; creation of royal counts among Saxons in 782, 113; authority of, to punish criminals and execute judgments, 138; liberation of cities from rule of, 150; jurisdiction over free persons in immunities, 158; duty to levy army in county, 158; rights and duties in Frank Empire, 164; office regarded as benefice or fief, 167; supervision by *missi*, 183; jurisdiction over cities of Teutonic kingdoms on Roman soil, 213; establishment during middle ages in Westphalia of county courts under the chairmanship of free counts, 254

County courts, how constituted, 229; in Westphalia during later middle ages, 254

Court, duty of defendant to appear in, when summoned, 38

Court of Common Pleas. See Common Pleas, court of

Courts, organization of, in Frank Empire, 134; capitulary of Charlemagne regulating attendance of freemen by, 134; important changes in procedure of, in Frank Empire, 135-36; execution of civil judgments, 138

Courts, tribal, 34 ff.; *echte dinge*, 35; *bot dinge*, 35; *afterdinge*, 35; jurisdiction of, 35; powers of presiding judges, 36; finding of judgments in, 36, 37; purpose and functions of early courts, 67

Courts and procedure, 34-44; procedure in early German courts, 38; formulation of complaint and answer, 39; oath and oath-help, 40, 41, 42, 43; purpose of procedure, 43; settlement of disputes out of court, 43; important changes in procedure in Frank Empire, 135-38; ecclesiastical courts, 202, 203; trial by jury, 210; modern developments, 212; *consulatus maris*, 225; *vehm* courts, 255, 256

Crimes, 24-28; origin of criminal law, 24; crime distinguished from tort in early German law, 25; punishment of criminals, 25, 209, 210; jurisdiction over, 156, 158, 179, 186, 193, 194, 195, 227. See also Jurisdiction, criminal

Criminal jurisdiction. See Jurisdiction, criminal

Criminal law, origin of, 24; during later middle ages in Germany, 250, 251
Criminal procedure, in Frank Empire, 139; in ecclesiastical courts, 202 f. See also Courts and procedure
Cujacius, criticism of glossators, 268, 269, 272
Custom of Paris, 238, 243
Cyprus, feudal law of, 175

Decalvatio, definition of term, 99
Denariales, or "penny freemen," 112
Disintegration, period of, 149 ff.
Dominium eminens. See Eminent domain
Dominium utile, right of, 171
Donellus, *Commentaries on the Civil Law* by, 272
Dower right, origin of, 49
Droit d'aubaine, origin of, 117

East Germans, racial division of, 6
East Roman Empire, xviii
Ecclesiastical courts, jurisdiction of, xxii, 184-87, 192 ff.; procedure of, modeled after that of late Roman Empire, 202
Ecclesiastical establishments, grant of immunity to, 155, 156, 157
Ecclesiastical law. See Canon law
Echte dinge, 35; attendance by freemen without special summons, 35
Economic conditions, of early Germans, 8 ff.; in Frank Empire, 106-14, 161; in Europe during later middle ages, 258, 259
Egriga, revision of Reccesvind's code by, 96
Eminent domain, right of, 171
England, development of central lawmaking organs in, xx; feudalism in, 170; introduction of trial by jury, 210, 211; reformation of court procedure, 212; commercial law part of common law, 218; jurisdiction of ecclesiastical courts in, 227; establishment of shire courts, 229; origin of court of common pleas, 232, 290; study of law books of Justinian, 258; theory of continuous empire not accepted in, 261; establishment of learned judiciary, 261, 262; influence of Roman law on English law, 290-92; institution of Justices of Eyre, 290; study of Roman law at Oxford, 290; development of English common law, 290; Court of Common Pleas, 290
Equality oath, 32
Erbpacht, its conflict with Roman law, 284
Especulo, the, 276
Ethelbert, law of, concerning marriage by sale, 49
Ethelred, law of, concerning payment of *wergeld* in cases of seduction, 49
Eurich, code of, 95; military tenures, 160
Ewa, meaning of, 66, 125
Excommunication, penalty of, 178

Fæth, 29
Faida, 29
False Benedict, 189, 190
Family relations, 47-53; husband and wife, 47-50; father and child, 50-51; guardian and ward, 51, 52; the sib, 51, 52; kinship through the female line, 52, 53
Father's power over children, 50, 51
Fehm. See Vehm
Ferdinand III, study of Roman law in Spain fostered by, 276
Ferdinand and Isabella, unification of Spanish monarchy in fifteenth century by marriage of, 151

Feud, defined, 29; prosecution of, 30; substitution of composition for, 31
Feudal law, xx, xxi, 153, 173; compilations of, 174, 175, 248, 249
Feudal system, origin and development of, 23; 154–60; immunity from payment of taxes and personal service, 155, 156, 157; decrease in number of small landholders, 157; service to be rendered by retainers, 160; based on military service, first developed in Frank Empire, 161; fighting prelates of later middle ages, 161; feudal tenures in Frank Empire, 161–65; fully developed feudalism, 166–75; reversion of fief to feudal superior in certain cases, 167; feudalism in Spain, 168, 169; in England, 170; eminent domain and practical ownership, 171, 172; system of primogeniture, 172; compilations of feudal law, 173, 174, 175
Feudal tenures, 23, 60, 159; in the Frank Empire, 161–65; abolished by revolutions in eighteenth and nineteenth centuries, 173
Feudalism. *See* Feudal system
Fides facta, explained, 64
Fief, source of revenue, 167
Filii alicuius, fijos d'algo, belonging to lower nobility in medieval Spain, 168
Fiscus, lands of, immune from payment of taxes and personal service in Roman Empire, 155
Folgeras, 22
Folkmoot, 17, 18; procedure, 18, 19
Forisbannire, 35
Forms of legal acts, 45–46; self-mortgage, 62, 64
Forspeaker, functions of, in Frank Empire, 137
Forum judicum Gothorum, 100
France, development of états généraux, or estates general, in, 152; local and customary law in later middle ages, 236–39; compilations of laws, 237, 238; organization of royal courts with appellate jurisdiction, 239; revival and reception of Roman law, 271–73
Frankalmoign, religious, charitable, and educational services by special feudal tenure, 164
Frank capitularies. *See* Capitularies
Frank Empire, xix, xx; historical data, 101–5; developments from fourth to sixth centuries, 101–2; conversion of Clovis to Christianity, 101; victory over Visigoths, 101; conquest of Thuringians and Burgundians, 101–2; annexation of southeastern Gaul, 102; conquest of Bavarians, 102; annexation of Langobard kingdoms in Italy by Charlemagne, 102; unification of empire under the Carolingians, 102–3; conquest of Lombards, Saxons, East Frisians and other Germanic tribes by Charlemagne, 103; coronation of Charlemagne at Rome as emperor, 103, 104; division of empire in 843, 104; reunion of empire under Charles III, 104; final division of empire in 888, 105; origin of present France and Germany, 105; economic and social conditions, 106–14, 161; legal developments, 115–23; right of Germanic tribes and Romans to live under own law, 115 ff.; conflict of laws, 117–23; the written laws, 124–33; courts and their procedure, 134–46; organization of courts, 134; origin of *schöffen* courts, 134; important changes in court procedure, 135–38; inquest procedure, 141–46; roots of

feudal system, 154; immunity of fiscal lands and ecclesiastical establishments from payment of taxes and from personal service, 155; feudal tenures, 161-65; Christian church in Frank empire, 180-90; ecclesiastical legislation, 181; jurisdiction of church, 184-87

Franks, establishment of tribes of, along lower Rhine, 73; conquest of northern Gaul by, 80; Visigoths expelled from Gaul by, 80; overthrow of Burgundians by, 80

Frederick I, *Landfriede* of the emperor, 25; special rights conferred upon students and professors of Bologna by, 266

Frederick III, summoned to appear before the *vehm*, 257

Freedmen, status of, 11, 12

Freemen, duty to attend courts, 108; military duties, 108

Freigraf, chairman of county courts in Westphalia during middle ages, 254

Freischöffen, members of Westphalian county courts, 254

Freistuhl, 254

Frisians, under Roman rule until end of third century, 73, 74; compilation of laws, 130, 131

Fronurteile. See Holy judgments, 34

Fuero jusgo, 100

Fuero of Huesca, 243

Fuero of Leon, 242

Fuero of Nagera, 242

Fuero of Tudela, compilation of feudal law down from *Fuero* of Sobrarbe, 174

Fuero real, 242

Fuero viejo or Old *Fuero*, 242

Gau, German division of tribe, 14, 15, 37

Gau court, 36

Gaul, invasion of, by Vandals and Swabians, 78

Genserich, treaty between Valentinian and, 78

German customs, adoption of, in Roman army, 77

Germanic kingdoms on Roman soil, 78-84

Germany, historic significance of final division of Frank Empire in 888, 105; imperial diet or *Reichstag* during thirteenth century, 152; local law in later middle ages, 247-52; reaction against lawlessness, 253-57; revival and reception of Roman law, 258-62; theory of continuous empire, 259-60; establishment of learned judiciary, 261, 262; reception of Roman law, 279-87

Gesithas, royal retainers of earliest Saxon period, 160

Gewer, 46, 50, 54

Ghibellines, protagonists of Roman law in Italy, 269

Glossators, in Italy, 265, 267, 268; method of instruction by, 267; criticism, 268

Goldschmidt, cited, 220, 221, 225

Goths, migration of, 71; attacked by Huns, 78

Grand coutumier of Normandy, 237

Gratian's *Decretum*, 205

Gregory VII, enforcement of clerical celibacy under, 192

Gregory IX, digest of papal decretals under, 205

Grundbücher, land books kept on lot and block system, 250

Gundobad, compilation of Burgundian law by, 87, 88, 125

Half-free class, *wergeld* of, 112; manumission by church, 112; by testa-

ment, 112; by the penny (*per denarium*), 112
Hand wahre Hand, old German rule of, 55
Hanseatic League, commercial and political power of, 216; development of court of appeals promoted by, 235; protection of independence and trade, 253
Hapsburg, establishment of the house of, 280
Henry I, reign of, 149
Hermandades, establishment in Spain of, 254
Herzog, authority of, 16
Hispana, important collection of decrees of church councils and of papal decretals, 189
Hofrecht, treatises on manorial law, 249
Hohenstaufen, downfall of the imperial house of, 279
Holy judgments, 34
Holy Roman Empire of the German Nation, 105, 150, 244, 260, 261, 280, 283
Holy *Vehm*, organization of the, 254. *See also Vehm*
Hospes, 82
"Hospitality." *See* Quartering of troops
House carls, 22
Huesta, compilation of, 275
Hufen, defined, 107
Hundred court, originally both sacral and political body, 34; procedure in, 34; jurisdiction of, 35; majority of controversies settled by, 35
Hundreds, division of the *pagus* into, 15
Huns, migration of the, into central Europe, 78
Husband and wife, establishment of relationship of, 47, 48; payment of composition by abductor, 47; legal position of wife at early Roman law, 48; morganatic marriage, 49; power of husband over wife, 50

Iberians, original population of Spain, 89; Basques, descendants of, 89
Illegitimacy, 199
Illyrians, conscription by Romans of, 76; rivalry between Germans and, 76
Immunity from payment of taxes and from personal service in later Roman Empire and in Gaul, 155; development of system, 155, 156, 228; ecclesiastical establishments, 155, 156, 157
Impedimenta dirimentia, 196, 197
Inbreeding or endogamy, cause of, during reign of Charlemagne, 109; during middle ages, 198
Inheritance to land, establishment of right of, 107. *See also* Succession
Innocent III, efforts to humanize laws of war by, 209
Inquest, development of procedure by, 141; employment of inquest procedure in Merovingian period, 141-43; origin and subsequent development, 143-46; in later middle ages, 202, 203, 254, 255, 256; superseded by jury trial, 210
Interest on loans, 211, 212
International law, influence of idea of a community of Christian nations upon, 105; influence of canon law on international relations, 208; international arbitration cases submitted to Pope, 209; efforts of church to humanize laws of war, 209; *jus gentium*, 218, 220, 223
Investitures, conflicts over, 192
Irnerius, glosses of, 265; participation in struggle between emperors and

popes over investiture of bishops, 266
Isidore of Seville, collected writings of, 189; "Isidoriana" falsely ascribed to, 189
Italy, invasion of, by Visigoths, 78; local and provincial law during later middle ages, 244-46; prevalence of local law over general law, 246; theory of continuous empire, 260; study of law books of Justinian in, 262; establishment of learned judiciary in, 261, 262; reception of Roman law in, 263-70; medieval law schools in, 263, 264, 265, 266; glossators, 265, 267, 268

Jerusalem and Antioch, assizes of, compiled during thirteenth century, 175
Jhering, on evolution of law, 45
Judgments, in early courts, 34 f.; finding of, 36, 37, 39; execution of, 44; sureties for satisfaction of, 44
Jurisdiction, civil, in immunities, 157, 158; its exercise by episcopal courts, 179; benefices, tithes, and other property rights, 193, 194; commercial courts, 227
Jurisdiction, criminal, in Roman Empire and in Gaul, 156; over free persons living in immunities, 158; trial of clergymen in ecclesiastical courts, 179, 186, 193; concurrent jurisdiction of ecclesiastical and secular courts, 194, 195; feudal courts, 227; local courts, 227; Westphalian county courts, 254, 255; *vehm* courts, 255, 256
Jurisprudence, beginning of modern historical, in France, 272
Jury, trial by, 210, 211
Jus albinagii, origin of, 117
Jus gentium, 218, 220, 223

Justices of eyre, instituted by Henry II, 290
Justinian, armies of, overthrow of Ostrogoths and Vandals by, 80, 85
Justinian, law books of, xxiv, 85, 173, 174, 179, 234, 236, 239, 246, 258, 259, 261, 262, 264, 267, 268, 272, 274, 276, 291

Kaiserliches Land- und Lehnrecht, 249
King, ownership of forest and waste lands in, among Franks and other Germanic tribes, 106, 107
Kings and princes, election of, among Germans, 16, 149, 169; in Italy and France, 149; difference between, 16; functions of, 17
Kingship, origin of, 16, 17; elective at first, later becomes hereditary, 149, 169
Kinship group. *See Sib*
Knecht, old German word for slave, 110; service in Frank cavalry, 163

Lag, words derived from the Indo-European root, 66; defined, 66
Landfriedensgesetze, land peace laws, issued during later middle ages, 251
Landrecht, compiled by Eike von Repkow, 175, 248
Langobards, invasion of Italy by, 80; migrations of, 80; legislation, 85, 86, 87; similarity between Lombard law and that of ancient Saxons, Anglo-Saxons and Scandinavians, 87; influence of Lombard law upon medieval European law, 87
Lantfrid, Duke, compilation of Swabian tribal law by, 130
Lantweri, military duty of, in case of hostile invasion, 162
Last will. *See Testament*
Law, evolution of, 45; divine origin of, 66; words used to designate, 66;

purpose of early law, 67; unwritten custom, 67; strict rules among early Germans, 67; act, not intent, determines crime, 67
Lawbreach, 32
Law merchant. *See* Commercial law
Law of the Seven Parts, 276, 277, 278
Law schools, establishment of, in Italy, 263, 264, 265; in Spain, 276; in Germany, 280; in the Netherlands, 287
Law speakers, functions of, 36, 37; in England, 232
Legal acts, forms of, 45-46
Leges Barbarorum, compilation by King Rothari, 86, 125
Legislation, Ostrogothic, Langobard and Burgundian, 85-88; influence of ecclesiastical principles upon modern, 211
Legists or civilians, defined, 204; supersede ecclesiastics in many branches of public service, 267; provisions against, in Barcelona, 275
Lehnrecht, compilation of, 175, 248
Leo XIII, digest of ecclesiastical law, superseding *Corpus juris canonici*, 207; submission of controversy between Germany and Spain to, 209
Leti, settlement of, in Gaul, 75
Leudis, defined, 111
Lex Alemannorum, compilation of Swabian tribal law, 130
Lex Anglorum et Werinorum, compilation of Thuringian laws, 131
Lex Gundobada, compilation of Burgundian law, 87
Lex Rhodia de jactu, 219
Lex Ripuaria, 129
Lex Salica, 125, 128, 129
Lex taliones, delivery of criminal to wronged party, 139
Liber Papiani, 88

Liber Sextus, compiled under Boniface VIII, 208
Libri feudorum, private compilation of feudal law made in eleventh century, 174
Liutprand, laws of, 86
Local law, 227-35; disintegration of political authority on the continent, 228; jurisdiction of manorial courts, 228, 229; after dissolution of Frank Empire, 230; in European cities, 230, 231; abnormal development, 232, 233; absence of trained legal experts, 232; development of appellate courts, 233; compilations, 233; use of subsidiary Roman law, 234; development of courts of appeal by city leagues, 235; France in later middle ages, 236-39; Spain in later middle ages, 240-43; Italy in later middle ages, 244-46; Germany in later middle ages, 247-52; reaction against lawlessness, 253-57
Lombard code. *See Leges barbarorum*
Lombard law, influence upon medieval European law, 87; status of aliens, 117; law school at Pavia, 264
Lynch law, among Saxons, Frisians and Franks, 26

Mægth, supervision over fatherless children by, 52
Maine, Sir Henry, on the development of law, 45
Maitland, on early legal development, 4; cited, 54, 55, 178
Malberg gloss, 129
Mancipium, 46
Mannitio, method of opening suit, 138
Manorial courts, jurisdiction of, 228, 229
Mansfield, authority on Roman law, 291
Manslaughter, 31, 32

Manumission of slaves, among Germans, 10, 11; among Lombards, 11; among Swedes, 11; in Iceland, 12; in Frank Empire, 112; by church, 112; by testament, 112; by the penny (*per denarium*), 112

Manumitted slaves, protection by former master, 10

Manus, 45, 46

Marcomanni, invasion of Italy by, 71

Marcomannic war, 71, 73

Maritime law, compilations of, 225, 226; *Costumes de la mar*, *Libro del consolat del mar* or *consulatis maris*, 225; *Charte d'Oléron*, 226; *Waterrecht* of Wisby, 226

Markgenossenschaften, 15

Marriage, development of law of, 198, 199, 200, 211

Marriage by sale, 47, 48; consent not required, 47; payment of price or *wergeld* necessary to establish marital relationship, 48; law of Ethelbert, 49; law of Ethelred, 49

Martinus, glossator of twelfth century, 265

Matrimonial cases, ecclesiastical jurisdiction over, 195 ff.

Mercantile law. *See* Commercial law

Merovingians, rule of, in Frank Empire, 103; royal ordinances (*auctoritates, edicta, præceptiones, decreta*), 131, 132

Metronymic system, 51

Migration of the peoples, 78

Military and political organization, 14–23; employment of cavalry as chief force in war, 162, 163

Milites limitanei, settlement of, along Roman frontier, 75

Ministeriales, knights of servile origin, 168; appointment of, to public office, 111; service in the Frank cavalry, 163

Mirror of the Saxons. *See Sachsenspiegel*

Mirror of the Swabians. *See Schwabenspiegel*

Missi, appointment of, by Charlemagne, to ride circuit and supervise administration of justice, 141

Montalvo, ordinance of, 242

Moors, overthrow of Visigothic king by, 90, 93; victory of Charlemagne over, 103; struggle of Castile, Aragon, Navarre, and Catalonia with, 151

Morganatica. *See Morgengabe*

Morganatic marriage, origin of, 49

Morgengabe or morning gift, 49

Movable property, 54–56; action for protection of, 54; Roman rule, 55; acceptance of German rule by continental countries, 55; French rule in eighteenth century, 55; acceptance of Roman rule in English law, 56; succession in case of death, 56

Mund, 21, 45, 46, 48, 50, 62

Mutterrecht. *See* Metronymic system

National law, development of, on European continent, 170, 171, 253

Netherlands, reception of Roman law in the, 287

Nexum, compared with self-mortgage, 62

North German Hansa. *See* Hanseatic League

Novels of Justinian, reference to, in Constitution of Roncaglia, 266

Nueva recopilación, 242

Oath-help or compurgation, 40, 41, 42, 43, 140, 256, 257

Odoacer, king of Italy, 77; overthrown by Ostrogoths, 79

Ordeals, trial by, 27, 28, 41, 44, 143; different kinds of, 41; Christian

ceremonies used in, 136; abolishment of ordeal of battle in France by Louis IX, 239
Ostrogothic Empire, extent of, xix, 79
Ostrogoths, subjection by Huns, 79; settlement in Pannonia, 79; invasion of Italy under King Theodoric, 79; extent of empire, 79; overthrow by armies of Justinian, 80; legislation, 85
Otto I, reign of, 149
Outlawry, 25, 26, 43, 67, 139; relationship between lord, vassal or kinsman and outlaw, 25; banishment *in sylvam*, 25; person and property affected by, 26; choice between composition and, 32; ordeal invoked to establish guilt in criminal cases, 41; resistance to arrest or distraint, 44; loss of connection with kinship group, 52; excommunication by church, 191
Oyez, origin of term, 35

Pactus Alemannorum, compilation of Swabian tribal law, 130
Pagus, division of tribe, 14, 15
Paris, custom of, 238, 243
Parliaments, development of, 152
Patron and client, relationship between, in ancient Mediterranean world, 10, 11
Pavia, law school at, 264
Peace, proclamation of, by priest, 35; to put out of the, 35; term used as equivalent by early Germans, 66
Peace money, payment of, 32, 33
Pepin, assumption of royal title by, 103
Perjury, 43
Personal law (*lex originis*), in Frank Empire, 116
Petri exceptiones, medieval Italian manual of Roman law, 264

Phillimore, cited, 291, 292
Pledge, historical development of, 61, 62
Pliny, quoted, 59
Pœnæ medicinales, or healing penalties imposed by church, 210
Polygamy, practice of, by German nobles, 10
Pope, recognized as first bishop in Christendom, 181; coöperation between church and state, 187; right of, to convoke Frank synods, 188; proceedings to depose bishops under control of, 189; head of organized hierarchy, 191; "universal ordinary" of all Christendom, 201, 202; submission of international controversies to, 209; authority over church lands during middle ages, 244
Portugal, separation from Castile in twelfth century, 151
Power, symbol of, in early German and Roman law, 46
Power of husband over children, 50, 51; over wife, 50
Primogeniture, 60, 172
Procedure. *See* Courts and procedure; Criminal procedure
Procuratores, functions of, 156
Prolocutor or forspeaker, functions of, in Frank courts, 136
Pseudo Isidoriana, 189, 190
Punishment of criminals, among heathen Germans, Scandinavians and Frisians, 27; idea of vengeance abolished in Roman law, 209; attitude of church, 209, 210

Quartering of troops upon civilians, 81, 82
Quod actoris interest, Roman phrase for damages, 211

Rachimburgi, selection by count of, in Frank Empire, 134; appointment for life, 135
Ravenna, law school of, 264, 265
Real property, historical development of permanent control of, 57–59; transfer or conveyance of land, 59
Reccesvind, compilation of laws by, 96, 97
Reception of Roman law. *See* Roman law
Recht, explanation of term, 67
Reformation, ecclesiastical unity of western Europe until the, 105
Reguli and *subreguli*, 16
Relations between Germans and Romans, 71–77
Religious offenses, jurisdiction over, 193
Repkow, Eike von, compiler of the *Sachsenspiegel*, 248
Retinue. *See Comitatus*
Revenge. *See* Vengeance
Richtsteige, treatises on procedure in territorial and feudal courts, 249
Ricos hombres, feudal magnates in medieval Spain, 168
Roman army, Germanizing of, 75, 76, 77; foreign-born citizens serving in, 75; recruiting of auxiliary troops from captives, 76
Roman Empire, full development of, xvii; centralization of administration during fourth and fifth centuries, 74; German tribes controlled by, 74; conquest of Ostrogoths and Vandals by Justinian, 80; invasion by Langobards, 80; immunity from payment of taxes and personal service in later Roman Empire, 155; Christian church in Roman Empire, 176–79
Roman law, compilation of, during fifth century, 88; based on handbooks of Roman law and code of Theodosius, 88; compilation during sixth century under authority of Alaric, 88; influence of theory of "continuous empire" upon reception of, at close of middle ages, 105; status in Frank Empire, 115; subjection of clergy to, 116; influence on Germanic customs, 120; recognition of primary affinity, 196; *sponsalia* not a contract, 198; activities of legists or civilians, 204; punishment for violation of social order, 208; its use as subsidiary law, 234, 258; revival and reception of, 258–62; in Italy, 263–70; in France, 271–73; in Spain, 274–78; in Germany, 279–87; in the Netherlands, 287; in Switzerland, 288–89; in Norway and Sweden, 289; in Denmark, 290; influence on English law, 290–92
Romans, relations between Germans and, 71–77
Roncaglia, Constitution of, 266
Rothari, compilation of German customary law by, 86

Sachsenspiegel, 9, 175, 248, 249
Sacral punishment, among early Germans, 27, 28
Saisina, 46
Sale, primitive, 65
Salian Franks, occupation of lands along lower Rhine by, 73
Sanction, in early society, 61
Santa Hermandad, law and order league in Spain, 254
Sarmatians, settlement of, in Italy, 75
Savigny, cited, 263, 268
Saxo Grammaticus, 20
Saxons, distribution of, in Germany during early periods, 73

Scabini or lay judges, in northern Italy, 244
Scandinavian sources of law, importance of, in comparative study of old Germanic law, 289
Schalk, old German word for slave, 110
Schepen. See *Schöffen*
Schöffen, 30, 247, 249, 254, 255, 256, 281, 282; origin of *schöffen* courts, 135
Schuldknechtschaft, defined, 62
Schutzzins, payment for protection, 114
Schwabenspiegel, 175, 249
Seasons, division of year by early Germans, 9
Seizin, 46, 50, 54, 58, 59
Self-mortgage, important root of early formal contracts, 61, 62
Serf. See *Villein*
Sermo regis, 35
Servi casati, housed slaves, status of, 111
Servi inquilini, status of, 111
Setenario, the, 276
Sib, importance of, in early German law, 51; disciplinary power over its members, 52; adoption into the, 52; decrease of public and private powers, 109
Sicily, Constitution of the Realm of, 245–46
Siete Partidas. See Law of the Seven Parts
Simony, jurisdiction over cases of, 193
Slaying, secret, 28; open, 28
Slav, etymology of term, 110
Slave, status of, 12, 13; improvement of legal position during Merovingian period, 110; in the later Roman Empire, 111; *servi casati*, 111; *wergeld* for household slaves, 111; slaves of kings and magnates made knights, 112

Slavery, establishment of, 13; slave trade in Gaul, during Merovingian period, 110
Social classification, among Germans, 9; amount of *wergeld* indicative of social status, 110–14
Sors, land ceded to German invaders, 82
Spain, invasion of, by Vandals and Swabians, 78; expulsion of Vandals from, 78; historical development in, 89–93; unification under single monarchy by marriage of Ferdinand and Isabella in fifteenth century, 151; development of *cortes*, 152; local law in later middle ages, 240–43; no general law at close of middle ages, 243; reception of Roman law, 274–78
Spiegel der deutschen Leute, based on Repkow's compilation, 248
Spirit of early Germanic law, 66–68
Sponsalia. See Betrothal
"Staff saying" or "bestaving," 39
Succession, to movable property, 56; to real property, 60
Summons, by complainant (*mannitio*), 138; by judge at request of complainant (*bannitio*), 138
Sureties, responsible for defendant's appearance in court, 43; for satisfaction of judgment, 44
Switzerland, reception of the Roman law in, 288–89
Sword-oath, retained by early Christians, 63
Symbolic acts, in early law, 46, 59, 60

Tacitus, cited, 5, 19, 27, 32, 34, 36, 47, 48, 49, 58
Tallage, contribution from villein, 167
Testament, succession to real property under feudal system by, 173; influence of church, 211

Teutoburg forest, battle of, 7
Theft, action of, for the protection of *seizin* in movables, 54; extension of conception of, 63
Thegnas, household retainers in Saxon England, 160
Theodosius, peace with Visigoths, 78; code of, 95, 179
Thinghelgi, 34
"Thirding" of land, 81, 82
Thuringians, union of tribes in central Germany, 73; compilation of laws (*Lex Anglorum et Werinorum*), 131
Toledo, councils of, 91, 92
Toro, laws of, 242
Torts, 24, 25, 28, 29-33, 63; fines or compositions to be paid for, 31; cases of "blood and honor," 31, 32; oath and oath-help, 40; execution of judgment, 44; outlawry for non-satisfaction of judgment, 44; capture of woman within the tribe, 47
Treason, 28
Tribal assembly, 17, 18; functions of, 18; meetings, 19; acting as court, 35; jurisdiction, 35
Tribal courts. *See* Courts, tribal
Tribe, formation of new, 18
Trover, origin of the action of, 55
Truce of God, 253
Turf and twig, transfer of land by symbol of, 46, 59

Umstand, participation in finding of judgment by, 38
Usatici of Catalonia, 242, 243, 274
Usuræ, change in meaning of, 211

Vacarius, lecturer on Roman law at Oxford during twelfth century, 290
Vandals, invasion of Italy by, 71, 90; invasion of Gaul by, 78; invasion of Spain by, 78; expulsion from Spain into Africa by Athaulf, 78; peace with Rome, 78
Vehm, German law and order league, 254, 255; development into vigilance committees, 255; procedure of *vehm* courts, 256, 257; disappearance of, 257; sporadic revival in Westphalia, 257
Vengeance, in feud, not breach of peace, 29; no basis for claim, 29; on kin of offender, 30; must be public, 30-31; importance in early criminal law, 209
Villein or serf, duties of, 167
Visigothic code. *See* Visigothic legislation
Visigothic kingdom, historical data, 89-93; Celtic immigration, 89; Greek colonies in Spain, 89; control by Carthaginians, 89; Roman rule, 89, 90; Germanic rule, 90, 91; orthodox Catholic creed accepted by Goths, 90, 91; councils of Toledo, 91-93; end of Visigothic rule, 93
Visigothic legislation, 94-100; Breviary of Alaric, 94, 95; Eurich's code, 95; Paris palimpsest of ancient Gothic laws, 95, 96; laws compiled by Chindasvind and Reccesvind, 96, 97; revision of Reccesvind's code by Egriga, 96; ecclesiastical influence, 97; Visigothic code in eighth century, 97-100; torts and crimes, 98; organization of courts, 98; judicial procedure, 99; translation of code, 100; influence upon early Bavarian law, 130; Visigothic code in Spain during later middle ages, 240
Visigothic rule, extent of, xix, 90
Visigoths, defeat of Roman army at Adrianople by, 78; invasion of Italy and sacking of Rome by, 78;

control of southern Gaul and greater part of Spain by, 80, 90; expulsion from Gaul by Franks, 80; defeat by Clovis, 101
Vogelfrei, 26
Vormund, 46

Wadiatio. See *Wed* contract
Wapentake, 18
War gear and house gear, succession to, in Germanic law, 56; oldest evidence of a distinction in the law of movables, 131
Wed contract, origin of, 62
Weichbild, compilation and treatise of Saxon laws, 250

Werewolf, 26
Wergeld, 9, 12, 21, 32, 47, 48, 49; increase in, among Franks, 108; amount of, indicative of social status, 110-14; for killing of slave, 111; for killing of nobles, 112, 113, 114
West Germans, racial division of, 6
West Roman Empire, end of the, 77, 78, 80
Wisby, *Waterrecht* of, 226
Wise men, functions of, 36, 37, 38, 40
Wite, 32
Witod, 66
Wood-walker, 25
Written language, slow development of, among Germans, 9

THE DEVELOPMENT OF EUROPEAN LAW

BY

MUNROE SMITH

A SERIES OF LECTURES DELIVERED AT
COLUMBIA UNIVERSITY